War Through a Lens

War Through a Lens

A Combat Team Photographer Looks at World War II

Clifford Bell

Tell Your Story Books
3408 Trenary Lane
Colorado Springs, CO 80908

Cover designed by: Tiffanie Davis

All photographs courtesy of the author

ISBN: 978-1-365-78240-4

Distributed by Lulu Publishing Services

Introduction

Clifford Owen Bell was one of my father's oldest friends. They met in the seventh grade in San Antonio, Texas, and remained friends until 2004, when my father died at eighty-two. I knew Clifford from the day I was born. We became especially close during the last fifteen years of his life, after he bought a computer and we began a regular email correspondence. I learned that, besides being an excellent photographer, Clifford wrote. I read several of his short stories, and thought them very good. But it was not until after he died in 2013, when I received his bequest of all of his writings, that I discovered the book he had written about his experiences as a still photographer with the U.S. Army Signal Corps in World War II. Like so many men who went through that war, Clifford did not talk about his experiences until late in life, and then only minimally.

In the years after the war he worked at various jobs, finally settling on surveyor for oil and gas companies. While he remained a confirmed bachelor, he enjoyed visiting with a select group of friends and their families despite, or perhaps because of, the tendency of the children to be rambunctious (present company excepted, of course). He could always be depended on to take snapshots at any family gathering. In his 50s Clifford decided he could make more money by wisely handling his investments than continuing to work, so he retired early. He spent the rest of his life taking pictures, painting, and writing; in other words, indulging the creative side that most of his friends never realized was such an important part of him. His book showed me a man I would never have suspected lived behind, or inside, the quiet, self-effacing man I knew all my life. I was drawn into the fascinating, at times truly horrifying, world of "him, taking pictures," and given a new perspective on a well-worn topic.

It suddenly dawned on me that he and men like him were responsible for all those war pictures I'd seen in old Life magazines; the movie men who worked alongside him made possible all the newsreels that preceded the feature film at the movies when I was a child. Wars continue to happen, and men (and women) continue to record them on film, in hopes that we will be able to see the truth for ourselves. The fact that he often felt he was not allowed to show that truth, however ugly, was one of Clifford's frustrations.

Most of Clifford's war photos have disappeared into a giant government data base which, unfortunately, was never indexed by photographer's name or even location or date. They are essentially irretrievable. But his story remains.

At one point Clifford suggested that perhaps, after he was gone, someone might see fit to destroy his book, since it had fulfilled its primary function, that of serving as a catharsis for all he had seen and felt. I trust that one of my favorite members of the Greatest Generation will forgive me for deciding to share his memories rather than bury them.

Melody Norman-Camp, Publisher
December, 2016

FOREWORD

The reason truth is more fascinating that fiction is that the reader can relate more intimately to real people involved in real situations, however bizarre those situations may be. The reader may think, *that could have been me.* Or: *I could never do that.*

A true story may very well have all sorts of strange twists that no fiction writer would dare use, either because those twists might not seem believable or because they disrupt the smooth flow of the narrative. Such disruptions may, however, serve to bring the situation nearer to the reader's personal experience.

Then there is the matter of endings. In fiction, the author can supply a neat, logical ending, whether happy or tragic. In real life the ending is seldom satisfactory. Indeed, most of life's episodes just play out in a frayed unraveling that can leave the participant, and any witnesses, feeling unfulfilled and unedified.

With these thought in mind, I decided to relate, as they had occurred, some of the more interesting incidents of my career as a soldier with a camera during the "Big War." I served as still cameraman in the three-man Combat Assignment Number One (as well as a couple of others), of the 163rd Signal Photo Company. In other words, if I'd ever had any children, and one of them had been curious enough to ask, "What did you do in the war, Daddy?" I would have been compelled to say, knowing it did not begin to convey the truth of the matter, "I took pictures."

What follows is the story of me, taking pictures. It is also, to a certain extent, the story of one of the great catastrophes of the 20th century: World War II.

1
Off to War

That living god, Emperor Hirohito of Japan, considered the intelligence reports of his military and diplomatic services and was convinced that the decadence of the United States had reached a level that made it fatally vulnerable to a carefully orchestrated stab in the back.

One quick and successful surprise attack left our naval defenses at the bottom of Pearl Harbor. All that remained to complete the full conquest of the enemy, i.e., the United States, was the easy occupation of the nearly undefended Pacific Islands, as well as the west coast of the American continent. Why the Japanese hesitated then, with sure victory at their fingertips, has escaped me, despite much reading on the subject. However, this sort of misjudgment was practiced at some point by every army engaged in the global conflict known as World War II.

On December 7, 1941, I, as well as millions of other Americans, was dazed and disbelieving at the enemy's first blow. Then, on the resulting wave of anger and patriotism, I was washed into the flood of young men pouring into the armed services.

When the clerk at San Antonio's old Dodd Field, which later became the reception center for Fort Sam Houston, asked me what I would like to do while I was working my way up to general, I told him I wanted to be an Air Corps photographer, with lots of stripes and flight pay.

*****

At the dangerous age of twelve or thirteen, I had read an exciting fictional story about a handsome young news photographer whose job was very glamorous and unlikely. Then and there I was transformed into one of those amateur photo bugs, complete with dangling miniature camera, bathroom darkroom, and a high nuisance factor. In high school, with still-undiminished enthusiasm, I talked the school newspaper into investing two-thirds of its fifteen-dollar operating capital in two cuts from shots I had made of the R.O.T.C. unit. After graduation I staggered through a year in a free-thinking photo school in Chicago, and several months in speculative free-lance picture shooting back home in Texas, until my father convinced me that I should quit playing around and get a job. After nine or ten months as a miserable clerk in a cut-rate camera shop I was ripe for anything, so long as it would shake loose that strait-jacket routine. I thought the Army was what I wanted, especially since I would be accomplishing two things at once: supporting my country's fight against a vicious enemy and climbing out of my own personal rut. In those days I was still learning, but not very fast.

*****

"What was your civilian job, soldier?"

My shiny new uniform still had deep packing creases in it, but despite its newness smelled to high heaven of moth balls.

"Photographer." (More or less.)

"Education?" (Hadn't really had it yet, but...)

"Photo school." (What it called itself in the catalog.)

"Hobby?"

"Photography."

"Second choice?"

"Signal Corps photographer." (My God! Was there a chance I wouldn't get it?)

"How about glider pilot training?"

"No, thank you, Sergeant."

I finally arrived, dusty and dazed from bouncing in the

back of a G.I. truck, at the orderly room of the 163rd Signal Photo Company, Fort Sam Houston Army Post. I was just five miles and a ten-cent bus ride from home. And I got to go through the same question-and-answer show all over again. This time, though, I wasn't standing before a reception center clerk feeling belligerent, but quavering in front of the company commander, Capt. Ned Morehouse, not yet known to me as "That Bastard".

"What classification would you like, umm...Bell?"

"Sir, still photographer, sir."

"Uh-huh. Well, what kind of film and filter would you use if you wanted to make a picture of that flag there with all the colors coming out white?"

"Áll...white, Sir?"

My hands were sweating, my knees were negotiating for a sit-down strike, and my mind was shooting off thoughts like a box of firecrackers. Mentally I slid up and down spectrograph charts like a jet-propelled roller coaster. Ortho...pan...infra red...no...ortho makes the blue white...the white, already white...red, red...red filter.

"Ortho film and red filter, sir."

The captain looked questioningly at the first sergeant sitting beside him like a young Father Time ready to chop down us poor mortals with a notebook rather than a scythe. The first sergeant rolled his eyes to the ceiling, then mumbled something in the captain's ear. Then he repeated it. The captain looked at me quickly and asked, "Can you drive a truck?"

*****

Nobody asked me if I could cut weeds, but that is what I spent much of the next several days doing, in a casual, G.I. sort of way. Meanwhile, "new" men kept arriving in small groups at all hours of the day and night. We veterans of three or four days took condescending pleasure in introducing ourselves and showing them how to arrange their foot lockers. Every new guy, of course, had to tell his lamentable tale of how he was snatched out of a five hundred dollar a week job and thrown into the Army. This outfit, as far as he was concerned, was only an overnight stop on the way to Officer Candidate School (OCS).

By some coincidence (you'll recall the question about could I drive a truck) I had been assigned a bunk in a section of the barracks populated almost entirely by truck drivers and mechanics. We were all in the Signal Corps, but there were a lot of different things you could do in the Signal Corps, including drive a truck. One man did claim he had been promised a job in the lab when it was formed. I put him down as a floor sweeper for sure. As for me, I was rapidly developing a terrific allergy to motor vehicles.

One evening after chow we were sprawled on the dry grass outside our barracks absorbing chiggers and dust. A fat man with a huge Roman nose was telling us how he had almost had Hollywood by the tail when he was unceremoniously drafted. Dirty rotten politics was what it had been. Suddenly a dust cloud led by a truck pulled up in front of the orderly room. We saw immediately that this was no ordinary bunch of bewildered recruits. Out of the back end of the truck piled a dust-covered parade of elegance. We counted them as they majestically dusted their pink pants with silver-braided caps. The big brass bars seemed to get in the way. All thirteen of them, wearing a uniformly dignified scowl, marched stiff-legged into the building. Not one looked our way.

These were to be our company officers, our supreme law-givers, our inspiration to great deeds, and they looked as raw as we had felt a couple of weeks before, when we raised our right hands and swore our lives away. Somebody swore now, this time with embellishments. The so-obvious OCS written in the self-conscious actions of these men painfully emphasized their attempt to look like West Point. It was nearly two years of headaches later before the last of them gave up and became human beings, and received their true evaluation as officers in the eyes of the enlisted men.

With the company strength almost up to the T/O (Army-speak for Table of Organization), classes were organized in wire splicing, pole climbing, telephone and radio procedure, etc. True, this was the Signal Corps, but in our captain's mind this was what the Signal Corps did. Apparently he had not yet learned the function of a camera. We were also busy learning military organization, map reading, military courtesy, the Articles of War, first aid, basic infantry maneuver, drill, marksmanship, sanitation and a myriad of other indispensable subjects.

Finally the company was split into classes to study mechanics, driving, lab procedure or photography, both still and movie. As my mind wandered during a lecture on the operation of the Speed Graphic camera I had been using for years, I realized that the G.I. truck was no longer a huge mechanized octopus with swivel-jointed tentacles reaching for my throat. I was safely on my way to doing what I wanted to be doing.

*****

I had been in the Army almost two months, and a lot of the fellows for even less time, when rumors started drifting around that we were hot for overseas shipment. We had two Speed Graphics and not a single movie camera in the outfit. Then, all of a sudden, we had cameras, film, lab equipment and gas-proofed clothes. The order came almost immediately for a move. A formation was called, all classes suspended, and every man put on packing detail. We began in mid-morning.

Fifteen or twenty huge packing cases at a time were lined up in front of the supply room, and two men were assigned to each. The supply sergeant called out an item from a list, and one article went into each box.

When darkness came, large photoflood bulbs illuminated the area, and the packing went on. Everything from fifty-caliber machine guns to chemical thermometers, one in each box.

We worked all night, in shifts, with only occasional thirty-minute rest stops. Officers began to growl at non-coms, non-coms growled at privates, and the privates growled at a thousand snafus. Everyone was dead from lack of sleep.

By afternoon everything was packed in the crates, the crates were loaded into trucks, and the trucks were loaded and wired onto flatcars in the post's railroad yards. The captain ordered us to be dismissed, but stay within the company area, ready to move out at a moment's notice. Fifteen boring hours later we climbed aboard the train.

The Pullmans were fairly comfortable with two in a lower and one in an upper berth and crap games all over the place. But it was a long trip, and we had no idea where we were going. When we started heading west, the bets were for the Pacific via San Francisco, but when we awoke the next morning heading east, the betting switched to England via New York.

Two days, two nights and two exercise stops brought us to a halt in the most forlorn-looking little village I had ever seen. We leaned out the windows and yelled at a barefoot native staring at the train, "Where we at, Pop?"

He grinned at us for a while, and then drawled, "This here's Bowlin' Green, Virginny. You boys gonna be in that there Task Force A?"

We hadn't known it until then, but apparently we were indeed part of Task Force A, at least for the moment. We were also in the middle of a thorny wilderness where we proceeded to spend the coldest two months since Valley Forge.

In our flapping pyramidal tents most of us slept "full field," with two pair of wool underwear, a wool uniform, overcoat, cap, socks, shoes and gloves under three blankets and many layers of newspapers. A good percentage of the company spent the winter a bit more comfortably as patients in the tent hospital a few miles away. At least they ate beef instead of horse, and walked on boardwalks instead of sloughing around knee-deep in half-frozen mud.

At the end of those two miserable months Task Force A pulled up stakes and moved out for the invasion of North Africa, but the consumptive 163rd retreated to Camp Sutton, North Carolina.

On the long truck convoy south we didn't talk much about missing the boat. I guess we all thought it was a little degrading. None of us realized until later the sitting ducks we would have been with only our less-than-two-months of training. Some were deeply disappointed at not getting into action yet, while others were offering up silent prayers of thanksgiving that they had been spared a little longer.

Camp "Sooten" it was called, and with good reason. Every morning, just after the whistle blew for first call, an epidemic of coughing would break out all along the rows of "winterized" tents. I remember the next six months as a time of handkerchiefs black with soft coal soot blown out from the lungs, of "chicken" being consumed at almost every meal, and of false alarms.

When we arrived we were told that this was to be only a temporary stop, and that we were still on the list for ship-out. Until we left, however, we were to be Second Army Special Troops. I believe when they heard "Second Army" most of the men who had been thankful that we weren't shipped out began to wonder if they'd been premature, for the Second Army was under the command of General Benjamin "Yoo-Hoo" Lear. Lear was famous for having punished a whole convoy of new trainees because of the enthusiastic expressions of approval, including whistles and calls of Yoo-Hoo!, directed at a group of young women by some of the trainees. His training of soldiers emphasized protocol, manners, and neatness. The arrival of his official enforcement teams (aka the Gestapo) removed all doubt from our minds that this was not going to be a party. They went down on hands and knees to look for cigarette butts under tent floors, and asked questions which couldn't have been answered by an officer fresh out of West Point. I'll swear they smiled to themselves as they wrote nasty little notes in their books. If ever men put their hearts and souls into making themselves hated, these men did.

All the indecision and wheel-spinning that took place during the next six months appear, in retrospect, to have resulted from the Army's being overwhelmed by the sudden weight of undreamed-of masses of raw material being dumped onto an already shaky system. In its applications to me personally, my life was summarily handed over to an ROTC play-soldier: our company commander, "That Bastard."

Why, in the months to follow, I did not develop a consuming hatred for life in the Army, I don't know. I believe Morehouse to have been unqualified for his job: insufficiently trained, inexperienced, and unequipped intellectually. He appeared to us at the time to be sadistic, but it is clear now that he was only pitifully incompetent. At times, when he was frustrated, the shriek of his high-pitched voice assaulting the ranks of a hundred-plus men evoked, not consternation or fear, but rather an almost uncontrollable urge to laugh. He would have turned purple to hear and see the many mimes and mockeries that his sometimes bizarre actions inspired.

*****

Our chief occupation now, next to picking up matchsticks in the company street, was packing and unpacking the company equipment. We were alerted and unalerted so many times that we almost lost faith in rumors. All the while, though, an undecided sort of training program was going on within the company. Every day we would fall into formation, segregated by groups—motor pool, lab crew and photogs—and march off to our classes. As photogs we took turns working in the lab and going out on assignments shooting camp training exercises, usually engineers building a bridge. That way we built up quite a stack of useless pictures of unneeded bridges.

A few days before Thanksgiving, I was given a furlough, thanks to our kind, generous captain. When I requested fifteen of the eighteen days I had accumulated, he explained, without specifics, that I was a very important cog in the company machinery and asked me what was my name again? I was given all of seven days to ride a day coach a thousand miles, relax, have a good time and get back. Four days spent on the train, and three to do anything I wanted.

*****

A group of five or six men came into the company one day, and were assigned a tent to themselves on the back row. At first they had very little to do with the rest of us and stuck pretty close together. Their acceptance by the rest of us was slowed somewhat because their tent was always getting "Excellent" on Saturday inspections, and being held up to us as an example of purity.

One of these excellent characters was a shy-looking man with already graying hair who rose to an impressive six feet four inches off the ground. His huge frame was extremely loose-jointed and men stared as he lumbered along the company street in four-foot strides. He sported a big mustache, a pipe, and always a shy smile. He talked in a slow drawl that practically everyone in the outfit had a try at imitating. His name was Cecil Lannigan, he seemed to be a very nice guy, and he was assigned to the movie class. He was to play a large part in my overseas experiences.

2

Progress

The call came at last, and this time they meant it; we were shipping out. With some trepidation mixed with considerable relief, we made the trip to our embarkation point.

I am hardly the first to describe the cattle/slave/troop ships that served as transport across the Atlantic: the baking heat, the smell of sweaty bodies, the incredibly cramped quarters, or the hunger and boredom that we lived with for thirteen unforgettably miserable days. We were allowed to breathe for two hours a day on the weather deck. The rest of the time we spent lying in our bunks in the stinking hold, two decks below the water line. Twice a day we stood two hours in line with perspiration dripping onto the sloppy deck to get a skimpy meal so bad that we threw two-thirds of it away. At first we were sold candy, and while that lasted, few men went for chow.

Two inevitable products of the Army, rumors and crap games, got plenty of exercise during the voyage. Most of the rumors had us landing in India. I bet on that one too. I had a dog-eared and closely guarded little map, torn from a magazine toothpaste ad, on which I plotted our approximate positon each day, based on the intervals at which the clock was changed. This gave me only the approximate longitude, but I figured from the heat that if we were not going due east we must be angling southward.

We were ordered to keep our clothes, including life belts and canteens, on at all times. The first sergeant would climb around the dangling barracks bags and through equipment-clogged aisles growling at everyone to put his clothes on. And we would...until he was out of sight. It was torture to wear heavy clothing over bodies covered with heat rash. We figured if we were torpedoed and still alive, which was highly unlikely, we would still have time to dress, shave and play three hands of stud poker before we could get out, if the "abandon ship" drills we had been having were any indication.

Our convoy was large, and the voyage a simple exercise in monotony. The only suggestion of submarine trouble came almost as a welcome diversion. It occurred one afternoon when the men of our compartment were inhaling their two-hour ration of fresh air on the jammed weather deck. The first thing we noticed were three of the little submarine chasers bearing down at full speed upon a spot about a quarter-mile off our port side. While we watched from the crowded rail, two frail-looking little airplanes were catapulted from a cruiser ahead of us. They also headed for the same apparently empty spot, and beat the boats to it. The planes dropped one depth charge each. Then we were past the show, and it was out of sight. We never heard anything official about the incident, but it was rumor bait for days.

Soon after this touch of excitement, we awoke one morning to the news that we were now alone, deserted by the entire convoy except for one small corvette. During the night a boiler had exploded, killing one sailor, and we were dead in the water. Two days later the engine had been repaired and we had caught up with the convoy. We had all done a little extra sweating.

Our compartment was lucky enough to be on deck when the convoy passed Gibraltar. This was the first land we had seen in a long while, and it meant a lot, even though we were three thousand miles from home.

I don't know what I expected to see when I stepped off the ship in Oran, Algeria, but what I did see wasn't it. All Africa had ever meant to me were Arabs sitting on white horses outside striped tents in the Sahara, or black people running through the jungle. The only people I saw now, besides hundreds of other G.I.s, wore berets and argued in violent French. I was a bit disappointed at this, but I was amazed at the huge, bustling port, with what looked like hundreds of ships unloading thousands of trucks and tanks and mountains of boxes. This was amid a chaos of half-sunken ships, wrecked buildings and gigantic broken and twisted steel loading cranes.

While we were sitting on the dock in formation with our barracks bags, waiting for trucks to pick us up and trying hard not to look too green in front of the men working there, I heard my name spoken by a voice I didn't recognize. I turned around and found a face I also didn't recognize smiling at me. The face's owner held a clipboard in his left hand; his right hand was close against his side. My lack of recognition must have shown on my face.

He laughed and said, "Remember me? Leroy Hudson? The back of Mrs. Gold's algebra class?"

Then I remembered him. But he looked ten years too old.

"Oh, my God, yes. Leroy! How long you been here?"

He looked a little sad when he answered, "Oh, I came in the first day. How's things in the States?"

I said, "I don't know, about the same, I guess." To me it seemed unimportant. After all, the war, which was the important thing, was here. I had yet to learn that this was a very important question, and deserved a much better answer.

He glanced down, looked back up.

"I'm going back in a week," he said.

With us just arriving, it seemed incredible that anyone was going back already. I didn't know yet that there could be only one reason, so I blurted out, "You are? How come?"

Leroy lifted his right arm about three inches and said, "I got hit the first day, a bomb, right over there by that ramp." I looked quickly, then stared. The heavy steel of the thing was twisted like a pretzel. It seemed impossible that anyone within a quarter-mile could have lived.

"After I got out of the hospital they put me in this port

outfit until they got a ship going back," Leroy said.

I was thinking hard what to say next, but I am sure it would have been foolish. I was saved the embarrassment when somebody banged a carbine against my helmet and I saw we were beginning to move off.

"Well, so long, Leroy; good luck," I said quickly, and staggered away under my barracks bag, feeling stupid.

I never met another person I knew, or even anyone from San Antonio, while I was overseas.

*****

We stood jammed amid our equipment in the back of open trucks as we drove through the city at forty miles an hour. All along the way dozens of filthy, ragged young boys lined the roads yelling, "Hey, Joe, cigarette, Joe?" as they waved the V sign at us. There were also a few young hags giving us the V sign, and some of the men swore they meant "two dollars." They may have.

About fifteen miles of narrow road after we left Oran, we saw a group of buildings. Our driver pointed. "That's you guys' camp."

As we wound through the large camp over roads a foot deep in fine, powdery dust, we saw that the buildings we'd seen were being used as warehouses and administration units, but the pyramidal tents where the troops were living didn't look all that bad. They had wooden floors and screened sides, very similar to those we had left at Camp Sutton. But we kept riding until we started passing through rows of very old, uninhabited tents, leaky and leaning, with neither floors nor screens.

Oh, well, we told each other good naturedly, we won't be here too long, so it won't be too bad as long as it doesn't rain. The hot sun and deep dust certainly didn't conjure up visions of gully washers.

But we still kept riding. Finally we were completely out of the camp area on a flat, dry stretch of land that reached to the horizon without so much as a lump to break the monotony. Well, at least we wouldn't be crowded. This was the African desert I had looked for, only it wasn't sand. It was just ordinary dry dirt that didn't furnish nourishment for even the hardiest weed.

The ground was almost covered with little round balls. A Brooklyn boy picked one up and held it under his nose.

"What 'n hell 'er deese?" he asked of the world at large.

A West Virginia cook looked at him disgustedly and answered, "Them's goat pills. Ya want some salt?"

It was nearly dark when we lined up for chow. We found out then that we were to get three C-ration units a day, plus one canteen of water. After about a week, the water ration was increased to two canteens a day. Later we got all the water we wanted, except for bathing, but the C-rations went on for some time. Truthfully, the Cs didn't taste bad at all for the first three or four cans. Later, however, I joined ten million other men in a wholesale dislike of them.

The second revelation of the day was that we were to sleep right there, dust, rocks, goat pills and all. The ground was hard, the rocks were sharp and always in the wrong places, and the night was cold. Nevertheless, I finally went to sleep, contentedly feeling sort of brave about all these hardships and ready to bear up under the difficulties now that I was "overseas."

Another thought that came to me then, and over and over in the nights following, was the question of how I would react to combat. I didn't deny to myself that I would be frightened. I had been frightened before, but I had never been through anything as fright-provoking as war. Taking for granted, then, that I would be afraid, would I freeze? Lose my head? I didn't think I would, but how could I be certain? If I didn't freeze or lose my head, would I be able to push myself on into greater danger if the occasion demanded it? I didn't ask myself to be a hero (whatever that was), but I was determined not to disgrace myself.

In the morning we awoke to find everything soaked from the heavy dew. The only things not wet were the C-ration biscuits, and they were oh-so-dry.

That day we got a truck-load of those pyramidal tents to keep the dew off us. (A pyramidal tent had a roof that rose to a center point—like a pyramid—with "walls" reaching straight down to the ground from the edges of that roof.) In a couple of weeks another outfit moved out and we raided their area for the homemade beds they had left behind. It wasn't a bad living after that, except for the dust, the flies, and the boredom.

The captain explained to us a new idea someone had given him, that war was nine-tenths waiting and one-tenth violent action. In keeping with this theory, he inaugurated a training program. The violent action phase consisted of a mile run before breakfast, and the waiting phase consisted of doing nothing at all for the rest of the day. The run was supplemented at intervals by extra-curricular activities in the local bars and pleasure houses. If it had not been for the soldier's natural prejudice, K.P. would have been almost welcome, and we didn't mind guard duty at all.

We began to learn the real Army there in that desert. We learned to trade with the Arabs who hung around the boundary lines of our company's area, things like candy and soap for eggs and "purple death" wine. We learned to carry on conversations with them using pantomime. We learned to bathe out of a helmet and to make a sleeping bag out of blankets. We saw fighter planes strafing practice targets in the desert, and we saw the wreckage of airplanes which had crashed when the fighting was still going on in that area. We also learned about North African rainy seasons.

The deep dust turned into the same amount of mud, and it got deeper with every daily rainfall. Trucks bogged down, clothes mildewed, and we were issued grease for our shoes with orders to use it. We found that with a short section of web belt stuck in the can of grease we had a smoky but usable lamp.

The beginning of the rains also ushered in the malaria season, and we were issued one Atabrine tablet every other day. The pills tasted terrible, and the ground around the eating area where the things were passed out began to take on a yellow tint from tossed-away pills. We were warned that anyone who came down with malaria and did not have Atabrine in his bloodstream would be court-martialed. We did not know then that Atabrine would show up in a blood test minutes after it was taken.

Another reason for throwing the pills away was that some men were taken by violent nausea a few minutes after swallowing them; some even lost their whole meal. Even dysentery was blamed on the pills.

Whatever the cause, amoebic dysentery soon became a byword in the company. At practically any time of the night you might wake up to that clump-clump sound made only by a sleepy soldier running for the latrine in unlaced G.I. boots. If you happened to be lying awake nursing stomach cramps and wondering how long you could hold out, when one of these nocturnal pilgrims came back muttering to himself, the standard greeting was, "Did you make it?"

Sometimes the answer was 'no'...with elaborations.

At the peak of the dysentery epidemic a large group of men would gather around the orderly room for sick call, with a trickling stream of others flowing to and from the latrine. A truck made regular ferry trips every four hours to the hospital dispensary, where the suffering would get a dose of sulfaguanidine powder, followed closely by a dose of paregoric. After two days of this treatment the dysentery would be stopped cold and, likely as not, the same victims would be back shortly for CC pills[1] as a remedy for the resultant constipation.

Undoubtedly the millions of flies on the food were the real reason for the epidemic. It was impossible to keep them

---

[1] *A cascara-based medicine used as a laxative.*

away. If you kept a constant fanning with one hand while eating with the other, they would simply fly under the swaying hand and light on the food. The only way to make them move after they had settled was to touch them with a finger. Even then, after one tight circle, they would dive back and land in the same spot. The technique for getting the food to the mouth consisted of a couple of furious passes through the air with the fork trailing a comet's tail of flies, and then a quick dive into the mouth. Even so, many a fly met a violent death as the ivories converged at an inconvenient moment. A not-very-successful scheme to outwit the flies was to place something especially appealing to them beside the mess kit as a lure. However, when this morsel was completely covered by flies on top of flies, those left were only too willing to take up the second choice in the mess kit.

At meal time these devils were especially irritating, but they reported for duty at all times of the day. It was a never-ending battle of swinging, swatting and blowing to keep them off your face and hands.

The Arabs' method of dealing with this scourge was an amazing sight, and I never ceased to be intrigued by it. With rigid faces they completely ignored the flies, allowing them to wander peacefully over eyes, nose and mouth.

*****

Also swarming around the company area, like the flies, were ragged Arab men and boys. Most seemed to speak French and Spanish, as well as Arabic, so some of the men were able to talk with them without pantomime. The Arabs usually got the better end of our trading deals. They were, however, considered untrustworthy, and finally the captain gave an order than none could come within the company area. After that most of them quit coming around—all except for "A-rab Joe," a waif with no discernible home or family connections.

Joe must have been about ten years old, and he had a

mania for imitating everything he saw us do. He learned to salute, stand at attention, parade rest, and to drill to his own unintelligible commands. He dressed very simply. His entire wardrobe consisted of an inverted blue barracks bag with holes cut out for head and arms. The yellow lettering of the former owner's name, serial number and shipping code added a touch of chic across his back. This refreshing little character was always happy and willing to exchange his whole English vocabulary—which included the most select of military profanities—with any enlisted man. Of officers he was deathly afraid, and he could recognize one from as far away as he could see him.

After it became evident that, orders or no orders, Joe was there to stay, the mess officer suggested that at least he could be cleaned up a bit. Joe happily consented to a bath in the water left over from washing the mess kits. The idea caught on with him, and every morning he could be seen diligently scrubbing his hands and face with water and G.I. soap.

At the end of our stay, Joe stood in the deserted company street, tears streaming down his cheeks, and held a stiff salute as the trucks passed by on their way out of the camp. We were going to miss him, too.

*****

Our first glimmer of the vastness of the war had come in Oran. Besides the uniforms of nearly every Allied country with troops in the fight, we met civilian refugees from France and Spain, and almost every European country. They swarmed the narrow, crowded streets babbling away in what to us were exotic-sounding languages.

The city itself was the dirtiest we'd ever seen, but then, it was also the first city we had ever seen that had been through a war. Outside of the port area, which had been almost destroyed by Allied bombs clearing the city of enemy troops before the landing, the city was hardly touched by the physical violence of war. Emotionally and economically, however, it had been hit hard. The civilians were frantic to make all the money they could from the soldiers in order to buy life's necessities on the black market. This created a surly atmosphere that was hardly improved by the actions of the troops. The soldiers had no respect for the civilian population because the civilians swindled them, and because the civilians resented this lack of respect they worked all the harder at their swindling.

Beyond the city, away from the filth and stench, a well-paved highway led along the edge of tall, beautiful rock cliffs overlooking the Mediterranean. After a short time, the cliffs dropped away and wide, sandy beaches appeared. The locals had had their beaches taken over by the Army, and USO clubs had been set up. There were two beaches available to us. One, with a dangerous undertow, was for the enlisted men; the other, without an undertow, was for the officers and nurses. During the warm weather, we made almost daily trips to the beach, for the sake of both cleanliness and exercise. The dust on the roads effectively nullified the cleanliness.

After two months we were fed up with the boredom of living in a desert with almost nothing to do. We were pretty well used to the life, though, and didn't suffer physically from the lack of permanent barracks with flush latrines and ceramic wash bowls. But when the order came for another move we were glad to pull out our frail roots and be on our way.

Naturally we were not told where we were going, but it didn't take much guessing to figure it would be Naples.

Down at the harbor, the drivers were put onto one ship along with trucks loaded to the gunwales with equipment. The rest of us boarded another ship the next day. Our barracks bags were loaded into the hold, so all we had to carry on board was a full pack with two blankets, helmet, carbine and canteen. These weighed only about fifty pounds, and that was a fortunate thing because we boarded by climbing a cargo net draped over the side of the ship. To make it even more interesting, we approached the ship, which was anchored in the middle of the harbor, in landing barges. A rough sea made it necessary for us to get set up and then wait for the craft to be lifted to the top of a wave before grabbing onto the net and scrambling up like a monkey on a string. Some of our heftier members almost didn't make it.

The trip as the Navy's "guests" wasn't bad at all...mainly because it lasted only four days. The voyage was extremely uneventful, other than the poker game in which I filled an inside straight. We spent most of the time we weren't playing poker watching the antics of our porpoise escort.

In the early afternoon of the fourth day we were assigned the task of climbing down the same cargo nets we had struggled up before. As the landing barges raced each other for the shore, we got our first look at Italy. What we saw seemed to be a small town beginning about fifty yards back from the water and spreading up the side of a steep hill. On the peak, alone, stood a large building covered by a camouflage paint job that looked phony even at that distance.

As we stepped out of the barge onto smooth, dry sand, we heard an explosion down the beach. Someone from another outfit had just stepped out of a barge onto an old mine. He and two other unfortunate soldiers were saved the worries of combat.

We had the local peddlers outnumbered as we swarmed up the sand, but not by a comfortable margin. Our defenses had been shattered by four days of shipboard chow, so we gladly surrendered, trading our cigarettes for apples and nuts, as well as coral necklaces that couldn't be eaten, but might come in handy at later bargaining sessions. Not yet knowing the market value of cigarettes, we were unmercifully overcharged.

Finally the barges brought our barracks bags and, loading them onto our already overburdened backs, we staggered off into the town. With the help of our G.I. Italian phrase books, we learned from the natives that this was Bagnoli, on the outskirts of Naples. The sun was hot, our loads were heavy, and our legs were weak from four days of non-use. Morehead, carrying a two-pound pistol on his belt and not a heavy thought on his mind, led the struggling, sweating formation up one street and down another, from one side of town to the other, and finally up the hill to the entrance gate of the big, camouflaged building at the peak. There we stopped and lay panting in the shade of a stone wall while our illustrious captain went inside to make arrangements for our billeting.

There was a large statue of a Count Ciano in front of the main building, the one we had seen from the barges, and we learned that this building, along with others that we could now see, were what was left of a slightly bombed and now-defunct university. It was being used for billeting new arrivals as they came in from the ships. We were herded to our assigned quarters, a huge room on the third floor of the main building, with solid marble floors that were to double as beds. Here we were scheduled to wait until the ship carrying our drivers and the trucks and equipment came in.

The men who had arrived a few days before we did told us that every once in a while there were air raids at night. Our first couple of nights we didn't have anything disturb our sleep but aching hip bones and cramped shoulders. In the middle of our third night I suddenly came out of the fog of sleep with whistles blowing, people yelling "Air raid!" and our captain running wildly around the room screaming at the top of his voice. I dressed in no time flat, having been sleeping minus shoes only, and dashed off with the crowd in total darkness. It was impossible to do anything but flow with the stream down three flights of stairs and across the grounds to the huge tunnels used as air raid shelters.

While crossing the grounds we could see searchlights and a few bursts of ack-ack (anti-aircraft fire) over in the direction of Naples. The only danger to us was being trampled on the stairs. After we stood around for half an hour in the tunnel cursing the no-smoking order, or maybe sneaking one anyway, the call "All clear!" began its relayed course back from the entrance. Then we filed back to our blanket rolls to try to finish out a restless night's sleep.

After that first one, the alarms began to come thick and fast—two, three, even four times nearly every night. It seemed that we spent most of the hours of darkness trudging to and from the air raid shelters.

We were ordered to dress completely for each performance with helmet, carbine and gas mask. We soon found, however, that it was hard to enforce the order in the blackness of the night, so first the gas mask and later the carbine stayed behind.

The first few nights of these raids, we saw the search-lights and heard the ack-ack about once in every four alarms. The alarm was given according to radar and, more often than not, the enemy planes never got through the defenses around Naples, or they were after another target. Therefore, after the novelty had worn off and the alarms had become no more than a very inconvenient nuisance, we were given the privilege of staying in the sack until the ack-ack actually began. Later on, the room was not even checked to see that everyone was out during a raid. The closest to our building that bombs were ever dropped was on the coast road about two miles away.

One night during a raid I found myself stalled at the door waiting for the jam in the hallway to clear enough for me to push into the stream of men. The ack-ack had already begun and by the flashes of light through the windows I was able to recognize a fellow still photographer named Larry Jones standing beside me.

"Damned lot of nonsense, huh?" I growled at him.

"Yeah," he answered sleepily. "All they want is those ships in the Naples harbor."

We stood there a while longer without speaking. Suddenly Jones shifted from one foot to the other and said, "Look, let's go around to the back behind those bushes and watch the fireworks. If it gets rough we can always go in that other shelter over the hill."

"O.K., let's go," I said.

After we got down the stairs and out the front entrance, we ducked out of line and around to the side of the building. At the rear was a clump of bushes, and beyond that the grassy top of a little hill. Here we seated ourselves and contemplated the display of lights, flashes and arcing paths of tracers as they made their thousands of glowing red streaks across the inky blackness of the sky. The immensity and violence of the gigantic show was overpowering but its remoteness gave me a feeling of peace.

"Beautiful," I said, "but scary."

"Yeah," Jones answered. "Like sitting up here on a cloud and looking right down the throat of hell." Jones was revealing an unexpected poetic side. But he was right.

"Yeah," I said. "Kinda makes you think things you never thought before." I was thinking out loud here. "Like maybe if we're here in the middle of something so much bigger and hairier than we ever thought about, then why shouldn't there maybe be something even bigger and hairier than even this, somewhere else? Like a real hell?"

Jones considered this. "Umm. Maybe we're getting a sneak preview of the really big show."

"Could be," I speculated. "But then if there is a hell, on the flip side there's got to be a heaven, right?"

A new idea was being planted in my mind, or maybe it was a new question. For as long as I could remember, I had accepted a social type of religion, practicing it in the usual one-day-a-week fashion. There had always existed, however, a little blank spot inside me. I had never bothered to try to analyze this incompleteness until now, when thoughts of death began to invade my mind.

Tonight it was made real to me for the first time that death was not always something that happened to someone else, and it occurred to me that whoever was running this chaotic world was going to be an important consideration in my plan of operations for the foreseeable future. For the first time I had no doubt that there was Someone up there, somewhere, running the show, wars and all.

3
On the Job Training

The ship carrying our drivers with the trucks and company equipment didn't arrive within the few days allotted. The best rumor had it sunk in the Straits of Messina. From the rumors you could almost get latitude and longitude. As time stretched on, the boredom and air raids were interspersed with short hikes in company formation around the countryside and nightly expeditions, in small groups, into Naples.

We found Bella Napoli a bit cleaner than Oran, at least on the main streets. The people were better-dressed, but we were swindled and stolen from with the same frequency as in Oran. Rumor had it that the Military Government (MG) had estimated that eighty to ninety percent of the female population between the ages of twelve and seventy were active prostitutes. The venereal disease rate was so high that we had to stand inspection before we left the company area to make certain we were carrying a prophylactic kit and condoms.

The most disgusting part of the whole thing was the pimping. A soldier could not walk ten steps down Via Roma without being asked at least twice by ragged little gamins, "Hey, Joe. Ficky-ficky my sister? Wanna eat? Wanna drink? Wanna ficky-ficky?" After the propositioned soldier had said no three or four times, if he was saying no, he would begin to get angry, at which point the little imps would turn loose a well-stocked vocabulary of mixed English and Italian profanity while keeping just out of reach.

After a little over a month, the drivers joined the company with trucks, equipment, and long stories of sweating out thirty-odd days aboard a Liberty ship, during which time they had done everything there is to do aboard a ship except join the Navy.

When our truck convoy started north we had the feeling that we were finally going to get something worthwhile done. For better or worse it was the end of the long period of training and waiting. No more dry runs; it was live ammunition and "fire for effect." I don't think I was the only one fighting a little unraveling of his blanket of confidence.

We didn't just drive up to the front lines and go into action, however. The only thing that looked like combat during the trip was the posting of aircraft lookouts, two in each vehicle, who wouldn't have known a P-51 from a Jap Zero, despite all our aircraft recognition classes.

We had been told that the front was only thirty miles away—though it was still moving in those days—so we were surprised when we drove what seemed like twice that far. Finally we came to a halt and deployed and camouflaged the trucks amid a group of trees beside a small river. Within plain view was a fairly large town atop a nearby hill. We wondered then, and I still wonder now, why we didn't billet there. However, that night we unfurled our bedrolls in and under the trucks.

Nature worked in beautiful coordination that night. With the darkness came the rain and with the dawn came the rainbow. Also, with the fertile ground we were parked on, came nearly a foot of soft mud. When I jumped over the tailgate of the 6x6 truck I had been sleeping in, I almost fell into the river, which by now had become a muddy torrent. During the night the stream had eaten away its bank and was now within inches of the truck's left rear wheel. When we returned from breakfast we found the truck with a twenty-degree list to port and still sinking toward the slowly caving bank of the river. We saw at a glance that to try to drive it out would be fatal, so we frantically chained another truck to it, with which we hoped to pull it out of danger. Then we had two trucks bogged three-quarters deep in mud.

By noon we had both trucks winched out and on solid ground, ending our formal introduction to Italian mud. Since then I have driven the same type of truck over hundreds of miles of Central American jungle trails during the rainy season with relatively little trouble. I therefore blame the large number of military trucks I saw stuck in Italy to Italy's incomparable mud. Besides its gooeyness and stickiness, it could approach four feet in depth in many places.

Thousands of colorful words have been written and spoken to describe it, but none have approached the elegy it richly deserves.

*****

A message came to the company from Army Pictorial Service Forward (APS), the handful of cameramen and drivers who had covered the picture story of both the African and Sicilian campaigns, as well as the Italian campaign up to this point. The message called for one team consisting of movie man, still man, and driver with vehicle. These were to be the first men in our outfit to see combat. I was elated—despite suffering with a bad cold—when Lannigan (the big, shy, slow-talking guy who had been around since Camp Sutton) and I were picked to go. Our ride was a weapon carrier, driven by one Snuffy Owen. This was the first time we had operated in this streamlined formation, which was being used by the APS but had not yet been named. We were later given the designation of Combat Assignment Team Number One—CAT-1.

Deliriously, we flung barracks bags, bed rolls and camera equipment into the truck and started out within the half hour. Only once more during the course of the war did I pack that fast...and that was for the exact opposite reason.

Darkness descended about halfway to the bivouac area of the APS unit, and Snuffy drove the unfamiliar roads in blackout. When we arrived, a corporal of the guard showed us a tent on the side of a hill, and there we spread our bed rolls on the wet ground and went to sleep immediately.

For me, sleep lasted about an hour. I awoke with a horrible feeling of nausea and gripping pain in the stomach. My "bad cold" had become something much worse. I retched, shook with chills, and made trips to the latrine at thirty-minute-to-an-hour intervals until five o'clock in the morning, when I finally fell asleep.

I didn't get up for breakfast, and was sound asleep when someone came into the tent and asked if I was Bell. I didn't feel like anything human, but I told him I was.

"Well, you're going out on a job this morning with Lt. Stone and the major wants to see you now," he informed me.

I didn't know Lt. Stone from Lt. Adam, and I didn't even know there was a major around. I pulled on my shoes painfully and fell over a tent stake on the way out. At the bottom of the hill I saw Lannigan talking to not one but two majors, and two lieutenants. Walking as straight as I could, I stumbled up and saluted the group in general.

"Bell?" one of the majors ventured.

"Yes, sir."

"Well, good morning. I'm Major Betts. I just wanted to welcome you and Lannigan to the outfit. You're going out with Lt. Stone on a Christmas story this morning. He'll tell you all about it." After a beat he added, "If you need any socks, we got in a bunch yesterday."

"Thank you very much sir," I said, meaning it. He hadn't said, "You're one helluva looking soldier," but I knew that was what he meant.

We got a jeep to pull the weapon carrier out of the mud and sat waiting for our Lt. Stone. When he finally came and introduced himself, almost the first thing he said was, "Don't call me 'sir'." We figured there might be advantages to working detached from the headquarters unit of the company.

As we drove to the infantry outfit where he had already arranged to shoot the story, Stone explained it to us.

"If we can get some good stuff on the G.I.s getting Christmas gifts now it will get to the States in time for the papers to use it on Christmas. Use your own ideas, of course; it's your story. But here's an idea I had." He went on to detail a whole series of shots as if he were describing pictures already made. I saw that he wouldn't really appreciate any large-scale deviations. My stomach was still in open revolt and my brain was functioning in weird ways, so I decided to stick as closely as possible to his outline, if I could remember it. And I did, except for one shot, and I still have the clipping of that picture from a New York newspaper—my first published shot from over the waters. Despite having deviated from The Plan, I got a note from Stone a month or so later congratulating me on the story.

On the road back to the bivouac area, the lieutenant told us that a fellow photographer, Max Osborne, had recently been killed when he took shelter in a house during a bombing attack and the house received a direct hit. His body and his camera had been found in the rubble. I had not known Osborne well, but I could feel the war becoming more real.

Just as Stone finished telling this story, we saw a low-flying airplane approaching us in a parallel path about half a mile away.

"Watch him, watch him," the lieutenant breathed tensely. As the plane reached a point almost opposite us, it started a bank to the right directly toward us. At the same time it dipped its nose slightly. The noise of six machine guns cutting loose mixed with the whining roar of the diving plane was the most terrifying sound I had ever heard.

"Duck!" Stone yelled, but we were all out of the truck before it had stopped sliding in the dirt.

Happily, there were two stone pillars marking the entrance to a side road, as well as several other large stones. We were each flat on our faces behind a stone shield within two seconds. The plane, an FW-190, continued its strafing run until it was almost overhead; then, inexplicably, it lifted its nose and roared over, hardly more than fifty feet directly above us.

Here was my first taste of actual combat, and I was too green to be frightened. My only emotion was one of high excitement. I was thrilled with the sense of danger, just as I had once been thrilled by drag-racing the family sedan. We were all shaken, but I was trembling not with fear, but with a stupid sense of elation.

After the plane had roared over and disappeared, we were left to wonder why we had been targeted. When we climbed back onto the road and looked around, we saw what we had missed in the excitement. Directly across the road from us were large red crosses painted on the roofs of hospital tents. This was our first lesson in the nature of the Luftwaffe. To us, the Red Cross symbols signified "Hospital." To the German fliers they represented big, easy targets.

*****

To say we were untrained for our jobs as illustrators of a war is a grievous understatement. We were rehearsed in military discipline, calisthenics, wire splicing, close-order drill, and so on. But no one had taught us about this particular team way of operating because, until now, it had never existed. The only team organization we had ever had in the States was as a fifteen-man (or thereabouts) self-contained unit equipped to shoot pictures and then process the film and file it. This wholly impractical method of operating was never attempted in an actual combat situation. The higher-ups were so out of touch with reality that they ended up having no part whatever in the final formation of the three-man CATs. This arrangement simply evolved naturally under fire.

So far from practical involvement was the administrative control that even by the end of the war, more than two years later, they had never discovered a way to insure that those of us in the field got food or gasoline. We bummed both from whomever we could. The Headquarters unit (HQ) continued to receive rations in our names even though we might have been a month and a hundred miles away. The lab and clerks back at headquarters ate very well and we managed to survive in the field by grubbing food whenever and wherever we could.

As for work assignments, we made our own except for occasional special projects. This was simply because no one else was in touch with the immediate situation in our area. Because of this freedom, we worked harder and longer than we would have if we had been given a rigid schedule to follow. We avoided any unnecessary contact with our company headquarters for fear of being entangled in G.I. "chickenshit." We even devised our own uniforms to a certain extent because few people knew who or what we were, which was the way we preferred it. We found civilian tailors to alter our issued uniforms. We invented identification sleeve patches and had them made by civilians. We never wore any rank or unit designations on our uniforms. We painted our jeeps with identification that might indicate either Army or civilian correspondents.

And with all this unconventionality we did a damn good job.

*****

Our new team lived with the APS group in their informal camp for several days, riding with some of their veteran teams around the now-quiet sector, meeting regimental and battalion officers of the 45th Division to get an idea of how the experienced teams worked. Their procedure was simple and was used by all the 163rd teams later on, when they were not working on a specific job or didn't have one lined up.

The first stop was the division's G-2 (Intelligence Center) to find out where the most pictorially interesting action of the day was likely to take place. Second stop, battalion CP (Command Post) to narrow down the sector of interest. Third, company CP for the straight and pointed dope, information and advice as to where to go to get pictures and where to go to get shot at. Preferring the former, this is usually where we left the jeep, providing we had been able to drive it that far. From then on it was usually leg work and luck.

One day we heard through the rumor channels that several more teams had been sent out from the company. Then, abruptly, APS was retired from the sector, our team was pulled back to the company CP, which was now installed in a deserted convent in the little town of Caiazzo. We were issued a brand new jeep, told that the 45th Infantry Division was ours to cover with one other team, and sent out on our own.

Our first concern was to find someplace relatively safe to sleep. This meant either a place that would be out range of all the heaviest artillery, or one so unimportant that it wasn't likely to be bombed, shelled, or strafed. We found an unused house in a little town off the main highway and unloaded our duffels. To call the place a house might have been an unwarranted compliment, but it suited our purposes. It had once been a two-story affair, but now most of the roof and half the upper floor was gone. We didn't intend to use that part of the house anyway so we didn't care if it leaked. What the downstairs room we settled on had was a fireplace and two windows. No furniture, no floor. There was a haystack next door and we brought half of it in—under the screaming protests of our civilian neighbor—and spread it on the floor for a mattress. Next day we scouted the area and made some good contacts, by means of bull sessions, with men in the ration and gas dumps.

Among Lannigan's talents was an easy ability to shoot the bull. This was despite being a basically shy man. This knack came in so handy that when we returned to our little hay-lined nest that first day we had the jeep loaded down with rations and four extra cans of gasoline, to say nothing of the good will and buoyed egos left behind for future reference.

After a fairly good supper of food heated in the can at the smoky fireplace, we slept well, considering the occasional firing of heavy guns somewhere nearby.

It took a long while to prepare a decent meal with the

minimal cooking equipment we'd been able to scare up, so we were still at breakfast the next morning when we had a visit from the new team assigned to the 45th Division with us. They had learned our whereabouts while attempting a touch at the same ration dump we had hit the day before, and they wanted a conference to coordinate the stories we would tell to cover our scrounging. We could lose our meal ticket if anyone started checking up.

I'm still not sure how the Army expected us to eat. At times it might have been possible to go on the rations list of some other outfit but, usually, we moved so often and ate at such irregular times that the idea would have been impractical. We were carried on our company headquarters' ration list but the only way our own mess could have fed us would have been to issue us K-rations for two or three months at a time. We lived in fear that some little second lieutenant would notice and decide the Army had to have a regulation to cover the situation.

Both teams finally agreed that the best solution to our common problem was for the other team to move in with us. They did so gladly as they liked our home better than their own.

The new team consisted of Vicelli, Italian-speaking movie man with a tendency to suffer from very convenient migraine headaches; still photographer Larry Jones, my fellow philosopher on the hill at Bagnoli; and driver "Pop" Ericson, a slow, silent, very independent Swede. With plenty of good, dry Italian wine we were a happy group, with fierce nightly arguments about everything from Technicolor technique to Jones' third wife.

The morning after the other team moved in Lannigan and I invited the others to ride up to regimental CP to see what was going on with our war. Vicelli complained of a headache brought on by the frequent firing of "Long Toms" the previous night, but Jones was eager to go. We were taking only one jeep, with Snuffy as driver, so Vicelli and Ericson stayed behind to prepare dinner.

The only way to reach the CP was to make a dash over about ten miles of "Messerschmidt Alley." This was the G.I.s' name for it, borrowed from a similar strip of dangerous real estate in North Africa. Our local brand consisted of a twenty-odd-mile section of the highway from Caserta to Venafro, running straight as an arrow along the flat floor of the valley, with almost no roadside cover. We had been told that in the first days after this ground was taken from the Germans it was impossible to drive from one end to the other without being strafed. The strafing had decreased because of the many anti-aircraft guns strung along the valley, but it was an unwise soul who limited his 360-degree vision by driving with his jeep top up, even in rain, snow or hail.

The four of us reached Venafro safely with no more excitement than a few minor skids on the mud-covered pavement. We made the usual mad dash through the town. Venafro was an unhealthy place in those days. When they had nothing else to do, the German artillery whiled away the time lobbing shells over the mountain into the town at sporadic intervals. BBC radio called it "the hottest spot on earth."

A few miles past Venafro we reached a very small town, deserted except for the CP, and left the jeep beside a building on the town square. Snuffy stayed with it and Lannigan, Jones and I walked the half-block to CP. Before we were well into the building, a four-shell barrage dumped its last explosion on the building beside which we had left Snuffy and the jeep.

The same thought hit the three of us at the same instant. "Snuffy!"

I took off at a run, cocking my camera shutter as I went out the door, with Lannigan and Jones breathing down my neck. When we reached the square we saw nothing but dust and smoke, with a single ragged wall standing above it. As the smoke cleared, we saw the jeep, looking unharmed except for a shattered windshield and a negligible hole here and there. But Snuffy was nowhere to be seen.

We were standing there feeling varying shades of dismay, and wondering what to do, when we heard a "Saay…" and saw a pair of eyes looking at us through the narrow slit of a basement window fifteen yards down the street.

When he came up, Snuffy examined the jeep and reported that it had received only superficial wounds. The battle scars would look good the next time we drove into the company HQ area.

Back at the CP again, we talked with the G-2 officer, then proceeded on foot, with a mortar platoon lieutenant as guide, about a mile over rocky foot trails and up a high hill to an artillery OP (Observation Post—everything in the Army gets reduced to initials.). The last hundred yards or so the lieutenant instructed us to keep low at all times and to make a running dash past the open places. He explained that Germans were about a quarter-mile away, on the next mountain over.

We stared long and hard at the other hill from behind our rocks and bushes, but were unable to see any movement. We decided that since we were risking our necks just being there, it would be a shame to go back without some pictures. Before we could do anything foolish the lieutenant saved the day by crawling up behind us and saying, "Look, fellows, if you want, I can call for a few rounds of white phosphorus on the side of that hill yonder. It sure looks pretty and ought to make a good picture. What d'ya say?"

We quickly agreed and pointed out a spot where the white bursts would look best against the dark side of the hill.

"O.K.," he said. "I'll fire the battery three rounds at thirty-second intervals. That ought to give you enough smoke."

He crawled back about ten yards to the field telephone and then yelled to us, "Hey! The name of the battery goes along with the pictures, don't it?"

We yelled back that our stuff would not be accepted without full information in the captions, though it went without saying that the captions would not declare that the pictures were staged.

We heard him give the order and almost as soon as he had crawled back to us the four flat "pock" sounds of outgoing mortar shells came from somewhere in the valley behind. The shells swooshed over us and dropped just where we wanted them.

Our cameras were ready and as I clicked off about four shots with my Leica I heard Lannigan winding off a long scene with his Eyemo. Jones, seven or eight yards to the left, was working a Graphic. Just as the white smoke drifted far enough to be out of the way, four more shells landed in the same area. I did my best to catch the brilliant flash at the instant of the explosion while the long plumes of snow-white smoke were still arcing out like the shimmering petals of a giant marigold. Beautiful, deadly stuff. It was a fine display and made for good pictures. Considering that it was a good experience for green photogs, we didn't regret what it had cost the taxpayers back home.

That night we watched from the front of our house the most intense part of an all-night barrage being thrown at the neighboring hill, Monte la Difensa, which became known as "Million Dollar Hill." We learned later that for several weeks artillery of all sizes, mortars and even 40mm and machine guns, had been brought up and placed in position for this one show. The plan was to dislodge the Germans, once and for all, from their dug-in positions on this small mountain. Someone estimated that the ammunition spent during that night had cost about a million dollars, hence the name. Nobody had actually figured out the cost, but it was a nice round number.

In the days following the Battle of Difensa, the First Special Services Force (SSF), as part of the 36th Division, along with British troops, took this mountain, as well as Monte Camino and the adjoining ridges. However, the front bogged down for another week or so, except for small night skirmishes. In one of these the hill on which we had made our white phosphorus pictures was taken from the Germans. The next night there was another skirmish and the Germans owned it again. Too often, that's war for you.

Our lieutenant friend with his mortars had been in on the attack, and the next time we saw him he laughingly said, "Remember those WPs I fired for you? Well, you got yourselves fifteen Krauts in a dugout. When we were up there the other day I saw 'em. Burned up like G.I. toast."

The ammo hadn't been wasted after all, and we could now claim five of the enemy apiece.

*****

Our CPLO (Corps Photo Liaison Officer) was a Lt. Southworth, who had been in charge of our training unit before CAT-1 was detached from company headquarters. He had a brilliant mind but was undoubtedly misplaced as a tactical officer, another example of the clumsiness of the Army at work. Before the war, he had been a technician in the experimental laboratories of the largest photographic manufacturer in America. He began writing a deeply technical book on film emulsions and, as time went by, began to retreat into it more and more, giving only the barest minimum of attention to his military duties. His outward eccentricities became more pronounced until it seemed that he was holding a complete breakdown away by sheer power of will. Fortunately, he had no lack of that.

Southworth was not the only one in our outfit who experienced this type of wound. Though the combatant element of our company suffered an extremely high rate of physical battle casualties, there was an even higher rate of mental wounds. A man did not have to see combat to be affected. Regimentation and confinement are not the natural states for man or beast. Birds kept in cages develop a variety of behavioral problems. Dogs go crazy in confinement. Men without freedom of movement or the freedom to think and act for themselves try to drown their frustration in pleasure or hard work, to compensate for their lack of freedom with bragging and self-aggrandizement, or to displace it with an addiction to religion, alcohol, drugs. Often it becomes necessary to up the dosage for the same effect, until this method of coping moves outside the bounds of acceptable behavior.

*****

About this time a letter came for me from Marie, a girl from home whom I had almost forgotten. I had gone with her on and off for a number of years, and had once been briefly in love with her. It was a very nice letter, even if inspired by the "Write a Soldier" posters. The fact that she coyly mentioned that she had been engaged but had broken it off made the whole thing more interesting. My greatest amusement, as it was for every other G.I. I knew, was receiving letters, so I decided to send a reply immediately. I made my letter sound as if I had been thinking only of her since we had last parted, though I couldn't remember when that was. I begged her for a picture of herself and asked if she still baked those wonderful cookies. I don't think she knew a pie pan from a coal bucket, but in about three weeks, almost record time, I had an answer full of tender phrases, snapshots, and an assurance that cookies were on the way.

Feeling a little guilty, I wrote another letter that retreated a bit in style and gained a lot in sincerity. Her next was also toned down a bit, and from then on a very nice correspondence continued, becoming a little warmer with each letter, but remaining truthful. Before I left Europe I was pointing at the snapshots over a mug of beer and saying, "*Ja das ist mein Liebling in Amerika.*"

*****

Lagoni was a little town on a hill surrounded by mountains, and could be looked down upon on two sides by the

Americans and two sides by the Germans. The Germans held the town itself, which was a shambles, but it would offer wonderful pictorial possibilities if someone could reach the top of the nearest mountain and stick a camera over long enough to photograph artillery shells landing, then get back without being picked off by a sniper or wiped out by German mortars.

At regimental CP I learned there was an artillery OP on top of a mountain, but I was not permitted to go there in daylight. When I insisted on finding some way to get the pictures, the major I was talking to phoned the captain of the infantry company holding that sector. He was told there was a place less than a hundred yards away, well covered by trees, where one might go unobserved by the German emplacements. The major informed me and added, "Come see me—if you get back."

I write this as ample proof of my ignorant foolhardiness at the time. Later, I would never have considered taking such a risk without a guarantee of the most sensational and newsworthy pictures.

Lannigan stayed home sick that day. I gave Snuffy the choice of staying at the CP in comparative safety or going with me to drive the jeep. Intelligently, he stayed. I drove the jeep as close to the company CP as I could and left it. A lieutenant offered to take me to the spot where I was to get my pictures. We started up the rocky, slippery trail. Halfway up the mountain, he turned off toward the cellar of a house, which was all that was left of a group of farm buildings. Jumping in, he pointed up the mountain and said, "Just follow the trail. It'll lead you right there." I had thought he was going to take me all the way.

For the first time I began to worry. With a man who knew the way, all was right; but I hadn't even seen a map. There was not a soul in sight on the entire side of the mountain. The deathly quiet got on my nerves. The only sound was a distant background rumbling of artillery fire. Having come this far, I couldn't turn back now, so I panted on upward, slipping and stumbling.

The trail grew dimmer to discern and after a while I realized that for some time I had been following my imagination. When I looked around, I could not find the slightest trace of a trail among the rocks. Looking up, I saw that the side of the mountain had become so steep that I could no longer see the small saddle I was aiming for. I began to get genuinely scared. If only I could see at least one person in an American uniform, I could ask the way and everything would be all right. But I had not seen a living creature since the lieutenant deserted me. The quiet pressed on my eardrums, and the sound of my own heavy breathing deafened me when I tried to listen.

Then I thought of mines, and I began to inspect closely every inch of ground before stepping on it. This made the going slow, which irritated me.

Heading straight up the mountain, I hoped to regain sight of the saddle formation with the promised grove of trees on it. I developed the habit of taking ten steps, inspecting the ground closely before each one, and then standing still to look and listen a few seconds. I was shocked when I looked up after finishing a set of steps and saw at close range a gory sight. What had once been a mule now had its head, neck, and shoulders blown away. Blood spattered the rocks, and bits of flesh and entrails hung from the scrubby bushes.

That was the clincher. I turned around on the spot and headed down the mountain. About a hundred yards down, I came across the loose ends of a telephone wire. I recognized it as American, thanks to Basic Signal Corps Training class, and began following it. An explosion behind me, followed instantly by the whine of heavy metal flying overhead, made me fall instinctively forward on my belly. A few seconds later another landed farther to the right, and then another a little farther on. Since the shells were falling farther away each time, I decided to run for it. As I scrambled downward amid sliding rocks, disregarding the thought of mines, the explosions began walking back toward me. They were now on direct level with my position. Clearly, this was the appropriate time for a miracle. As my feet slipped from under me, I tumbled amid a landslide of rocks, down the steep slope. Blindly, I clawed for a handhold with my right hand while clutching my camera desperately with my left. I landed with a grunt in the middle of a sandbagged pit among a surprised three-man mortar crew. This was obviously no time for introductions. We all huddled in a tangled mass of arms and legs while rocks rained down and explosions straddled us.

When it was over we sat up, and the three men looked at me. I waited for someone to ask me what the hell I was doing there, but they didn't even look curious. I asked, instead, "Where's the trail back down, fellows?"

One of them pointed over the side of the pit with a thumb and said, "Right there."

It was a different trail from the one I had come up. It didn't lead past the company CP. I was so chagrined that I didn't want to tell anyone about my failure to reach the mountaintop. When I finally managed to stumble on my jeep, I packed up my camera and got in, ready to call it a day. However, I wasn't the one calling the plays that day.

Driving back, I heard the sound of an explosion very close to the road. Looking back, I saw dirt settling to the ground and a cloud of gray smoke rising about fifty yards away. It struck me that this road might be under enemy observation, though I hadn't bothered to notice on the G-2 map. I determined then and there to find out just how fast that jeep could go. As I gained speed, I heard another explosion behind me. I couldn't tell just how far away; I was too busy driving to look back. The next one needed no guess; I saw it. Silently, a couple tons of dirt lifted from the ditch beside the road, no more than ten yards ahead of the jeep, and shot straight up. Almost immediately I was beside it and the jolt of the blast hit me. When I was past, I had a good load of dirt in the jeep and on me. Evidently the shell had sunk too far into the soft, wet earth to allow shrapnel to fly in any direction but up. There may have been other shells thrown at me, but I was cursing too loudly to hear them.

When I got back home I found that the other team had just returned from the CPLO's place. Lt. Southworth had told them that he had been at the Corps HQ arranging an investigation and search for the body of Pete Ratoff. Pete, the younger brother of Hollywood movie director Gregory Ratoff, had come into the company with the first arrivals at Fort Sam Houston. He quickly became one of the best-liked men in the outfit. His bald head, smiling face, and thick accent had been a natural for comedy, and his wit made the show complete.

He had his own prescription for photographic art. The last time I saw Pete, he was shooting street scenes in a picturesquely blasted little town. He was doing the same sort of thing at another location when the Germans began to bomb it. His body was never found, as far as we knew. What was found was his camera, set on a tripod and still running on its electric motor.

During the month we had been living in our half-gone, straw-lined little home, the Vicelli/Jones/Ericson team had completed two stories, both of which required driving south rather than north. One was a Red Cross doughnuts-and-smiles ceremony, and the other was the repairing of a railroad. This not-very-impressive track record was due to Vicelli's ailments. He divided his time between having an examination at every field hospital he could find, sitting around the house complaining of terrible pain, and making trips back to the company headquarters to tell of his battlefield exploits. Jones often rode with us to shoot what film he could without cutting in on my stories. Finally, their team was called back to the company HQ. Vicelli was sent to a hospital and transferred out, Ericson became a Corps courier, and Jones accepted a job in the lab.

By this time the front had moved up a couple of miles, and we felt we were losing too much time on the road. We decided to look for a more convenient place, farther up.

That evening, at the CPLO's house, we and another team that was assigned to the division flanking ours decided to join forces, find a house, and move in together to share foraging and mess duties. The other team barely contained the larger-than-life characters of Bob Heller as movie man, Yale Lapidus as still man, and Reno Frate as driver.

Heller was the only born comedian I have ever met. If there was a situation that Bob could not meet with a wisecrack, I never saw it. I was to see him white with fear, wisecracking. I saw him groaning in pain, wisecracking. He was a natural at imitating other people's voices and expressions. Accents were meat for him.

Yale Lapidus, whose trademark was a dripping nose controlled by an ever-present roll of toilet paper stuffed in his field jacket pocket, liked to have his name accented on the first syllable rather than the usual second. If you put the stress on the "i", he would only grin and giggle through his teeth. He would grin and giggle through his teeth on almost any occasion, whether it was the hottest point of an argument or the high spot of a joke. He had an even temper, and sailed along peacefully through storm and calm. The only thing capable of bringing him out of his tranquility was an argument on the relative merits of the Rollieflex as opposed to the Speed Graphic. He was a Rollie man to the core, but managed to use the Graphic with unusual success throughout the war.

Reno Frate was an insatiable souvenir collector. He was Italian-born, with a hardly understandable accent. His mania for collecting souvenirs began with pistols but later included German prisoners, at which he proved surprisingly good. His "collecting" ultimately included hot machine gun slugs in inappropriate places, though fortunately they were not fatal. His favorite pastime was firing his pistols out the window at tin cans. This was naturally somewhat disturbing to the native population.

With these characters under the same roof only a fool

would expect a dull moment, and the dull moments never came.

*****

I was intrigued for some time by what appeared to be an ancient little town high on the mountainside above the road we traveled nearly every day. We learned that it was called Sesto Campano. One morning we drove up the winding road leading to the town. When we arrived we looked it over, with an eye to protection from artillery fire. The town was in a sort of step in the mountainside, and the peak rising above it faced the German lines. It seemed completely immune to artillery except for long-range howitzers, and it had no military installations, so we considered it as safe as you could get.

Later we took the other team up for their approval. Our resident Italian, Frate, did the translating. He summoned the mayor of the town who showed us the unoccupied and unfurnished lower floor of a house. It wasn't the Ritz, but we took it.

The town certainly measured its age in hundreds of years. The solidly constructed houses had walls over a foot and a half thick, and were built of gray stone in the ancient architecture of that part of the world, which gave the facades a foreboding drabness. The interiors, however, filled with furniture appearing almost as old as the houses, were ornate to the point of giddiness

The cobblestone streets were narrow. Many were built on such steep slopes that they consisted of steps, for at least part of their length. Open sewers ran down the middle. On each side of the streets rose the outwardly austere houses, built one against the other, so it was almost impossible to tell where one left off and the next began.

On one side of the town, the steep mountain rose at least two hundred feet to the peak. On two sides were sheer drops varying from two or three hundred feet on one side, to about fifty on the other. The cliffs on the shallower side were reinforced with huge rocks forming a sort of wall beginning at the bottom of the cliff, continuing up to the level of the town, then built up some fifteen to twenty feet higher as a thick wall.

Had Sesto Campano been defended by the Germans, it could have held off an infantry attack almost as well as when it had been built long ago, with a very similar purpose in mind. However, in this war, it had not been touched. While we were there it was strafed only once by a single German fighter plane, for no apparent reason, but that was the extent of any kind of invasion.

So much the better. I often thought, as I gazed out over the ancient piazza, that large modern cities should be destroyed rather than a small piece of living history such as this little town. The cities could be built up again in much the same style, and probably with many improvements. But this could never be replaced. Though I saw numerous historical "sights" later on, I never had the same feeling for them as I had for Sesto Campano.

I could never imagine gladiators clanking around in armor in the Coliseum, but I could see, with my own eyes, burros loaded with twigs stumbling up the cobblestone streets of Sesto Campano. I didn't have to close my eyes and imagine magnificent stone columns; I could walk on top of this wall and poke my carbine through the loopholes where long-gone soldiers of the Roman Empire had rested their *ballistae*.

We came to know several of the townspeople quite well, and had a civilian visitor or two nearly every night. They were always willing to return friendliness if we offered it first, and we were invited into their homes on many occasions. The mayor made weekly visits to ask if we were comfortable, or if there was something he could do for us.

The only person to behave in a manner that reminded us of the denizens of Naples was a young woman of about twenty-two or twenty-three. She said she had recently come from Rome to stay with her uncle's family. It was never quite clear how she had managed to get through both German and American lines.

She invited us to her uncle's house several times and asked for chocolate and cigarettes, which we gave her and which she always put away for future use. When she began to ask too many questions about subjects we couldn't see should interest her, we half-decided she was a spy (albeit a pretty inept one) and plied her with a constant stream of outlandish misinformation

We had the occasional guests from the company, curious about our little town and our relatively plush life. If they stayed only a day or so, they only had to help with the cooking and dishwashing. If their stay was protracted, we subtly suggested they get out and scrounge their share of the chow.

To brighten our diet somewhat, we made contact with the town baker, a middle-aged lady who was only too happy to bake cakes and cookies for us in exchange for a little sugar and baking chocolate. We also gave her powdered eggs and salt. She furnished the flour, knowledge, work, and oven. Her flour wasn't perhaps the best grade for cakes; it was probably intended for dark Italian bread. But to us the cakes were amazingly good. No matter how large she made them at our repeated requests for more quantity, they never lasted more than one meal.

During this time, because of the different development techniques for movie and still stories, Bob Heller and I worked together on occasion, while Lannigan would go with Lapidus. One day Heller and I went out to get what we could on a pending attack against another worthless, but defended, hill. We arrived early in the morning at the company OP we had chosen as the most likely spot to get good pictures.

The OP was on the top floor of a two-story house in a deserted and nearly-destroyed village on a hillside. It was about five hundred yards across a narrow valley from the German positions on the hill just opposite. It was within perfect observation range of the enemy. Perhaps the only reason the Germans had not blasted it with artillery shells was that they had not yet noticed the observers' scopes staring at them from behind thick curtains covering the windows. Even so, the situation was tenuous at best.

A heavy haze hanging in the valley was an advantage in terms of hiding, but also a great hindrance to the post's own observations. With the naked eye we could see the flashes of mortars, machine guns, and rifles from the German troops at the top of the hill opposite. The Americans working themselves slowly and painfully up from the floor of the valley were barely visible.

It was possible to peer through a crack in the curtain and see glimpses of the action in which men were fighting and dying, but it was utterly impossible to get it on film. We watched what we could see of the battle for a while and realized that there would be no pictures for us thatmorning. Heller and I decided to leave, as each additional person in the OP increased the chances of its being discovered. To go back, we had to climb a trail over the top of the mountain behind us and on to the road where we had left the jeep.

As we climbed the rocky trail, Heller panted, "Damn shame about that haze. Perfect place to shoot from there."

"Yeah," I panted back. "Grandstand seat."

Then, as if on cue, a quick series of about eight loud explosions behind us sent us sprawling. We lay, face down, hiding under our helmets while rocks rained from the sky. When the noise finally stopped, Heller looked up, still on his stomach, and said "Hey, you know what I'm thinkin'?"

I was having the same thought. We scrambled to our feet and ran farther up the trail to where we could look back toward the valley through the scrubby trees. Through a thin cloud of dust we saw that the building we had just left had disappeared into a pile of rubble.

I touched Heller's shoulder and said, "Let's go." I felt a little sick.

*****

Time was passing quickly. Even though we wrote the date on our captions every day, we were almost surprised to find it was only three days until Christmas. We had no plans yet for a celebration and couldn't think of much to do anyway. We could remind each other what day it was and sing a couple of carols to the tune of an extra bottle of good, dry Guinea red. Instead, Lannigan and I decided to turn in the best Christmas picture story made that year in Italy. Most of the other teams had the standard stories in mind—church services, gifts from home, fancy turkey dinners in the rear areas. We found something different: a turkey dinner was to be cooked in a rear area and carried to the front line for the men engaged in combat. These men had been living for days in mud and snow with nothing to eat except cold K-rations.

After talking to the regimental chaplain who was arranging the meal, we began shooting early the morning of the twenty-fifth. We started with the kitchen where the food was cooked near the regimental CP. The meal consisted of hot canned turkey, peas mixed in mashed potatoes, cranberry jelly, peach cobbler, and coffee. These were dumped into separate thermal cans and piled in the back of a jeep.

After shooting these scenes, we followed the jeep over the mountain roads until it went as far as it could. Here the cans were taken out of the jeep and lashed onto the backs of mules. Shooting pictures all the way, we followed the mule team up and down rocky trails, forded a river, and finally came to a little ravine. This was as far as a mule could go. The cans were transferred from the backs of mules to the backs of men, and the spirit of Christmas staggered up the ravine.

When we finally arrived, the only people in sight were the men who had carried the cans, the chaplain, and ourselves. The chaplain, having sent out a messenger, explained the situation to us. It was dangerous for men to congregate in one place. They had to feed the group a squad at a time.

The first squad of ten or twelve men straggled in. The prayer offered by the chaplain was punctuated by intermittent machine gun and mortar fire from the ridge just over our heads.

This was it, the picture we wanted: Christmas in combat, 1943. This was the scene to reach the hearts of people sitting at home warm and comfortable, safe and prosperous, stuffing themselves.

It was an enormous contrast, but the two scenes were joined by prayer to the same God. The men knelt in mud-caked uniforms, bearded and dirty, with that tired look that gets into the eyes of men long in combat. Helmets were respectfully removed in spite of the danger of mortar shells. Rifles covered with dried mud, though, were still slung on sloping shoulders. And there were the food cans in an olive drab line with the carriers standing behind them, heads bowed, serving spoons in hand. At the front of the group stood the chaplain, marching through with his flock, helmet in hand, asking the Prince of Peace to be there in the midst of war. And He was, I knew.

I watched the men slide down into the ravine one at a time. Each did roughly the same thing. When he reached the bottom he would stop a few seconds and slowly take in the whole scene. Then he would walk over to the cans of food and look in. Next, he would walk away a few paces and sit down to wait. The expression on his face never changed. I was still green. I expected to see a big smile light up each man's face as he learned what was in store. I was disappointed. Tired men don't smile easily.

But I realized I was seeing something one seldom sees outside the boundaries of war: complete acceptance of a situation, good, bad, or worse. I made the mistake of thinking it resignation at first, but it was something better than that. This was not giving up, the folding of hands and drifting with the current, this was a virile and strong-willed determination not to be licked, to save energy for the thing that counted. These men accepted snow, mud, frozen hands and feet, the necessity of sleeping in a water-logged foxhole, the ever-present likelihood of being killed or of killing other men. They had stopped "sweating it out." If they were to be relieved, they would be relieved. Of course they counted the days and complained when they could get together, but it didn't eat at their minds.

This acceptance was a child of necessity, probably the necessity of keeping one's sanity. Its depth must include not only acceptance of the hardships and utter boredom of living under conditions undreamed of before, but of personal danger, fear, the sight of friends killed and mangled in the fury of exploding shells, and of killing other human beings without benefit of personal animosity.

Therefore, when these men were confronted with a short chance to relax, to think of something else and to have the real food they had been dreaming of, they were able to accept it quietly, without undue emotion. They accepted the chaplain's prayer in the same way.

In the line the men carried neither packs nor mess kits. The flash of any bright object was enough to bring down an artillery barrage. For this reason, no mess kits were brought with the food either. Therefore, as each man passed through the line, he held out the torn-open waxed container of a K-ration dinner or the steel shell of his helmet. For utensils, folded pieces of paper or cardboard were used. I made several close-up shots of men eating in this manner. I wasn't offered a smile nor did I ask for one. In fact, most of the men hardly seemed to notice what I was doing.

This is how I found it from then on. Those men who were most closely exposed to death and hardship, those men who had learned to accept war and danger as another state of living, were never surprised by the presence of photographers. They were not even curious. With their profound acceptance, all persons who shared their situation were leveled to the same category.

*****

As we bounced back over the rocky mountain road after finishing our Christmas story, we began to think about our own celebration. We would take the next day off and call it Christmas. Lannigan's idea of a celebration of any kind began with chow, so we stopped by the ration dump to see our good friend, the sergeant in charge. The sergeant was in fine red-wine spirits and gave us the biggest frozen turkey he had left.

Merrily we headed home bearing what we figured was quite a triumphal acquisition. When we walked in the door, carrying the frosty carcass like a treasure chest, we were astonished to see two beautiful naked birds even larger than ours lying in state on the table, surrounded by four broadly grinning faces. The other team, accompanied by fellow photographer Sammy Goldstein, had got the jump on us.

While we were figuring up how much turkey each of us would get when the three birds were divided seven ways, three other men stomped in with a frightened, squawking turkey on the hoof.

It began to look like a white Christmas after all.

Four big turkeys, though, were a little too much even with our large appetites. We decided to have only the three frozen ones, which were already thawing. We put the live one in a coop outside that was already occupied by our neighbor's two scrawny chickens. Then we tramped en masse across the street to see our friend, the baker. As usual, she was quite willing, for a cut, to bake us a couple of cakes, size extra-large, plus the turkeys, in her bread oven.

The next morning after breakfast Lannigan, the self-appointed chef, drew up a list of the things we would need for the dressing and fixings. We headed out and when we got back, with only a few substitutions, we had all the makings. Frate and Lannigan washed their hands, rolled up their sleeves and went into the huge borrowed bowl up to the elbows. The rest of us stood around tossing out advice from the sidelines. By seven in the evening, we had all the canned vegetables opened and heated, coffee made, and the stock of wine up to the inexhaustible level, even with the considerable nipping that had been going on all day.

And then came the turkeys.

I can't remember ever eating a better meal.

When most people think of Christmas away from home, there is usually an element of homesickness in the musings. Naturally I thought of what it would be like at home. I remembered past Christmas celebrations—the tree, the gifts, the dinner, the congregation of family and friends. Then a question came to me: *Would I enjoy this Christmas at home while all these other men were here?* The answer was an emphatic *No*.

This was the second wartime Christmas away from home for most of us—the first had been spent in North Carolina—and it wasn't quite as hard to take as the first, especially since we had finally found some sense of purpose to our army lives. Homesickness is a disease that can only flourish in solitude and, heaven knows, none of us had that this Christmas.

By this time, of course, the Christmas festivities had been completed in Tunis, far to the south and across the waters. Winston Churchill had had his own fine meal. Around his table had sat Generals Dwight Eisenhower, Harold Alexander, Maitland Wilson, and other important people. While we relaxed that afternoon in Sesto Campano, we could not have dreamed that our lives, or deaths, had already been decided there across the Mediterranean as those great men planned to launch something called "Operation Shingle."

4
With the Rangers

What is war?

The American civilian of World War II, who stayed home safe and comfortable, might speak of noble sacrifice by gallant men, then go on to speak of the home front: rationing and hoarding, black markets and inconveniences, tears of parting and tears of grief, rousing speeches, parading soldiers, contributions to hundreds of charities, and bundles of cast-offs for deserving people. He would speak of heroics on the other side of the world, and of a country's pride. War, to him, meant patriotism and sacrifice.

His words would be meaningless to me.

A newspaper correspondent who had wet his feet in the marshy filth at the edge of war might answer with a thousand adjectives describing terrible scenes of enemy bombers, searchlights and anti-aircraft guns, falling bombs, broken buildings and broken flesh, women and children dying pitifully and without explanation. He also might speak of high strategy and show me on a map why certain men had decided certain other men must die. Clearly, war for him was horrible necessity and horrible death.

Finally, I could have asked the combat soldier. Surely he, who had lived in the entrails of the beast, who had been a part of it, who had created it and absorbed it, could give me my answer. But *he* would not speak.

No one can imagine the scream of a falling bomb, the flutter of a mortar shell, the swoosh of an artillery projectile, or the zip of a machine gun bullet. The sound might be reproduced artificially, but it would be meaningless outside its deadly context. A person might quiver in fear at the bottom of a muddy foxhole. He might even clutch the dirt in his fingers and push his face into the ground while praying aloud. But he could never reproduce in his imagination the genuine anticipation of violent death.

One can feel a momentary fear in a speeding automobile, yet unless this fear is sustained and recharged for days and weeks at a time, he cannot have an inkling of the combat soldier's emotion.

Whatever it is that makes a man's complexion take on the hue of a corpse, that gives his eye that blank stare, makes him smile as he contemplates the shredded stump of his leg in anticipation of a trip home, that makes him curse the mention of flag-waving patriotism and makes him fight and die for foreign real estate he never wanted; all of that, too, is a part of war.

Machines are also part of war. From the tenderly cared-for rifle of the slogging infantryman to the delicate mechanisms of sleek death from the air, machines are the hands of war while men are the brains. Machines are loved like wives and hated with the fury of the soul. Machines can protect a man's life or mangle his body.

War is hatred of the enemy, and love of companions. War is fear of death, yet war is valor in battle. War is every emotion man is capable of, yet war is also morphine. It is precision of planning, yet endless confusion. It is exhaustion, yet the zenith of alertness. War is life and war is death.

War is all these things, yet its full nature must remain hidden beyond the light of expression. The men who serve know only that it is impossible to reconstruct in memory the things they swore they could never forget.

*****

Soon after New Year's Day, which passed without a side glance, we were told at division CP that soon the whole 45th Division was going to pull back to Naples for a rest, now that

Naples was ours. That would leave us without an outfit to cover, and we did not like the thought of "breaking in" another group of officers in the replacement division. We had put in considerable time and effort cultivating a cooperative relationship with our current officers, and depended on the story tips we received from them.

At the same time more and more teams were being ordered back to the company. This began to look strange and, even stranger, the first teams called in had not yet been sent out again. We worried for another week or so without official news. Finally it came. We, too, were to report to company HQ within three days.

The return was like a family reunion and made us feel a little like conquering heroes. After we had carried in our stuff, we went to report formally to Capt. Morehouse.

The man who seldom wasted a smile on a mere enlisted man returned our salutes with a grin.

"Have you been assigned quarters?" he asked in an almost-friendly voice.

We told him we had.

"Well, as soon as you get your equipment arranged, turn your cameras in to Camera Repair for a checkup. After that just take it easy. You won't have any duties for a few days."

"Sir, could you tell us how long we'll be here?" Lannigan asked.

"I don't know yet." The answer didn't sound sincere.

"Will we go back with the 45th, sir?" I asked.

"We'll have to see." After a pause, he added, "I understand from the lab that you two have been turning in some good work." I think my mouth hung open a little. I had never heard him compliment man nor beast. I dusted a speck of dust off my sleeve, where I would have been wearing my PFC stripe if I had ever bothered to sew it on.

"Thank you, sir."

"Well, that's all. Just take it easy for a few days and don't worry."

With that we were brushed out of the office wondering, more than ever, what was going on.

When I turned my camera in at Camera Repair, the repairman looked at it and pretended to pull his hair out.

"My God!" he screamed. "What the hell ya been doing with this camera?"

"It's muddy up there," I answered. "Besides, what's wrong with it?"

"Nothing," he grinned, "except it's dirtier than hell. You should see some of them that's been coming in."

He took the lens board out and began to dismantle the front shutter.

"The boys at the lab say you and Lannigan been shooting some damn good stuff."

At that moment I felt that it all just might be worthwhile after all.

Walking toward the lab, I met Bernie Kline, one of the men who had come back to the company from the Army Pictorial Service. Bernie was one of the best cameramen in the outfit. I considered him a good friend even though we had known each other a comparatively short time. After we exchanged greetings, he smilingly said, "I hear you're quite a hot operator around the front."

"That's a lot of shit, Bernie," I said seriously. "You know what goes on up there."

He was serious, too, when he said, "Yeah, I do, and I'm telling you to take it easy."

Praise is praise, and a good reputation is a good thing to have, but all this seemed a little out of bounds. As I walked toward the lab I wasn't exactly worrying, but something seemed not quite right.

At the lab, I met Larry Jones at his new job of contact printer. When I greeted him he hardly smiled. He looked straight at me a while before saying simply, "Hello, Bell." There was something in those words that sounded almost like pity.

"How ya like your new job?" I asked warmly.

"O.K.," he answered slowly, and then added, "You don't get shot at here."

I couldn't think of an answer to that one, so I asked, "How's my exposure been coming lately?

"'Bout right." He was still looking at me a little too closely. I couldn't figure what was wrong with the man. "Want to see some of them?"

"Yeah, sure," I answered eagerly, glad of something to break up this odd conversation.

He led me into the next room, closed the door and turned on a white light. The room was exclusively for the lab's dry work and files. We were alone. After shoving a numbered list of work orders at me and pulling a box of negatives off a shelf, he leaned back on the edge of the work bench and resumed his contemplation of me. I tried to ignore his eyes as I thumbed through the stack of negatives. Finally, he broke the spell.

"I been watching your stuff, Bell."

"Yeah? How is it?" I almost didn't want to hear his answer.

"I don't like it." He was dead serious. It surprised me and I turned to meet his gaze.

"How come?" I asked.

"Look, Cliff, I've been up there and I know what's behind these shots. Believe me, it's not worth it."

So that was it.

"No, Larry, you've got the wrong slant. When you were there, I didn't know what was going on. I've got better sense now." It was the truth; I was learning fast.

"Don't give me that crap. I've been watching your negs all along." He sounded almost angry. "I'm telling you, take it easy or you're going to get tied up in a mattress cover one of these days."

O.K., he was right. Every day I had been at the front I had

been realizing it more and more. But what the hell can you do? It was a trap. You had to get pictures, and the only ones worth getting were in places where the shooting was. Take it easy—sure. But how?

More teams came in during the next few days. Cameras and jeeps were put in tiptop condition and we had orders to turn in any clothing or equipment that was not in good shape. We were all doing a lot of guessing as to details but it didn't take a crystal gazer to know that something big was brewing. We figured it would be a new beach landing somewhere, and we were pretty well convinced that it would be in southern France, or Greece.

In the meantime, we did just as we had been told, and took it easy. Most of the time we didn't even bother to get up for breakfast. During the day, we either wandered around the company area getting in the way of the HQ people who still had a job to do, or walked around exploring the little town of Caiazzo. At night, there were long and loud bull sessions, poker games, visits to the homes of the local people, or maybe visits to the usual dives for the usual reasons: red wine, homely women, discordant song.

Just as we were beginning to get sick of inactivity, the word was posted on the bulletin board, along with a list of about twenty names, to report to a particular schoolroom on the second floor of our building the next morning at eight o'clock. The names Lannigan, Owen, and Bell could not be missed. That night, the floor seemed particularly hard and I got very little sleep.

The next morning, every man whose name had appeared on the list was there ahead of time. No officer had shown yet, so we relaxed around the room, sitting on the little school desks, on the window sills or, in the accepted G.I. manner, on the floor. The talk floating around was quieter and less lively than the usual. It was almost dignified. We all had our own ideas as to why we were there, and we were waiting to see how right we were.

I had my back to the door talking with Art Eliot, a movie man who worked with Bernie Klein, when the room suddenly became quiet. I broke off in mid-sentence. Turning, I saw a strange captain we didn't know come through the door. He walked around to the teacher's desk and dropped a pile of papers on it.

"All right, men," he announced, sweeping the entire room with a slow, deliberate gaze. "Sit down and let's have a roll call."

After reading off the list of names, he looked the room over again before beginning. "I guess you men have a pretty good idea of what this is all about, but I'm going to make it official. It's going to be an amphibious landing. Where, I can't tell you. I don't know either."

Well, there it was—official. I didn't feel any different, though. Maybe I was a little relieved now that I knew what we were in for, but that was all. It was bound to be rough, but so would anything we got. Maybe I wouldn't come through it, but if I did, it would have been an experience worth having.

The captain talked on for several minutes about supplies, team lineups (our team was still intact, thank heaven), equipment, and so on, then asked for questions. There were none. We didn't know enough about the deal to ask questions.

He resumed talking. As he explained the details of our assignments and operations, he came to the part where the word "volunteer" cropped up. As that sank in, I found myself unable to look at Lannigan. Then as the words "jump with the paratroopers" floated across the room, I felt a drop of cold sweat trace a course from my armpit to my elbow. When the captain asked to see hands, I kept mine firmly where they were. I found I was looking across the room over the tops of heads. There wasn't a sound—and no hands were up.

"O.K., men. That's all," the captain said briskly. He picked up his papers and walked out of the room. Nobody else left.

My nerves relaxed as if an electrical circuit had been broken. I leaned back in my seat and looked at Lannigan. He was looking at me, so we just stared at each other a few seconds. Finally I said, "My Gawd, I was scared you would stick up your hand."

Without a smile, he answered. "Maybe you think I wasn't sweating about you."

We both knew that neither of us was going to let the team be broken up by anything we could control.

Pushing his way through the crowd with an ear-to-ear smile, Snuffy came up. "Boy, I'm glad you guys didn't hold up your hands," he said.

When we got back to our room we were met by one of the orderly room clerks, who was looking for us.

"Ah," he said, "here you guys are. Capt. Herbert wants to see you in his room right away."

"Who in hell is Capt. Herbert?"

"He's in charge of you guys. Didn't you know it?"

"Never heard of him. Where does he live?"

"Third floor. Top of the stairs."

Now, what the hell can this be, we asked each other as we climbed the stairs we had just come down. The only reason I could imagine for the officer in charge to want to see us was that we were being dropped from the operation. I couldn't tell if what I felt was relief or disappointment.

The door at the top of the stairs was open, and inside we saw a man bending over in the process of packing or unpacking a foot locker. He heard us as we stopped at the doorway and looked up. We saw a pair of silver bars on his collar and asked, "Captain Herbert?"

"Yes, come in." He motioned with a shirt and went on packing. "Sit down." He pointed to his folding cot. "You're Lannigan and Bell?"

"Yes, sir," we answered together, and sat down on the cot.

"Have you got all your replacements on your salvaged clothing yet?"

"Yes, sir," said Lannigan.

"Have you got your cameras back from Repair?"

"Yes, sir," I answered. I wished he would get to the point.

He tied two socks together. "They tell me you two have been doing some good work lately." He took a pair of pink trousers out of the foot locker and tossed them on a pile of other clothes. "Did either of you volunteer to go with the paratroopers?"

"No, sir." Heaven help me, I thought.

"Good," the captain said, and stood to face us. "It wouldn't have done you any good anyway. I've got another job lined up for you two. I'm assigning you to cover the Rangers."

So this was what all the flattery had been leading up to. This was the biggest tribute of all, but maybe the last. I felt a little weak, despite knowing we were being honored with the job of going on an assault landing with the toughest of all elite Army units. All we knew about them at that time was that they had been trained by the British Commandos to be an advance strike force behind enemy lines. Most people we knew spoke of them with respect, but not a lot of envy. It seemed to be considered something of a suicide outfit. Certainly it incurred a lot of casualties. Through all my other feelings, though, I felt pride at being placed in a class with these highly-trained professionals, and pride can hold you together when all else fails.

I had no illusions. It was going to be rougher in the first few hours of this landing than it had been in all the rough spots I'd experienced so far. But this superior officer had said "assign," not "volunteer. I couldn't back out, which made me confidently fatalistic.

Before we left the company to join the Rangers at their training area, a couple of pictures were taken of our team, along with our newly washed jeep. As I grinned at the camera, I had the fleeting thought that they would probably hold these pictures for Public Relations Office release as soon as they got word that we had been killed in action.

Me, Snuffy Owen and Cecil Lannigan, with his ever-present pipe.

*****

At Ranger Force headquarters in suburban Pozzouli, north of Naples, we were left strictly alone as far as the Rangers' training activities were concerned. We never received an order, since we were not attached for administration, nor were we ever offered suggestions, requests, or even information. I sometimes wondered if anyone knew we were there. We asked for and received a schedule of the training activities and, from that, were able to plan our own shooting schedule. Unmolested and unassisted, we went happily about making our story.

We had heard these men were tough and now we had proof. The physical training we saw made our own basic training seem like the local fat ladies' exercise class. A daily schedule included such things as rifle calisthenics for an hour before breakfast. After breakfast, two hours of heavy physical exertion, including violent games on the sandy beach and group exercises such as lifting, passing, and throwing huge logs. After that, a hike in the mountains behind the beach until lunch. After lunch, another hike of about fifteen miles, mostly at double time. From then till supper, firing on the range with everything from M1s and tommy guns to bazookas and mortars.

The Rangers' weapons were light and small, and every man knew how to use them all, as well as most of the enemy's, though each man was given the opportunity to choose his own personal weapons. Seeing a Ranger with an M1 rifle slung on his shoulder, a .45-caliber pistol on one hip and a bayonet on the other, with a hunting knife in his boot, you could be sure nothing was there for decoration.

The officers were young, and their commander, Lt. Col. William O. Darby, was the youngest of his rank in the Army. These officers were just as tough as the men under them.

In theory, every man was a volunteer, but in talking with them, we found that a large number were really refugees from the stinking repple depples—the G.I. term for Replacement Depots—of North Africa. These camps were where replacement troops, some barely out of training camp and all very inexperienced, waited to be assigned to fighting units. The depots were little more than ill-run supply dumps of human pawns. So, bored, essentially ignored, and when not ignored insulted, young soldiers jumped at the opportunity to volunteer for the roughest outfit in the Army. Once in they had not found the going any easier physically, but here they had an outfit of their own to take pride in, a fine young tradition to build and uphold. They got decent treatment from their officers. All things considered they, they were satisfied.

We had a fulltime shooting schedule that could last as long as two weeks, but we expected the embarkation order at any time. We took shots of the physical training, hikes, and range firing. These were all old and generally uninteresting subjects, but the way the Rangers did them was unusual. For instance, they did not fire their weapons in handbook style. We saw snipers' rifles adding up amazing scores. We saw M1s fired from the hip. We saw mortars fired by only one man, who held the tube that was resting on the ground with one hand, while loading it with the other.

We got an inkling of what we were in for when the training program gradually began to stress street-fighting techniques. This particularly unpleasant type of personal mayhem was one of the specialties of the Rangers, but I had never witnessed such intimate barbarity, and it left me with a very poor impression.

The climax of the street-fighting program was to be a simulated battle in the next town, Bagnoli, where our company had originally landed. Simulated it was to be, at least as closely as the Rangers ever came to simulating such things. They were to use live ammunition fired into the air, and concussion grenades instead of the fragmentation kind. It promised good pictures, so we were out bright and early.

We deployed at the waterfront and worked through the town. With one squad to a street, we crouched in doorways and dashed across street intersections, with men firing into the air when imaginary snipers were pointed out. Some of the men thought it a terrible waste of ammunition to fire at nothing, so telephone wires and ceramic insulators were "accidently" clipped off all over town.

When the squad I had joined came to an open square with a little park in the middle, the squad leader gave the signal to halt. The men took cover in doorways and niches. I went up to the head of the column to get a shot of the men as they made a dash across the open space. First, several smoke grenades were tossed out to screen the movement.

In an actual situation, the bushes in the little park might

have hidden a machine gun, so the squad leader threw a concussion grenade into it. The grenade went wide. It skidded along the sidewalk and across the street to the feet of three children who were there in spite of previous orders and ample warning. The explosion broke plate glass windows halfway down the block, scattered merchandise into the street, and knocked the legs out from under the children.

I started toward the spot, racking out my lens for a close-up as I ran. Just when I rounded a corner at full speed, a hidden man let out a long burst from his tommy gun tilted up from the hip. The stream of bullets must have passed a foot above my head, and for the next week, everything I heard sounded as it if were coming through a telephone with a bad connection.

When I got to the place where the explosion had occurred, getting pictures was out of the question. A huge crowd of wailing Italians had appeared. Two of the children were only frightened. The mother, who had allowed them to stand and gawk in the middle of a military maneuver, was in hysterics. The third little girl had a few cuts on her leg. She was carried, scared and screaming, into a G.I. ambulance that had been standing by waiting for this, or something similar, to happen.

When the show was over, the battalion was assembled. They marched back to Pozzuoli at double time two thirds of the way, led by an officer who had been taken to the hospital the day before with two broken bones in his left foot.

*****

The next day, Lannigan, Snuffy, and I went a few miles up the beach to cover preparations for the 1st Battalion's practice combat landing. When we arrived, several men were in the process of burying T.N.T. charges at twenty-foot intervals along the edge of the water. Several rows were placed at right angles, leading across the beach to the steep incline about a hundred yards back. These, when fired by a remote electrical detonator, were to represent the mines we might expect when the real thing came off. Of course, these too were not strictly toothless.

Three machine guns, located strategically on the top of the bluff, were to furnish realistic battle noises and form a close tracer crossfire above the men's heads as they came up the beach. To make it even more realistic, men would stand at the top of the bluff tossing down concussion grenades, rolls of fused primer cord, rockets, flares, and tear gas grenades. We could see it was going to make a pretty picture. The only thing wrong was that it was all going to happen in total darkness.

We planned to shoot this show from the shore to get an idea of what went on, and then come in with the 3rd Battalion in the boats on the next practice. From what we saw that night, however, we realized it would be murder for an open camera to go through that mixture of sand and water. We would have no resulting pictures of the second practice, and would risk not having an operable camera for the real landing. The cameras would have to stay home during our turn at the practice landing.

The moon was rising earlier every night, and was high already when the sun set. If we had known anything about landing operations, we would have realized the significance of that. We knew only that we were able to make out the long white tails, preceded by dark blobs, as the barges rushed to the shore. It occurred to us that German observers would be able to see as well as we could.

The first wave of barges hit the beach together. They formed a front about two hundred yards wide. Men poured out as the nose ramps dropped. Some jumped to the beach dry while others waded in through chest-deep water. We could see them only faintly in the dim light, but suddenly they were lost amid flashes and the roar of exploding T.N.T. mines. Then machine guns cut loose, and a hail of grenades and flares rained down among the running men. I held my shutter open until I was sure my film registered the planned chaos. Streaking tracers, arcing rockets, and dozens of miscellaneous explosions illuminated the dark. I had time for one more shot before I was in the middle of the battle. Men rushed past in the dark with rifles and tommy guns. A tear gas grenade exploded somewhere nearby. With my eyes streaming water, I grabbed my camera and stumbled blindly down the road. Somewhere behind me an extra-loud explosion went off. Rocks rained down.

The wind cleared my eyes a bit, and I sat down beside the road to light a cigarette. A man came panting up the hill and pushed through the bushes behind me. When he saw me, he sat beside me to catch his breath.

"Getting any pictures?" he asked. I recognized him as one of the men I had talked to in the chow line.

"Yeah, a couple," I answered. He was soaking wet.

"Get your rifle wet?"

"Yeah, damn it. Fell down gettin' out of the boat. Got my cigarettes wet, too." This sounded like a hint so I handed him my pack. He took one and lit it from mine.

Lannigan came striding up the road, and dropped down beside us. He took out his pipe and said, "Did you get your stuff?"

"More or less," I answered. "You?"

"Couldn't see much, but I got something on the film." He stoked his pipe in his usual leisurely manner.

"Look," our drenched companion said, then hesitated. "Are you guys in the Rangers?"

"No, we're Signal Corps," I answered.

"Oh, you're attached to us, huh?" he theorized.

"Nope," said Lannigan, with his pipe still in his teeth. "We're just along for the ride."

"Then you're nothing?" The soldier was confused.

"Just say we're in the Rangers temporarily," I said.

He leaned back and laughed. "Yeah, just say you're in the Rangers for the rest of your life."

Lannigan caught the joke and began to laugh with him. I tried to join in, but I suddenly felt cold, and shivered from the inside out. I knew there was only one way to look at your chances: in the most fatalistic way possible. But joking about it didn't seem to ease my mind.

On the schedule for the following morning were further landing practices, minus fireworks, for the purpose of perfecting the technique of hitting the beaches from the landing barges. Lannigan and I stuffed our cameras, film, and essential accessories into our packs and went along for the training rather than the pictures. Even though our area of expertise was photography, we weren't exempt from doing a little shooting with bullets instead of film. Practice might come in handy should the need arise. We wanted, at the very least, to be introduced to the formalities.

We loaded into the barges from the beach, backed off, and splashed out into the harbor. We circled until all the other barges were loaded, then swung into formation. At the signal to go, the barges roared at the beach, ten abreast in four waves. We were crouching low and ready to dash out as soon as the ramp door dropped. After a few tense minutes we felt the bottom of the boat slide up onto the sand. The door in the nose dropped with a loud clang and we jumped forward. With the powerful engine roaring as the pilot held the barge in position, we ran out the open front of the craft and jumped into ankle-deep water. As we splashed up onto the sand, we fanned out until the flanks of our group met with those of the other groups who had poured out of their barges at the same time. In a solid front, we lunged through the barbed wire entanglement, and headed up a fifteen-foot bank. Without a hitch we completed our exercise just in time for evening chow. Next up would be the real thing.

We drove into Naples for the evening. The Arizona Club, a G.I. hangout and saloon in a basement off Via Roma, was very popular with most of the Rangers, so this is where our tent mates steered us. We spent the long evening drinking some vile mixture that tasted like low-octane gasoline, talking in pantomime with a flock of painted ladies and dodging bottles as they sailed across the room at head level. At about one o'clock someone began punching holes in the ceiling with .45 slugs.

By this time the world was beginning to look as rosy as the three-quarter exposed bosom of the blond dangling from my left shoulder. The MPs, now on the way, seemed inconsequential. I remember objecting violently when a first sergeant dragged me out the back door. After that I recall lighting cigarettes for two good buddies who appeared to be Moroccan soldiers, and later singing "*Roll out the Barrel.*" This was done in three languages simultaneously with a drunken French captain and an ancient, wrinkled Italian woman in an air raid tunnel. Lannigan and Snuffy were asleep in the jeep when I found it, but I have yet to be convinced that I drove it home.

I was awakened next day by the rattling of mess kits heading for noon chow. The thought of coffee came to me like water to a man dying of thirst. Half-dressed, I stumbled to the chow line with my eyes half-closed. There, I met Lannigan.

He greeted me with a grin. "So you finally got up." I hated him. No one had a right to be so cheerful at a time like that.

"Yes," I growled, "but I'm going back to bed."

"You can't," he said.

"Don't make me suffer. Why the hell can't I?"

"You gotta help waterproof the jeep."

"Waterproof the jeep," I repeated.

"Yeh." He said it again, "Waterproof the jeep." He was dead serious.

"I'm sick," I said.

With a good chow of hot Spam, stewed tomatoes, fruit cocktail, and coffee, I recovered amazingly fast. Snuffy had been working most of the morning gumming up the engine of the jeep with some sort of pliable asbestos preparation. There was still quite a bit of work left for us, however, and the three of us worked until almost dark before the job was finished.

That night, reserve candles were burned all over the

area. By dim light, everyone sorted the few essentials we would need and put them in backpacks. Everything else went into the barracks bags, which we then painted with our assigned code numbers. Lannigan and I felt unfortunate that we were unable to take more than a clean set of underwear, a couple of pairs of socks, and a toothbrush. The rest of our packs were crammed with film and cameras. However, when we saw other men carrying mortars, radios, and machine guns, as well as their personal items, we realized we were fortunate.

Late that night, we sat around the tin-can stove burning up the last of our wood and talking. A detail came into the tent and issued each man three D-ration chocolate bars and three boxes of K-rations. This was to be our food ration for the first two days after the landing. There was absolutely no room in our packs, so we determined to carry everything in our pockets. Especially the chocolate.

Up at five-thirty next morning, our team was near the front of the chow line instead of in our usual place at the tail end. There was a feeling of tension among the men. There was very little talk. Personally, despite a dark dread that made my insides feel heavy, I wanted to go quickly and get it over, one way or another.

Soon after breakfast, the order came for the drivers to load up. We tossed our barracks bags, along with camera cases containing all the equipment we were not going to carry on our backs, into the jeep and tied a tarp over them. Then Snuffy drove into the line of vehicles. We shook hands and the line moved out. As we watched him drive off in the convoy, we wondered if we would ever see him or the jeep again. The three of us had made a plan. As soon as the jeep came off the ship, Snuffy would find the PRO (Public Relations Office) at Force CP. That was where we would meet him, or at least try to leave a message for him.

Lannigan and I had talked with the G-2 major and made arrangements to go in with the second of the three waves, which were to hit the beach at two, four, and six a.m. We picked the second wave as the one most likely to serve our purpose, which was to get pictures and stay alive while doing so. The first wave would land in total darkness. So besides being more dangerous than the second, it would offer no opportunity for pictures. We might not live through the second wave's landing if the first had served only to wake up the enemy. However, if we got in safely, it would give us a chance to get our bearings and be ready to make pictures of the third wave, which would come in with early daylight. The disadvantages of our landing with the third wave would be our inability to get pictures of the men coming up onto the beach and, because of the light, the fact that we would make a target for strafing and bombing airplanes while still out on the water.

We were allowed to keep a bed roll that would be loaded into the hold of the ship we were to go on; so after breakfast we rolled them up (around a large core of film), sat down on them and smoked cigarettes until eleven o'clock. At that time we were issued cold Spam sandwiches and reconstituted lemonade since the kitchen had been folded up and loaded that morning.

The order came to fall in with everything we had—full packs, arms, and bed rolls. Thus loaded down, we marched about a mile uphill to the 4th Battalion area, where we were to leave the bed rolls. Only by wholesale puffing, sweating, and struggling was I able to keep up with the Rangers' hard pace. However, when we finally reached our destination and I came out from under my heavy bedroll, I was pleased to notice quite a few red and shiny faces being swabbed with handkerchiefs.

From there it was another two miles or so to the dock where we were to load and, just from habit, the whole battalion traveled most of the way at double time. At the pier there was the usual hour or two of waiting, so Lannigan and I slipped off our packs and got shots of the loading up, which was really the beginning of the story we had been sent to cover.

Finally our unit began to load and we stepped onto the

LCI—Landing Craft Infantry, or amphibious assault ship—which was to ferry us out to our British troop carrier, the Winchester Castle. The spirits of the men perceptibly improved as the shore faded away. At last we were on our way, and it was a relief from the monotony of waiting.

Rangers loading up for amphibious assault of Anzio. Due to censorship regulations, we couldn't give exact location so it was "somewhere in Italy."

As I went about the craft shooting pictures, I found myself picking out faces in my viewfinder and thinking, "Will this man be alive tomorrow?" Finally the thought occurred to me: "Will I?"

After transferring from the LCI to our ship, Lannigan and I were assigned a cabin with two bunks to ourselves by someone who evidently mistook us for civilian correspondents. Almost immediately the call for chow was relayed along the passageways. Supper, as anyone who has ever been a guest of the Royal Navy knows, consisted of mutton and tea.

After chow, cases of hand grenades were broken open and set in the passageways where one and all were invited to help themselves to as many as they felt willing to carry. I took two and hooked the handles under my cartridge belt with a fervent hope that I would not have to use them.

A little later, the call was passed for all troops to get in small groups for a detailed briefing. Lannigan and I waited for our turn and then went into a large cabin that contained a large-scale relief model on a table, and numerous aerial photographs on the walls. A lieutenant from G-2 briefed us.

"We are going to hit a little town called Anzio, south of Rome," he began. I wrote the name down so I didn't have to trust memory when making out my captions. "The rocket barges will soften up the beach from midnight till oh two hundred, day after tomorrow. The first wave will hit at oh two hundred, the second at oh four hundred, and the third at oh six hundred. The first phase of the attack will be the beach; the second: the first street back from the beach, here." He pointed to the street on an aerial map. "The third will be the railroad tracks, here. Force CP will be here, in this hotel, after the third wave lands. By then the first wave should be in the third phase. The 3rd Division will hit south of the town at oh six hundred, and the British at the same time on the north. Till then, it's all our own show."

Much later we learned a bit more of the larger picture. The landing forces were commanded by Maj. General John P. Lucas, C.O. of VI Corps. The forces included the U.S. 3rd Division, the British 1st Division, U.S. 504th and 509th Parachute Infantry Regiments, the British 2nd Special Services Brigade, two commando battalions, and the U.S. 6615th Ranger Force, reinforced by one three-man photo team.

Forty-eight hours was supposed to take us into the Laziali Hills, and beyond that to the three thousand-foot Alban Hills, considered the key to Rome. Then, so the thinking went, the German XIV Corps, with its supply and communications lines cut, would be all but defenseless. The next simple step was for the 36th Division—still not up to strength after its disastrous landing at Salerno and consequent bloody fighting up the Italian boot—to join with the rest of II Corps and the British X Corps on the southern front. They were to make a frontal attack on the main German defense, the Gustav Line, in an attempt to cross the Rapido River and work up the Liri Valley.

After what was assumed would be the inevitable German withdrawal and a quick link-up with the Anzio Forces, there would then be an easy sweep up Highways 6 and 7, right into the Eternal City. Instead, inexcusable bungling by Lt. General Mark Clark, commander of the Fifth Army, resulted in one of the war's bloodiest massacres, beginning at Cassino. Thirty-two thousand men were to bleed and another seven thousand to die on the Allied side alone. The 141st and 143rd Regiments of the 36th Division were virtually wiped out.

The idea for an amphibious assault had been born in the mind of politician Winston Churchill, and forced on the military commanders who were nearly one hundred percent against it. Churchill was also the man responsible for the disaster of Gallipoli in World War I some twenty-odd years earlier. What we didn't know now was that Clark never had any faith that the operation could be successful. General Lucas, working under Clark, was also convinced that it would fail. General George Patton flew from England to Naples to say goodbye to Lucas, believing that his old friend was sure to be killed.

British intelligence had informed Clark that the German 29th Panzer Division, which had been stationed at Anzio, had been sent up to the Gustav Line, leaving behind only a few engineers. Clark ignored the information and left Lucas orders only to "seize and hold a beachhead." The road to Rome was virtually undefended for two days after the landing, but the landing force stopped and dug in. Lucas' strategy (following Clark's vague orders to the letter) was to establish a beachhead and sit tight until enough supplies and reinforcements could be brought in to launch an overpowering attack against any possible defenses. What he apparently did not consider was that while we waited the Germans were going to be rushing in troops to contain the landing forces, and that they would then be in a much better position in the mountains looking down on the Allied troops.

Clark's ambiguous orders gave no direction at all. Later, when the operation was criticized by Churchill, British Generals Harold Alexander and Henry Wilson, and American General George Marshall, Clark placed all the blame on Lucas.

Even as late as early February, force strength favored the Allies, at one hundred thousand men against the Germans' ninety thousand. On the Allied side, there were generally full units that were fully equipped, while the German opposition was composed of assorted portions of many different units quickly flung together with whatever equipment was at hand. Later it was known that the Germans were almost ready to break down when, on Feb. 2, Clark ordered VI Corps to dig in and hold a defensive line.

Churchill later said he had hoped "that we were hurling a wildcat onto the shore, but all we got was a stranded whale."

Clark attempted to defend himself by saying had the landing force advanced into the Colli Laziali, and possibly on to Rome, it would have been destroyed. Few ever agreed with him.

It hardly seems possible for any operation to succeed with its leaders convinced of its failure in advance. Neither, surely, can timidity ever be a helpful trait in a combat commander. If this timidity includes hesitation in removing a subordinate he feels to be incompetent, it is even more unacceptable.

*****

"As for resistance," the G-2 lieutenant was finishing up our briefing, "there are indications that the beach is armed."

That was what we had been waiting to hear. It seemed more like a sentence from a judge than the explanation of a job to be done. I thought of the beautiful and inspiring movie scenes, dramatically lighted and accompanied by stirring background music, where the grim-faced but tender-hearted commander looks emotionally at his men and says, "Men, this is it." In comparison with our cheerful, friendly lieutenant who might just as well be discussing a football maneuver with his team, the Hollywood version seemed ludicrously funny. By God's grace we were spared the full picture, which we only later learned. Dog-faced soldiers were not supposed to understand politics, so we were not told that we were to be pawns in Churchill's game called Operation Shingle, or that our lives had been turned over to a man named Clark who was about to demonstrate his incredible incompetence.

It was hard to sleep that night. As I lay in my bunk with my head propped up on a kapok life jacket, my caption book in my thigh pocket kept jabbing me in the leg. I pulled it out and began to write, hardly knowing what I was putting down. Then I dropped the book on the deck and drifted off into a sound sleep.

In the morning I picked up the pad and reread what I had written the night before. It was a very bad poem, the first and only poem I have ever written. It was so bad I wanted to laugh, but the words meant too much to me at the time. Instead, I shuddered a little.

> Once again on the briny deep
> With a rolling deck beneath my feet,
> Film, not food, bulges my pack,
> Hurting my feet and bending my back.
> Where we'll land, we really know not
> But wherever it is it's sure to be hot.
> With visions of rockets, tracers and flak,
> The past seems bright but the future black.
> So to that beach where the Jerrys play
> Heaven will guide our LCA.[2]
> And in my foxhole wide and deep
> I'll wait for Snuffy to bring that jeep.

---

[2] *Landing Craft Assault. In the event we were transported in yet another type of barge, an LCM (Landing Craft Mechanized.)*

The next day the ship was far out to sea and heading almost due west. Lannigan and I took a number of shots around the decks of the men, and a few group shots with the commanding general, the ship's captain, and several other staff officers gathered around the relief model that we brought out on deck for that purpose. Then we wrapped our cameras in waterproof gas capes and put them back in our packs.

At midnight the moon had already set and the landing barges came alongside our transport, which was now lying dead in the water. The first wave began to load into them. I watched the other men for an indication of emotion. I felt that these men, being more experienced in such operations would, by their actions, give me some indication of what to expect, and therefore, how to act in this critical situation. I saw no emotion I could classify and I began to feel terribly alone, as if all these men possessed a secret that I must know to avoid an approaching catastrophe. However, upon examining my own thoughts, I found that they were about the same as they had been all along. I wasn't frightened and I wasn't excited. The same dull dread still weighed down the bottom of my stomach, but nothing more. And maybe it was the same for the others.

5

The Pyrrhus and Clark Expedition

At oh one hundred hours, Jan. 22, 1944, a large group of highly trained Rangers and two photographers—also, after several months in the field, highly trained—gathered in the ship's large dining hall. There we sat on the mess tables in the dark of the blacked-out ship, silent, longing for a forbidden cigarette, for nearly an hour. Then, slowly, the line began to move in a winding course through the ship along passageways, down ladders, and through bulkheads. We arrived at a large port in the side of the ship. It opened to darkness only a little less black than the inside of the ship. As the line moved up and we came to the opening, we reached out with a foot, found the rope ladder, and climbed down into the LCM that was going to carry us ashore to meet whatever it was we would find there.

We were packed into the barge much more tightly than on our practice landing, and I thought how it would take a lot longer to get out this time. Fortunately—or unfortunately?—Lannigan and I were near the front of the barge.

The bottom of the craft was lined with wooden boxes of some sort. When my toe found a cracked board, I pried it up and reached my hand in to feel. When my fingers touched a cluster of little metal fins I jerked my hand back and the words "mortar shells" came out involuntarily.

"Oh, my God!" the man next to me said under his breath.

One rifle slug or a tiny sliver of shrapnel from an artillery shell could easily blow us sky-high.

By this time the LCM was moving through total blackness. It was impossible to tell water from sky except in the one direction we surmised might be the shore. There, we could discern a faint and flickering glow, punctuated at intervals by dull flashes. We could hear nothing above the roar of the engine.

It seemed to me that at a time like this a person should have certain thoughts, but I couldn't think what they should be. Instead, I was very sleepy. I leaned my chin on the muzzle of my carbine and dozed off to the monotonous roar of the engine. When I returned to complete consciousness, I could tell by the luminous dial of my watch that we had been circling around the black, heaving ocean for well over an hour. The tempo of the engine's noise suddenly changed to a much louder roar. I could see that we were now heading straight for that glowing spot on the horizon. I began to hear faint explosions.

For what seemed a long while we watched the flashes grow nearer and nearer. Finally the officer in the nose of the craft said quietly, "All right, men, get down now." We crouched below the metal sides of the barge and waited. After a few minutes, the roar of the engine dropped, revved up, and died down again. Suddenly the craft hit something and it pitched up high to the left, then slid off and rocked in the water. The engine roared up again and once more a jolt told us we had hit another obstruction. The engine was quiet for a few seconds more and I heard a British accent say, "We can't put these men out here."

The boat backed, turned, and headed off parallel with the shore. Expecting the blast every second, I began to feel a wave of claustrophobia come over me in the bottom of the crowded boat. Someone else called out in a low voice, "Goddam it, let us out of this fuckin' thing."

Once again we felt a jolt as the boat struck something, but this time the engine roared, holding the nose against the obstruction. The steel door dropped with a loud clang. As one of the first men out, I found myself stepping into total blackness and immediately stumbled and fell headlong. Under my hands and knees I could feel that we were on a pile of large rocks. A series of thuds, metallic clanks, and quiet curses told me that I was not the only one to fall. Climbing on all fours, I reached the top of the pile of rip-rap and found a narrow concrete jetty running in to the shore. In a single line, well-spaced, we ran along the narrow strip of concrete. It ended on a broad sidewalk laid beside the street parallel to the beach.

The flashes we had seen from the water had turned into crashing blasts of artillery shells and small arms fire. I pulled aside and waited for Lannigan. When I saw a vague shape that appeared taller than the rest, I called his name and he stopped.

"What do we do now?" I asked him.

"Beats me," he answered. "Let's just follow these guys."

We could make out only two or three men in the darkness. They seemed to be heading south down the street, so we headed that way, keeping close to the buildings and walls along the sidewalk. As we passed a chest-high wall about two blocks farther on, someone suddenly cut loose with an automatic rifle. The slugs began to ricochet down the street all around us. Almost before we could think about it we were over the wall, headfirst. We sprawled in a long-neglected flower bed on the other side.

Lying there, a little reluctant to get up, we looked around to try to determine where we were. Behind us, in what appeared to be a large private mansion, we saw a glimmer of light.

"Let's take a look," Lannigan suggested. We walked up the steps and knocked on the door. The incongruity of such politeness never occurred to us. The light went out and the door opened. When the odor of disinfectant hit us in the face, we knew it was an aid station.

"Ya got somebody?" the man at the door asked.

"No, we're looking for Capt. Matthews," I answered. Matthews was the 1st Battalion medical officer we had talked with several times before.

"He ain't here," the man said.

The walls looked thick, so we went in and sat on the

floor. In the next room the medics were working on several wounded. There was nothing we could do until daylight, and this seemed to be a fairly safe place even though the windows and frames had been blown out. We took off our packs and got our cameras ready for action. Then we leaned back against the wall and dozed off in spite of the terrific amount of noise and the plaster continuously falling from the ceiling. Soon, however, we were forced to give up the remotest idea of sleep.

A man was brought in on a litter and laid on the floor. The medical officer went to work on the back of his head while aid men gave him plasma in the arm. Evidently there was not much to be done as the whole treatment was over within ten minutes. The man was left alone, groaning.

"Lieutenant from B Company," one of the aid men explained to us as he came over and sat down against the wall. "Got a machine gun slug in the head. He won't last another hour."

The man's groans became louder. His rasping breath became more and more erratic, then stopped. Someone shook the captain, who was sound asleep, and murmured something to him. With a tired groan, he got up off the floor and looked the patient over carefully. Finally, he tossed the blanket over the man's face. Going back to his place against the wall, he said to the other man sitting there, "Take it outside."

The silence was a relief.

Others now arrived in a steadily increasing stream. They were treated and lined up on the floor in the next room. Soon all the floors were crowded with the mostly still forms of men in a morphine stupor.

All the while, we could hear the steady rattle of small-arms fire just a few hundred yards inland. We knew that the action there was at close quarters. It was still too dark for pictures. We decided to stay where we were because we could not risk missing the all-important shots of the men in the third wave streaming ashore from the LCMs.

A few minutes before six, we left our packs, stuffed our pockets full of film, and went outside to get ready for the landing. Only the faintest trace of light in the east told us the sun was preparing to rise. We shivered in the pre-dawn chill. Occasionally we'd cower under the false shelter of the stone buildings along the street, as another loud explosion would bring down a nearby building. The noise of the small-arms fire was still almost continuous but had moved a bit farther away. However, the artillery was becoming a continuous roar and seemed to be getting bigger all the time. Several buildings near the aid station had been hit while we were inside, and the wreckage was nearly blocking the street. For the first time, we heard large shells fluttering overhead and exploding far out in the harbor, reaching for the ships.

By the time we heard the rumble of the barges from the third wave coming in, it had become almost light enough to make pictures, but not quite. This was a phase of the operation we could not afford to miss, so we opened our lenses wide, shot, and hoped we were getting something on film. The men jumped out and splashed up onto the mine-laden beach to narrow, white-taped paths the engineers had staked out. There was no small-arms fire. It looked almost nothing like a combat landing was supposed to look. Men were dying all around, but this looked like no more than a rather sloppy practice landing.

By this time, the sound of small-arms firing from just beyond the edge of the town had died down considerably. The crashes of artillery shell explosions had become almost a steady, deafening cascade of noise, and now a new element was added. The first of the German airplanes, fighters and dive bombers, began to strafe and bomb the town. Within an hour it was not possible to look up without seeing one or more of them circling or diving. The situation was getting close to unbearable, but there was no way to avoid the mayhem. Opportunities for fantastic pictures were everywhere.

From the time I left the beach after making the landing

pictures until two days later, my memory is a confusion of details. What I did, what I said, even what pictures I took, I cannot remember in any sequence whatever. As a whole, those two days live in my memory only as a depressing red haze. Visible through that haze I can make out little spots of a more brilliant red: the sound of a strafing airplane, the rising whine of a falling bomb, the shattered face of a dead man, the intense moment of waiting for a screaming shell to burst. And, always, blood.

The clearest thing remaining in my mind is the feeling of sadness that overwhelmed me and clung to me the entire time. Even now I cannot think of that period of time without the ghost of that deep depression reaching out and flooding over me. Sadness clouded my every thought. I was drunk with sadness. At times when I should have been frightened, I felt no fear, only an unbearable, crushing sadness.

It seemed terribly sad that these old buildings should be destroyed, that I, myself, should surely end my life here. It seemed unbearably pitiful that a once-beautiful marble fish pond should be cracked, dry and half-filled with rubble, that the lone arch of an ancient church facade should stand while the church was destroyed, that I should have a stranger's blood on my sleeve without knowing how it got there.

I walked down the street beside the beach until I came to a place where it was completely blocked. Turning to crawl through a space between two buildings, I traced a path through yards and gardens to the second street back. Here I met a group of men firing bazooka shells into a second-floor window of a house less than fifty yards up the street.

"Sniper," they said, in answer to my question. I waited with them while three others charged into the building and then, in a few minutes, reported from the window that the bastard was dead. Sadly, no picture.

I had never seen so many mangled bodies in German uniforms, but as I stepped around and over them they seemed no more significant than the other wreckage on all sides. Somewhere in the vicinity I took shots of Italian labor battalion stragglers being rounded up—cold, ragged, and scared. The Germans had used them and then abandoned them when they were overrun.

Back at the beach, I watched Luftwaffe planes bombing and strafing the ships far out at sea. They were too far away to get a picture.

In a little piazza, I ran across Lannigan sitting on the ground reloading his Eyemo.

"Getting anything good?" he asked, looking up with his pipe between his teeth. He looked sad, too.

"Scenery. Not much action. How about you?"

"Not much. Prisoners over there." He raised his chin and pointed with his pipe while he continued to thread film into his camera. I looked across the square and saw about twenty weary men in green uniforms lined up with their hands in the air while they were being searched.

I walked over to the group. I made a long shot and, picking out a couple of the worst examples, moved in for big close-ups. One man had a broken nose and cuts and bruises all over his head and face. Another was completely dazed and stared straight ahead without giving any indication that he saw me as I took his picture. White dust coated his entire uniform and his hair. I guessed he had been too close to the concussion of an exploding shell or bomb.

So intent was I on making this last picture that I failed to hear the roar of a diving plane amid the noise of exploding artillery shells until everyone, prisoners and guards alike, began to scramble for the doorway of the nearest building. Before I reached the door, the ripping roar of multiple machine guns blasted out behind me and little "spangs" and "spats" sounded almost simultaneously all over the little park. The combined roar and whine of the diving plane grew in a second to ear-bursting intensity, and then was gone almost instantly. As it swept over and up again, several machine guns and dozens of rifles in the town cut loose at it. I thought, no ack-ack yet, and wondered where in hell were our planes.

Over a rigged-up radio receiver, we heard later that bad weather was hampering Allied support. No one explained why the weather was bad only on the Allied side.

From then on, enemy planes were overhead all day, diving, circling, bombing and strafing. The return fire from the ground was mainly .50 caliber machine guns, which were being unloaded all day. I saw one plane go down trailing smoke as it disappeared behind the mountains. Its descent was followed by cheers from the ground, but it was a one-sided fight. There was no Allied plane over the beachhead for three days. During that time the official count of enemy sorties rose into the hundreds.

As Snuffy drove his jeep onto the 3rd Division beach at about eight o'clock that morning, a dive bomber laid a bomb directly on the pontoon pier behind him. He and the jeep were unhurt, but his was the last vehicle to come off the ship for several hours.

On the beach he met Yale Lapidus and Bob Heller, jeepless, and happily took them aboard. As they drove to the next town over, Nettuno, a formation of three planes flying at treetop level suddenly turned to sweep at an angle across the road. Looking them over carefully, Snuffy pronounced cheerfully, "Hmm, Mustangs." The reply came from eighteen machine guns pointed in his general direction. After a mass dive for the roadside ditch, and after a handy medic had reset Heller's dislocated shoulder, Heller looked at Snuffy and said, "Hmm, Mustangs, huh?" It wasn't very funny, but Snuffy heard it repeated for a long time.

*****

Walking along the little peninsula of land on the north side of the harbor, I made shots of the bomb-destroyed docks where the narrow strip of land had been almost completely severed by the bomb craters. Finding it impossible to pass this spot, I turned back to the mainland, where there were a few gutted buildings standing. As I passed these, I noticed a squad of engineers digging at the seemingly solid walls. Looking closer, I saw that they were uncovering huge hollows loaded with quantities of Italian-labeled dynamite wired with electric fuses and looking ready to blow at any second. Nervously, I took a couple of shots and walked quickly away.

Not long afterwards I found myself on the second floor of a three-story building, sitting on a set of bed springs talking to a lieutenant I had met back in Pozzuoli a lifetime ago.

"How come you guys are here?" he asked me.

"Because this is where the pictures are, I guess, Lieutenant," I answered.

"Uh huh." He seemed to be digesting that idea. "I guess so. We can let the civilians take care of the rear area, right?"

I realized he meant the civilian reporters and photographers.

A messenger came in the door and announced wearily, but with tension in his voice, "Two Mark IVs coming into town."

Across the room, a man laid his bazooka on the floor, leaned out the window, and looked up the street. The lieutenant pounded on the wall behind him with a rifle butt and yelled, "Jensen, get ready. Two tanks coming." Then, turning back to the messenger, "Go across the street and tell Sgt. Adams."

I looked at the window opposite ours on the other side of the street and saw the muzzle of a bazooka leaning on the window sill.

We waited ten minutes, fifteen minutes, and still could not hear the clank of tank tracks. The lieutenant opened a box of K-rations and began to eat slowly. I stood beside the window and watched over the bazooka man's head as far up the street as I could see.

After a half-hour, no one believed they were coming, so I lay down on the bed springs and immediately dropped off to sleep. Twenty minutes later I was awakened by a loud explosion and the sound of falling glass. Still half-asleep, I jumped up and ran to the window expecting to look out on a furious battle between tanks and bazooka men. I could not tell what direction the sound had come from, but I knew it was close because there was no sound of the shell's screaming approach before the explosion.

"Better get away from that window," a voice said behind me. I turned and saw a man looking in the door from the hallway.

"They're throwing eighty-eight[3] time fire," he said. He pointed out the open end of the hallway where there had once been a wall. By getting on the floor, I could see at enough of an upward angle to observe the sky above the town without exposing myself. The sky was dotted with fading black smudges, and another appeared while I watched. This added aggravation was to be with us for several days, and accounted for more small casualties than any other single weapon the Germans used at that time.

*****

The Ranger PRO officer had set up his office in what had once been the administration office of a large casino. It was now completely stripped of furniture, carpets, and window drapes. To get to the office, one had to cross the huge, high-ceilinged lobby. This was now turned into what one would probably call a hospital. Along the front wall, under the huge stained-glass windows, lay some fifty or so litters and blankets, their occupants bandaged and still. Some were partly or completely covered, while others weren't covered at all. I thought it was absurd to place wounded men where they would surely be showered with broken glass if a shell landed in front of the building.

---

[3] *The German 88mm anti-aircraft gun was also used to great effect as general artillery.*

Then I realized that no further harm could be done to these men. They were dead.

In a two-sided, partitioned section formed by blankets hanging on ropes, teams of men were working on two patients lying on tables. All around them on the floor lay others, silently waiting their turns. My rubber-soled boots slipped as I walked across the marble floor and I looked down. The floor was covered with a dark layer of blood, streaked and smeared by the boots of men walking through it. The medical officer at one of the tables turned aside to give an order and I saw that the entire front of his uniform was covered with a sticky-looking mass of blood. His bare forearms below his rolled-up sleeves were smeared with it and, as he shook his left hand, a spray of it was thrown to the floor. It was even on his face.

As I passed, I looked closer at the man lying on the table. His lower face and throat seemed to be missing. I recognized the torn uniform as that of a German officer. It seemed that these torn bodies were reduced to the same category regardless of the color of their uniforms.

Lannigan was not in the PRO, nor did anyone there know his whereabouts. Yes, he had been there earlier in the day to see if the arrangements we had made to deliver our film back to Naples were still in order. They were, he had been assured, and he had gone away again without saying where he was heading or when he would be back.

I went back through the Dante-esque scene of human carnage in the lobby, again feeling only a slight deepening of the sadness that would not let me go. I noticed that the German officer was making whistling noises through a tube that had been inserted into his throat.

At the far side of the lobby lay, on its side, the hotel desk. This area was now swarming with officers holding maps, papers, and colored pencils in one hand and field telephones in the other.

My first job was finished. I had seen and photographed everything of immediate interest in the town. Now I should get back to my job of photographing the activities of the infantry. This could be done only where the really close fighting was. Here in town, I had photographed a few hundred men who had died by artillery and air attack. I had seen a steady stream of others on litters, in jeeps and trucks, and a few walking in from the real front, now less than a mile away, but it was not the same. They were not physically fighting the enemy.

Newspapers, however, would be much more interested in the town than in pictures of men fighting in an open field, from behind bushes, and in ditches. Wrecked buildings and machinery were much more picturesque than mangled bodies. Pictures of damage could show the incredible violence of war without offending the delicate sensibilities of the readers. I already knew, with considerable cynicism, that one must be very careful about such things. Dead Germans, shown indistinctly, illustrated the grim victory of our valorous troops. But pictures of American dead were published only in exceptional cases, such as during bond drives, and then only the most peaceful-looking corpses were exposed to public view. Unpleasant reality was denied space. This fact we photographers knew and hated.

"To furnish the American public with a pictorial record of the war" was what we had been told was our duty. The falseness of the whole thing swept over me and my feeling of depression deepened till I wished to God I could sit down and cry. This business was affecting me more than I realized. Crazy thoughts of rebellion against the established regime flitted through my mind. What if I abandoned the whole structure of news policy and did nothing but make a "pictorial record of the war"? It was impossible, I knew, but what if I tried? What would happen if I made pictures only of bearded, dirty faces with tired eyes, of foxholes half-filled with icy mud, of boredom, of fright, of loneliness? Never mind the wrecked buildings, the burning tanks, the bursting shells. Never mind the misleading pictures of momentary laughter, the insincere applause of "liberated" people, all the good parts, and the bad parts only when they were spectacular. What if I were to try to show those glamour-loving flag wavers at home the difference between rationing and hunger, between restrained living and animal existence, between discomfort and misery, between insecurity and the threat of imminent death?

Such a thought was pointless. I knew very well what would happen if I suddenly became a Matthew Brady instead of a Salvador Dali: the Army wouldn't have any use for me, and neither would the general public. I laughed at myself, but cut it off quickly when I realized I was looking into the frightened eyes of a wounded man staring at me from a litter on the floor.

As I passed through that deeply depressing lobby, I looked at the faces of the dead and wounded and wondered if their fathers and mothers and wives had enjoyed the Fred Astaire and Ginger Rogers movie last Saturday night.

*****

I finally ran into Lannigan and together we ran across Capt. Matthews in his aid station in a two-story house near the center of town. Only two second-floor rooms were missing from the house. To reach the doctor's "consulting room," one had to pass through a small courtyard in front of the house where, laid out neatly in rows on both sides of the walk, were about a dozen burned and mangled bodies. On the small front porch, several litters were leaning against the wall and railings, where the fresh air would soon dry out the dark, dripping stains of blood.

Inside, the captain sat on the floor beside a still form on a litter, silently staring at the man's pale face. An aide held a plasma bottle while the liquid slowly drained through the rubber tube into the man's arm. Through the double doors to the next room we could see the floor covered with unmoving bundles of morphine-drugged men wrapped in blankets.

"Hello, Captain," I said softly.

He looked up quickly, and then stared at us for a long time as if trying to place us.

"Hello, boys," he said finally, his face falling back into an expression of utter fatigue.

"Lots of business for you today," Lannigan said quietly.

"Yeah," the captain returned. He let out a sigh, which sounded more like a groan, as he lifted himself to his feet and walked to the door where we were standing. "And I'm pretty damned tired. Where you fellows staying?"

"We don't have a place yet. Plenty of places, though, I guess."

"Stay here if you want to," he offered. "There's an empty room upstairs if you want to take the chance."

The "upstairs" feature was something of a negative recommendation. Artillery shells go through a roof like a knife through paper. Sometimes, also, they go through two or more floors with the same ease. But we were tired, and the fact that a solution to our problem was being offered to us decided the issue.

We carried our packs and cameras wearily up the long flight of stairs. At the head of the steps, just across the narrow landing, was a large window consisting of very small panes of glass in a decorative pattern reaching from floor to ceiling.

"Fancy dump we picked here, huh?" I said.

"I'm glad it's not in the room where we have to sleep," Lannigan grunted. This seemed to remind him of something, and he walked to the window of our empty room and began kicking all the remaining glass out of the shattered window.

We made the short trip down to the landing beach where, by now, the LCMs had brought in our bed rolls and dumped them on the damp sand. We rummaged through the pile, found our own with no trouble, and carried them back to the house.

By this time, the light had faded and our picture taking was over for the day. We left our equipment in the room and, taking a handful of caption blanks and our exposed film, we went back downstairs to begin the distasteful part of our work— deciphering our notes and writing "the ethically and factually precise captions" the War Department demanded for each exposure. We found a small wicker table and chairs and began our work while the captain went wearily on with his grim task on the floor beside us. On the other side of the room, two men sweated and cursed over a radio taken from an abandoned German scout car.

As I brushed fallen plaster off the table for the third time, a series of squeaks and squawks, and finally music, came from the radio. Triumphantly, the men spun the dial and after a few minutes had the BBC coming through from London, loud and clear. Immediately a little group of men gathered in a huddle on the floor around the radio and listened gravely to a symphony orchestra playing the "William Tell Overture."

Lannigan and I finished our captions with a relieved sigh and joined the group on the floor. We had to move once to make way for a litter being carried through from the group of wounded in the next room to the group of dead in the yard outside. Finally the newscast came. Calmly the announcer read, "Gen. Mark Clark's headquarters in Italy announced today that an amphibious landing is at this moment being launched behind the German lines at Anzio on the Tyrrhenian coast just below Rome. The Fifth Army spokesman announces that the landing procedure is going according to plan."

Behind us, the man lying on the floor groaned. The ragged stump of his left arm slowly dripped blood onto the floor as the doctor worked on it. I thought how nice it was that the general's plan was going so well.

*****

After the newscast, Lannigan and I went back to our table, wrapped the exposed film, labeled it, and tied it up in our red courier bag.

"Well, let's go," I said as I picked up my helmet and knocked crumbled plaster out of it.

"Wait a minute." Lannigan said. "Are you hungry?"

"No, not much," I answered. We hadn't eaten all day and I couldn't even remember drinking any water, but I still had no appetite.

"Well, how about coffee?" Lannigan insisted.

"Yeah," I answered. "I guess I could use a cup of coffee, but why?"

"Well, look," he said, "I'll take this film down to the CP, and you make us some Nescafe while I'm gone."

"O.K." I agreed, and he left. He was right, of course. There was no good reason for both of us to expose ourselves to whatever villainy the Germans were up to out there. It was simple military training.

In the kitchen, a little Coleman stove hissed away with its tiny blue flame under a canteen cup of steaming water. Several men sat on the floor or leaned against the walls drinking hot Nescafe and digging cold, sawdust-tasting meat mixture out of the little K-ration cans.

When the stove was available, I filled my cup with water and set it on to heat. I remembered that Lannigan had left his canteen and cup upstairs and went up to get it. As I climbed the stairs, a large artillery shell burst very close and I unconsciously slowed my pace. The next shell to fall shook the building violently, and loosened plaster fell everywhere. It sounded as if the explosion had been very close to the back of the house.

By now I had come to a full stop at the top of the stairs, tensed against the next explosion. Suddenly I realized I was staring directly at the huge multi-paned window, as yet undamaged, no more than three feet in front of my face. At the exact instant the realization hit me, I saw the whole thing disintegrate before my eyes. Something that felt like a solid wall hit me head-on. I felt myself rolling helplessly down the full length of the stairs. I landed in a heap and lay there trying to figure out what had happened.

A voice close to me asked, "You hit, fellow?" I looked around through the near darkness and saw one of the aides lying on the floor a few feet away.

"I don't think so," I answered. I didn't seem to hurt anywhere. Remembering the glass, I wiped a hand over my face and looked at it for blood. There was none.

The barrage was still concentrating on our area, and everyone kept on the floor, below the level of the windows. I lay where I had landed until I suddenly remembered the water I had on the stove in the kitchen. Crouching as low as possible and ready to drop flat at any instant, I dashed into the kitchen and snatched my cup off the stove. The water was boiling by now, so I sat on the floor and dumped in the coffee solvent and sugar cubes. I drank half and saved half for Lannigan, as I now had no intention of going back upstairs for his canteen until the barrage had stopped completely.

After about half an hour, the barrage seemed to shift a little farther down toward the beach, most of the shells landing in the next block. I made a quick dash upstairs, dug our two blanket rolls and cameras out from under the newly-made rubble, and ran back downstairs.

I had noticed an empty little room across the hallway from the kitchen, and decided to appropriate it for Lannigan and me. Kicking aside the litter of window glass and plaster, I dropped our bed rolls and knelt to untie the ropes holding my own. I was very tired and intended to lie down for a few minutes while waiting for Lannigan to return. As I knelt there, working on the hard knots in the rope, I gradually became aware of a peculiar smell. It wasn't a particularly strong odor, but as I gave my attention to it, it seemed to penetrate deep into my lungs, leaving a distasteful sweetish sensation that remained even when I held my breath. For some reason the odor brought a sharp increase to my ever-present sense of depression. Then, like a flash, a thought struck me: there was a ghost in here!

With this thought firmly imbedded in my mind, I went over the whole room, kicking aside plaster and glass, searching for blood on the floor. There was none. Inwardly denouncing the idea as nonsense and berating myself for letting an over-stimulated imagination run away with my common sense, I went back, untied my bedding, and rolled it out on the floor. But I could not bring myself to lie down there just yet, so I wandered back to the kitchen and struck up a conversation with one of the aides who sat there eating a disgusting piece of K-ration cheese. When the opportunity presented itself, I asked indifferently, "Why isn't anybody sleeping in that room across the hall?"

"I don't know," he said. "Ain't they? It's a good place."

"Maybe it's on account of the smell," I ventured.

"Smell? I didn't smell nothin'. We had some stiffs in there a while ago, but they don't smell yet."

So there had been dead bodies in that room. But that still didn't account for the smell. The door had been open all the while, and there was no glass left in the window, so the room should have had ample opportunity to air out. That hardly seemed important, though, because I was convinced that this was not an ordinary odor.

I decided not to sleep there yet, at least not alone.

*****

Now the barrage began to drop again and, as it slowly passed over our area, we lost a rear corner room on the top floor and a concrete shed in the backyard containing our only workable hydrant. After it had rolled over us, the barrage seemed to settle down into an irregular pattern, the center of which was about a block behind our house. Only occasionally did our area receive a hit, but during the night, the building directly behind ours was slowly chipped down from three stories to one and a half.

After half an hour of waiting for Lannigan, I began to worry. He could have been caught on the street by the barrage. I knew he would take cover and wait it out, but I worried, nevertheless. His coffee, which I had saved, had gotten cold, but it was possible that he had met someone who had offered him something to eat. I knew he could never turn down food.

When he still hadn't appeared after another hour, I began to debate with myself over the advisability of going to look for him. Reason told me, however, that there was absolutely no advantage to stumbling around in the dark in the middle of an artillery barrage when Lannigan was just as capable of finding his way as I was.

An hour and a half later, when the barrage had lifted from the area between the CP and the aid station and the only shells landing there were scattered two-forties at nearly one-minute intervals, and still Lannigan had not come, I almost decided that he was going to spend the night in the large air-raid shelter at the CP. I knew he could get blankets from the hospital there and would probably be more comfortable with a bunch of his friends, some coffee and food, than he would be in this exposed house.

I waited till about one a.m. without much hope of his return and then took my bed roll and spread it out in the former dining room among the wounded and the aides. Somewhere around five o'clock I finally gave up trying to sleep, went out to the front porch to sit on the steps and watch the continual flash and roar of artillery shells bursting in all directions. It was light enough to see where I was going at six o'clock, so I walked down to the CP on the beach road.

Passing through the casino lobby again, I noticed that the blood on the floor had become a little deeper, and it splashed up on my boots as I walked through it.

I went directly to the back of the lobby after I took a brief look around the huge room and failed to see Lannigan. Here, the wide mouth of a large cave opened into the side of the hill. The cave had probably served, at one time, as a wine cellar for the hotel, but it looked as if it had been considerably enlarged by the

Germans to serve as an air-raid shelter. It was now jammed with litters on which wounded men lay in long rows. Here again I noticed that sickening smell that I had come to associate with the presence of death. It even came through the strong smell of disinfectants.

I found no place where Lannigan might have spent the night in the cave, so I headed back through the lobby yet again, toward the PRO. Walking under the huge stained-glass windows at the front of the lobby, I suddenly heard the screaming roar of an airplane in a steep dive that had become so familiar and so dreaded in the last twenty-four hours. To a man, every person in the lobby who was capable of standing broke into a dead run for the cave in the rear. I was no more than halfway across the room when the scream had increased to what seemed its utmost intensity, and then broke into a crescendo of the ripping roar of multiple machine guns. Looking back, I saw the tall windows first give off little liquid-looking spurts of glass like bursting bubbles, then sag tiredly and fall in great shattering sheets. Simultaneously there was a noise like angry hornets bounding about the room, accompanied by little spurts of dust jumping out of the walls and floors.

I finally reached the PRO, and as if nothing had happened the major was heating a can of K-ration meat over a Coleman stove on his desk. He frowned at me when I came in, and said nothing to my "Good morning."

I said, "Sir, I'd like to know if Sgt. Lannigan left our film with you last night."

"Who? Lannigan? Oh yes, the photographer. No, he took it back with him."

"Did he say where he was going when he left, sir?"

"Going?" He scowled at me and hesitated before he went on, irritably. "Didn't you know he was killed last night?"

6
After Lannigan

I could feel the blood drain from my face. I wanted to vomit. *"...killed last night."* Lannigan ...*"killed last night."* The words echoed about the room, and the room was dark red. Suddenly the major was lying on the floor, face down—another interruption. Glass tinkled somewhere and a wind blew on my face. Killed last night.

The major looked up at me from the floor.

"Where?" I said.

"A block down the street."

I walked out of the PRO. Most of the front of the casino was missing, and a huge pile of stones lay in its place. There was blood on the stones and a dark pool of it on the ground. The red courier film bag lay on top of a pile of rubble. A medic gave me some tape and I patched the large rip in the bag's side. I noticed that several of the cans of movie film were deeply dented and knew they might have been ruined. I couldn't tell about my still film, but I didn't really care very much.

After turning the courier bag over to the major, I walked down the street, seeing nothing, hearing nothing, feeling nothing. I was emotionally exhausted. I felt no regret, no compassion, no fear, not even depression. Lannigan was dead, but the thought meant nothing. War is war, and if people get killed, they are only confirming the purpose of war.

Next it would probably be me. Certainly, I did not deserve to live if these others must die. Dying was the order of the day, so fall in and count off. I did not regret the past nor envy the future. I was lucky to be able to go out this way, doing my job, owing nothing to the world or my own conscience.

Suddenly I became aware of that odor again. This time it was stronger, so strong that I gagged. I coughed, but it did no good. The smell was not in my nose, it was in my mind. Half angrily, I turned back, determined to get at the cause of this sensation.

A few paces back, I saw the half-open doors of a private garage, and as I approached it I knew that inside I would find my answer. When I reached the door the sensation became so strong that I almost decided not to continue. I knew what I would see inside the building and I had no desire to look at more mangled and bloody chunks of flesh that had once been men. But I knew I must relieve my mind.

I pushed the door open and stood for a few seconds, while my eyes adjusted to the semidarkness inside. Finally I was able to see clearly four lumpy forms lying on the floor, twisted in various unnatural positions beneath blankets. The faces were covered, but the blankets were not long enough to reach over the boots that pointed stiffly upward at odd angles.

This scene was about what I had expected, but the intensity of the odor foreshadowed something worse.

Then I saw it. It was the second body from the right, the one from which a still-liquid pool of blood had crept across the concrete floor. The boots, white with the kind of dust that comes from wrecked buildings, reached far out from the bottom of the blanket. There could be no mistake: the boots were exactly like the ones I was wearing at that moment, and these two pair were the only ones I had ever seen exactly like that. I remembered the day Lannigan and I took our G.I. shoes to an old Italian shoemaker in Caiazzo and told him in pantomime just how we wanted him to re-do the tops of them.

Without realizing I was speaking, I heard my voice say hoarsely, "Good luck, Cece."

Back at the CP, I sat down on the sidewalk and leaned against what remained of the front of the building to wait for Snuffy and the jeep. Here I had a good view of the gigantic waterspouts caused by the artillery shells that fluttered directly overhead and exploded uselessly in the harbor.

As I sat there, a weak sun began to send its sad little rays through the gray overcast. The puny heat they gave somehow reminded me that I was very, very tired. If I had been capable of sleep, I would have slept there, but I could not bear to shut my eyes. When I attempted to, the red behind my eyelids sank deep into my brain and spread there like a blanket over my consciousness. The red was blood, and it brought back that horrible odor of death. The odor is unlike any other that I can recall in connection with the death. I have smelled it in places months after a body has been removed. I have smelled death where it has yet to occur. The night Lannigan died I smelled it even as death was happening.

*****

I sat against the smooth stone wall with my head leaning back so my helmet rested against it. I stared straight out over the water. I was tired and my eyelids felt rusty. It would have been an effort to shut them. Next to me men were eating K-rations, and the smell of the food irritated me. It was hard to remember when I had eaten last, but I mentally counted the forty-two hours since my last meal on the ship. It seemed as if at least a week had passed since I stepped out of that LCM, but I was not hungry.

The thought of food, as practically every thought did at that time, brought more memories of Lannigan. He had said more than once, "As long as you can eat, you can stay on your feet."

I pulled a D-ration chocolate bar out of my pocket, opened it and broke off a piece of the hard concoction with a rock. At the first bite I felt the filling come out of a tooth. Spitting out the pieces of chocolate and crumbled amalgam, I loosened my canteen to wash the remains out of my mouth. As I lifted the canteen and tilted my head back, I shut my eyes for a few seconds. Immediately the image of a pair of G.I. boots pointing upwards from beneath a bloody blanket flashed behind my eyelids with a cruel, glittering clarity. I gagged. Water poured from my mouth, nose and eyes. I gave up the idea of food for the time being. Panting, I leaned back again and resumed my contemplation of waterspouts.

A gentle voice beside me said quietly, "Bell?"

I jumped. *My God,* I thought, *I'm jumpy as a cat.*

Looking up, I saw a little red-faced man with captain's bars on his collar and a white cross painted on his helmet standing patiently beside me. It was the Rangers' Irish chaplain. He, Lannigan, and I had planned a news coup by getting the first pictures of the pope as soon as we hit Rome. Naturally, we planned to be among the first to enter the city.

"Hello, Padre," I said, attempting a smile while getting to my feet.

"You know about Lannigan?"

"Yes, sir."

"I'm really sorry," he said. "He was a fine fellow." I said nothing, and he went on, "I need some information about him if you can give it to me. What was his first name?"

"Cecil M."

"Sergeant?"

"Staff."

"Your outfit?"

"Hundred Sixty-Third Signal Photo."

"I'm taking care of the stuff from his pockets. If you want me to, I'll take his equipment."

"No, thanks. I'll take care of that."

"Well, so long, Bell. Thanks for the information." He hesitated, and then said, "You and Lannigan were pretty good friends, weren't you?"

"Yes, we were."

"Then, write to his wife."

"Sure, Padre," I said, rather unconvincingly.

My God! What would I ever say to his wife with a clear conscience? The very thought of sending her a letter full of childish drivel about his glorious death was repulsive. I'd have to say something about his being killed "in the line of duty" and, personally, I had never seen a man who purposely gave, or even endangered, his life for the sake of "duty." I have the utmost contempt for the fanatical zealot in a chivalric legend who goes down clutching a battle-rent banner with the cry of "Excelsior" on his lips. Lannigan was no fanatic. He was a level-headed, well-adjusted man. His death was unfortunate, but it was no sacrifice. He believed in the right of his superior officers to send him anywhere, at any time, within reason, but he certainly did not believe he was carrying the flaming sword of righteousness against the dark forces of evil. His country was threatened. It was up to him to help protect it. That was as complicated as it got.

I could never bring myself to speak of Lannigan's as a hero's death, though in my mind it really was nothing less. But there were neither medals nor acclamation to back me up. To his wife, he had undoubtedly been a hero long before this, and that was enough. But I was not going to write to her saying he had died while walking down the street with his camera, on his way to claim a cup of foul coffee a mere two blocks away. I couldn't tell her that his head had been crushed by stones and his body perforated by shrapnel and covered with rubble. Nevertheless, I resolved to ask her if I could do anything for her, and to say all the usual things that are expected in cases like this. I could do no less, but then, I could do no more.

*****

Still there was no sign of Snuffy with the jeep, so I decided to bring our equipment from the aid station to the CP to save trouble later on. As there was no way of getting a wheeled vehicle close to the house because of the rubble lying in the streets, it took me two trips to carry all of both Lannigan's and my equipment to the CP. I was panting and tired as I dropped the last bed roll on the floor of the casino lobby. Beat, I sat down on the soft roll of blankets, dropped my head into my arms and stared at the floor, seeing nothing.

Suddenly I felt, rather than heard, someone standing in front of me. Looking up, my heart failed a couple of beats as I saw the two most welcome faces I had ever seen. Standing there, smiling as if they had just pulled off a good joke, were my old friends Bernie Kline and Art Elliot. All at once, a warmth spread over my body, and I knew just how lonely I had been without realizing it.

"God, I'm glad to see you guys," I said, grabbing an arm of each.

"Been pretty rough here?" asked Bernie.

"The landing was a cinch," I answered, "but we've had artillery and air." My throat closed up at this point, but I had to finish. "Lannigan got it last night."

Neither said anything or even acted surprised, but I could see that both were deeply hit by the words. Finally, Bernie asked, "Killed?"

"Yes."

"I thought so, soon as I saw you," Art remarked.

"Damn." Bernie punched a fist into his palm. "That's tough."

For a few moments there was only silence. No one could think of anything more to say. Finally, Bernie broke it up by saying, "Well, let's go. Pratt's outside with our jeep. Snuffy's up the road with yours."

We drove from Anzio over to the next little town, Nettuno—the two blended into one another—and met Snuffy waiting in front of a large three story building that the civilian correspondents and photographers, who were just now coming in, had taken over. With him was the team of Heller, Lapidus, and Frate. I had to go through the ordeal of repeating the story of Lannigan's death. All of them took it pretty hard, especially

Snuffy.

The eight of us decided to stick together, and after looking over the civilian press building and finding it sadly lacking in charm, or even basic attractions, we started out to find a house of our own. We prudently headed for the outskirts of town, where we figured we would be at least a little safer than in the more important center. Actually, we may have been under less fire on the edge of town, but the difference was hard to distinguish. The beachhead was so small the Germans had little difficulty in working out a complete saturation.

We found an almost undamaged little house and immediately moved in. It consisted of four rooms of equal size, arranged in an exact square. The kitchen and the room next to it were connected by a door, and each of the two had a door to the outside. No one ever figured out which was the front or back of the house.

After knocking all the remaining glass out of the windows and sweeping the plaster off the floor, we left our equipment with Art and Pratt as guards, and drove back to town to hunt for bedsprings. There were quite a few scattered around in various abandoned houses. We also found two boxes of five-in-one rations someone had left unguarded on the beach. Five-in-ones provided canned meats and vegetables, canned biscuits, dehydrated soups, margarine, jam, cheese spread, cereal and pudding, all intended to feed up to five men. There were even cigarettes.

By the time we were completely set up with our sleeping arrangements, it was beginning to get dark, so we ripped open one of the waterproof boxes of five-in-ones and began to prepare a supper of meatballs and spaghetti from one can and creamed corn from another. I still had no appetite, but was determined to eat something if it choked me. When the smell of boiling coffee began to drift through the house I realized it would not be so difficult after all.

Despite the plebeian fare, this proved to be one of the

most memorable meals of my life, and I actually enjoyed it to the last hard biscuit. It had come at the end of a horrendous day, and it was my first food in forty-eight hours.

*****

That night was a horrible black thing filled with the noise of constant artillery bursts punctuated at an average of half-hour intervals by the sound of diving airplanes screaming headlong into a solid roar of machine gun fire streaking like a sparkling waterfall up to meet them. Through it all came the whine of falling bombs increasing in ear-splitting intensity up to the instant of their explosion. Sleep was impossible except in short snatches.

Most of the night I lay on my bunk, fully dressed, relaxed for a few minutes, then tensed in every muscle while I waited for the final crash, which terminated one of those long, nerve-shattering mechanical screams. Time after time, I got out of bed to brush off fallen plaster and dust and to walk to the door to watch the brilliant display of colored fires in the sky.

As the steady roar of an engine somewhere in the blackness above suddenly grew to a musical-like whine, a few machine guns on the ground would begin sending up long red threads of tracers. Almost immediately their staccato voices would be joined by an entire chorus to form a thunderous roar and streak the blackness with thousands of curving, crisscross lines of red fire, freckled with little blue-white twinkles. The long sustained roar was like a thousand waterfalls. The sound was almost physical, a heavy, crushing weight pressing on my chest. I wanted to yell and frighten it away, yet at the same time some part of me was urging it on to more red fire and louder noise.

During one of these orgies of fire and sound, I stood in the doorway, hypnotized by the unimaginable magnitude of the display. Far above, I saw a brilliant blue explosion, much brighter than the winking of the thirty-sevens. A shooting ball of fire emerged from the blast, streaming behind it a long fiery tail as it drifted down, exploding over and over again before it disappeared into a red glow on the horizon. For the first time I felt a strange exultation as I followed the flaming wreckage all the way to the ground.

A few months before, perhaps only a few hours before, I would have been surprised, and probably a little frightened, to recognize this feeling in myself. I would have been appalled to find satisfaction, even elation, at the spectacle of men dying horribly in a plummeting mass of burning wreckage. But with the memory of the mangled bodies of friends and compatriots fresh in my mind, and knowing that butchery had been perpetrated by those same Germans who were receiving their fair portion of devastation, I calmly accepted that my mind was beginning to give up its hold on centuries of civilization, and was yielding to the embrace of the gods of war.

"Burn, you bastards, burn," I whispered hoarsely into the blackness.

*****

Next morning, after a breakfast of cold canned bacon and egg mixture on hard biscuits and a good, hot cup of instant coffee, Snuffy and I began to search for the Ranger 1st Battalion CP. Luckily, we found it about three miles outside of town after having to hit the ditch beside the road only once as a strafing plane swept overhead.

The CP had been set up in a captured German command trailer. Here, only a hundred and fifty yards behind the farthest outpost, I found the most peaceful scene since I arrived on the beachhead. The men sat around talking, smoking, or cleaning their weapons near their well-dug fox-holes as if there were no war within a thousand miles. The peaceful quiet was disturbed only by the distant sound of artillery and the rustling sound of large shells as they flew high overhead on their way to the area towns and the harbor.

I didn't know then that this inactivity was caused not be the inability of the troops to overcome the German opposition, but by Clark's incompetence. Among other things, it resulted in what was essentially a rout in the nearby Cisterna area a few days later. For now, most of us simply welcomed the respite from the frenzy of the fight without realizing the tragic cost of a lost opportunity.

January 30, 1944: Four litter bearers carry a soldier wounded on the first day of the ill-fated offensive by Anzio beachhead forces in the nearby Cisterna area.

Mortar platoon moving up country road in Cisterna area.

The CP trailer was at the bottom of a slight depression in the ground, but otherwise the terrain was as flat as a pool table and almost as bare. A few miles away, however, steep mountains rose abruptly off the level plain and seemed to form an almost exact semicircle surrounding us on three sides. There, we knew, were the Germans. One could almost feel their eyes watching our every move.

I took a few shots of the men in their dug-in positions, trying to show the flat terrain occupied by the Americans and, in the background, the mountains occupied by the Germans. Then Snuffy and I headed back to town, where, though I hoped against it, I might be able to get a few good shots of the dive-bombing.

Figuring that one place was as good as another to get bombing pictures, we went back to our little house on the edge of town. I cocked the shutter and set my camera beside the door, where I could grab it on the run. Then I went inside to write the captions for the shots I had made earlier, and listen for the beginning of the ack-ack.

I didn't have long to wait before I heard the familiar whine of a diving plane and the solid roar of the machine guns on the ground reaching up to meet it. Snatching up my camera as I dashed through the door, I headed for the pit of a fifty-caliber gun about twenty-five yards from our house, and jumped in. The plane was heading in from the sea at a steep dive and seemed to be completely swallowed up by tracers. I took my shot just as it began to pull out of its dive. The bombs landed at the edge of the water and the plane zoomed up steeply, pulling up almost directly above us. The fifty-caliber beside me opened up with its deafening roar, and I saw the tracers ricochet off the armored belly of the plane. For several seconds the plane held its steep climb. Then it began a long, flat glide down toward its own lines, trailing a growing plume of black smoke.

The noise trailed off to a ringing silence.

"You got him, fella!" I yelled to the little man still looking over his gun at the disappearing German.

"I ain't sure," he answered, still watching through eyes squinted so tight they looked closed. "Anyway, he got back to his own lines."

I later learned to call the man with the good aim, as everyone else did, "B.B. Eyes," from a Dick Tracy comic strip. If this shot was confirmed, he had just added a fifth German airplane to his official credit.

Sitting on the edge of the gun pit, we began a conversation during which I learned that, according to official count, the beachhead had thus far received nearly three hundred individual air attacks.

"I wonder where the hell our planes are," I mused, not for the first time.

"I don't know, brother," B.B. Eyes replied emphatically,

"but the first one of the yellow bastards I see is going to absorb a whole belt of these fifties." Much later I watched him put about twenty-five rounds expertly through the space separating the first two patrolling P-50s we saw.

Somewhere on the beachhead, I knew, an officer in charge of our group of photo teams was supposed to have landed by now. I knew also that I should find him, report Lannigan's death, turn in his equipment, and get a replacement movie man. As much as I disliked the idea of working with another partner, I knew there was no alternative. Snuffy and I headed back toward the center of Nettuno, wondering where we could begin looking for a captain in charge of photo operations. For a start we would try Corps CP, if we could find that.

As we rounded the curve just before striking the beach road, there were yells and waving hands from another jeep passing in the opposite direction. Both jeeps skidded to a stop and backed up. We knew the other team and one of the men said, "Hey, Bell, Capt. Herbert is looking for you."

"Yeah? Where is he? I've been looking for him, too."

Boone, their driver, turned their jeep around and led us winding through the town, through a stone arch, into the large parking lot of some sort of factory. Two flights up, in the back of the building, we found the captain's room, cluttered with equipment and a bunk in one corner. When he saw us, Herbert smiled broadly and said cheerfully, "Hello, Bell." I don't know how he remembered who I was. We hadn't seen each other since he first informed us that we would be joining the Rangers' amphibious landing.

"Hello, Captain," I returned. "I have some film for you."

"Good," he smiled, taking the box and dropping it into a half-filled courier bag. Then, after picking up a handful of papers from his bunk, he headed for the door leading to the next room. "Come on in here a minute, Bell," he said.

The room contained a table, two chairs, and nothing else,

not even dust. Someone had swept the floor perfectly clean and I suspected it had probably been the captain. He sat down behind the table and motioned me into the other chair.

Herbert was an average-sized man with gray hair. He was probably a little over middle age and, in spite of the two silver bars on his uniform, could not help seeming somewhat fatherly. He had a passion for accouterments as I had already learned, having been issued such things as extra field bags, shoe wax, several gas capes for waterproofing equipment, photographic filters, cold weather combat pants, grease, etc., etc. Most of it was now scattered from Naples to Nettuno. Had I been a movie man, it would have been even worse, with at least fifty pounds of equipment added to my already heavy load. Evidently at the Training Film Lab the captain came from they didn't have to carry everything they owned on their backs.

For this and a few other reasons—such as his insistence on personally directing every shot made by photographers in his presence—he was considered at the very least eccentric. Some disliked him intensely. This practice of telling a photographer how to do his job was disconcerting and violated the unwritten law of the outfit, which said the time for criticism was after the final prints were made. By this time we were considered professionals.

The captain was himself a very good movie technician, however, and was so sold on the technique he had developed over long years of experience that he could see no other. In a career devoted to the making of movies, his knowledge of still picture technique had been neglected, but he insisted that all still photographers follow his own movie procedure. All the still photogs adopted the same course: listen attentively to his lectures, forget them immediately, and do as good a job as possible.

As I sat down in the chair in front of the table, the captain leaned over and asked, "How do you feel, Bell?"

I knew he was referring to Lannigan's death and I didn't

know what to say.

"All right, sir."

"That was a terrible thing, about Lannigan," he said. "He was a very good cameraman, and I understand he was very well liked among the men. However, such things happen in war and we must expect them and not allow them to affect us when they do happen."

Oh, Lord, I thought, what kind of eulogy is this?

He went on, "I know you and he were pretty close friends and I can understand how you must feel about it. Remember, though, that we still have a long, hard job ahead of us and you mustn't let what has happened affect your work."

"I just gave you two packs of film, sir," I said, feeling as if I were being reprimanded.

"Yes, yes. I know. That's fine. But if you want to, you can just rest until I get another cameraman to work with you. Sgt. Kreider, a very good man, is my supernumerary, and I think I will put you two together. He was supposed to come in yesterday, but I haven't seen him yet."

Kreider, I knew, was one of a small group of new men who had recently come from the States, and had not yet seen combat. I had not met him nor any of the other new arrivals, but I had already heard stories of their asinine behavior and condescending attitude. They had just come from the Astoria studios of the Army Training Film Lab and had firm, ready-made ideas on just how a war should be photographed. We all wondered how long it would take them to discover that the Germans were very camera-shy and refused to take directions from a G.I. photographer.

The prospect of being tied to one of these training-film technicians was dismaying. However, I knew that to attempt to argue with the man who had formulated the group's illusions would be foolhardy. I resolved to try subtle reasoning with Kreider and hope that the stories I had heard were exaggerated.

When Snuffy and I returned to the house, it was late

afternoon. As we drove up, we were greeted by the sight of men standing in knee-deep holes in the ground, cursing at rocks and tree roots as they swung picks and shovels. It was the remainder of our little family group in the process of carving out foxholes for themselves. Despite the physical work involved, the idea had a certain self-protection appeal, and soon Snuffy and I had borrowed the necessary entrenching instruments and were vigorously engaged in our own projects.

Estimating the distance that the stone wall of the house would scatter as it went down, I added about five paces and lined up a position giving a straight, unobstructed runway from the kitchen door. When I finished my calculations, I was standing with my back against the thin wooden wall of a small building about fifteen yards from the house. The flimsy building seemed to have been a two-room servant's quarter and general storeroom. Here, almost against the foundations of the structure, I began digging my hole. That the wooden wall might fall on my slit trench in case of a hit did not bother me because I felt I could lift the light boards off at least enough to get out. Also, I counted on the eaves of the roof to deflect at least the smaller pieces of falling flak which, during every raid, whizzed uncomfortably down from the bursting anti-aircraft shells like a steel hailstorm.

It was hard work digging that hole, and I constantly ran into large rocks and roots. By the time I had leveled the bottom off at a depth of two feet, I was ready to tell myself that if I went any deeper I was only increasing the possibility of being buried alive in case of a cave-in. I dropped the pick beside the hole and sat down on the edge for a rest and a smoke.

No sooner had I lit my cigarette than every machine gun in the area burst out in a furious roar. I saw a line of tracers streaming very close over the top of the house from B.B Eyes' gun, situated nearby. I jerked my eyes in the direction of fire and saw an airplane coming directly at me with a row of machine guns flaming in each wing. The plane was so low that it seemed to be touching the roofs as it streaked across the town toward me.

The next instant I was pushing dirt with my face in the bottom of my beloved slit trench with the roar of the plane feeling like a physical weight rolling over my back as it passed no more than fifty feet above me.

I was again digging with shining inspiration when B.B. Eyes came over to apologize for chipping tiles off our roof.

That night we all became disgustingly intimate with our engineering handiwork as we spent a large, harrowing portion of the dark hours shivering against the damp, cold dirt. Even with ignoring the lighter fracases, we still made the streaking dash from bunk to trench at least ten times between sunset and sunrise.

Immediately after breakfast we all headed for our holes, rearmed with picks and shovels, bursting with new ideas for improvements developed during the night.

By the time I had my hole down to three feet and the bottom lined with cardboard from the ration boxes, both the other teams had gone out to contact their outfits. Since the captain had told me to rest, I intended to take him literally. Still, I wanted to keep in touch with him in case any changes were to be made, so I called Snuffy, who was also finishing up, and we went in to wash up before paying a visit to the captain.

I was surprised to find Art in the house, lying on his bunk, reading, as I thought he had gone out with the other members of his team, Kline and Pratt.

"Hello, Art," I called through the door from the kitchen. "Thought you were gone."

"No," he answered rather weakly. "I don't feel too good this morning."

"That will teach you to put your pants on before you go out to lie in a wet foxhole," I kidded him.

I didn't doubt that he was feeling bad. For the last couple of days he had been looking pale and acting more jumpy than I had ever seen him. Well, he had reason, I thought, and didn't we all?

7
Prisoners

When I walked in the door of Capt. Herbert's squeaky-clean "office," he was in deep conversation with a man I didn't know. He looked up, gave his big smile and said, "Come on in, Bell, I'm glad you came. I want you to meet Sgt. Kreider. He's a very good cameraman and you two will work well together."

"*That, Captain, is a matter of pure speculation*," is what I wanted to say, but I realized that was unfair to the man who was going to be my teammate, for better or for worse, possibly so long as we both might live.

I should say that the sight of a pair of shiny tech sergeant stripes prominently splashed from Kreider's shoulder to his elbow contributed to my negative attitude. A tradition had grown up among the CAT teams that frowned on the wearing of stripes, no matter what the rank. The ranking man was recognized and accepted as the leader of the team, but the three men worked as movie man, still man, and driver, and cast their votes in that capacity. The constant reminder of rank was an unnecessary source of possible friction within the team.

Kreider came quickly across the room to me, extending his hand as he came.

"Hello, Bell," he said with a wide smile, "Glad to know you."

"Same to you, *Sergeant*," I returned as pleasantly as I could. But I couldn't seem to help emphasizing the word "sergeant." I saw him absorb the shock of it and felt sorry it had slipped out.

Sobered a little he went on, "I know how you felt about Lannigan but I think we'll get along all right. The boys at the lab were telling me you're doing damn good work and I'm glad I'm going to work with you."

He had hit me in a vulnerable spot, and if nothing else, I had to admire his tact. Involuntarily, I warmed up.

Back at the group house, I introduced Kreider to the other men and watched as everyone, without exception, glanced at the big chevrons on his sleeves. There were, however, none of the sarcastic remarks I had half expected.

This was when I realized just what it was that made a new man stand out so obviously. It had seemed strange before that I, and others who had seen even a couple of months of combat, were able to instantly recognize a man who had just arrived from the States. But I had never before tried to analyze the cause. This man was fated to assume a fairly important role in my immediate future, a future that I knew could come to an abrupt halt simply by allowing a combat-ignorant partner to maneuver me into committing the same kind of blunders I had made early on. I was now frantically applying myself to learning the smallest details of Kreider's character so I could tactfully lead him into our experience-built routine. I found in him the dozens of small details that distinguish newcomers from the "old timers," which all men seemed to become with miraculous rapidity if they managed to live through their first lessons.

The most obvious difference was dress, of course. Looking at Kreider, from the top of his brand new, unscarred helmet, through his clean, pressed new uniform, to his stiff, neatly laced leggings (I hadn't seen leggings since Africa!), it all screamed, "Rookie."

These physical things could be ignored, however, and still one had the urge, on seeing such a soldier for the first time, to ask, "How's things in the States?" After looking at Kreider for a while, I knew it was something in his face. He was a little under thirty years old, I guessed, older than I was, but there was something that made him look younger than any of us. I decided it was his eyes. They seemed to have a sparkle, a kind of life that

I hadn't seen in a long while. I was seeing the anticipation of adventure. I was worried about the situations such a state of mind could lead us into. At the same time, I felt sad that such enthusiasm was bound to die out in a very short while. It was this small thing alone, I realized, that makes a man look either young or old.

I didn't have a chance to talk with Kreider alone until after we had dinner and were out in the yard taking turns digging a slit trench for him. This was being done at my suggestion, and I knew that he considered it unnecessary and even a little foolish, but I counted on only one night to change his mind.

Finally, tired, we both sat on the edge of the hole to take a short break. After a silence, during which he appeared to be thinking hard, he said, slightly embarrassed, "Look, Bell, I realize that us guys that have just come in are green as hell about combat. We didn't even have any basic training in the States. But we'll learn pretty fast, working with you guys."

I said, "Sure, it won't take long. Without any basic training, you won't have anything to unlearn."

He went on. "I want you to be frank with me. Tell me when I do anything wrong."

Tell you when you do anything wrong! I thought. Brother, there's Hermann Goering's Panzer Division looking down at you from those mountains just waiting to remind you if you do anything wrong.

Evidently he had something else in mind. "A lot of the fellows in the outfit, not you guys here, but back at the company mostly, seem to be holding something against us." He sounded a bit peevish.

"O.K., Kreider," I said, feeling it was time to open up. "You asked me to be frank, so I will. First of all, you guys come into the outfit with a lot of stripes that might have been ours later on. Now we don't have a chance till our company T/O absorbs your rates and, the way it works, that will probably take a long time. That's always been a sore spot to the men, and you fellows hit it pretty hard. It's not your fault, but it's pretty hard to take. Nobody here wears stripes, and that makes it twice as bad to see yours flashing around."

Before I could go on, he stopped me with a surprised, "Why?"

"Why?" I repeated. "Because here we work as a team."

"But I wouldn't try to pull rank on anybody."

"O.K.," I said, anger deserting me just when I needed it. "Leave them on, then."

"No, wait a minute," he came back quickly. "Don't get sore. I just wanted to know. Go on with what you were saying."

"Well," I began again, "the way I heard it from the company, some of you guys have been saying that our stuff was no good."

"No, no," he came back, "it's not that. We just think the movie men don't shoot a complete story. When the stuff gets back to the cutter, he doesn't have enough film to put the whole story together. Now, guys like us who are used to shooting training films will send back the whole thing practically cut in the camera."

I decided it was a lost cause and went in to look for a poker game. The combination of lack of sleep, a bad case of nerves, and my jealousy of the glaring chevrons had brought to an abrupt close a conversation that might have been more beneficial for us both.

*****

That night Kreider learned to use a foxhole. The next morning he learned the meaning of the word "cover" when I pointed out to him (while we dusted off our clothes after a 109's strafing run in our direction) that his bush would not stop nearly as many bullets as my mound of dirt. When he professed interest, I explained that I had "assumed the prone position" before he had because I had anticipated the enemy by noticing an observation plane in a steep dive for the relative safety of a low altitude, that I had seen the plane before he had because I had looked in the direction of the sun first as the most likely direction, and that I had looked at the horizon instead of high into the air. His interest reassured me that he was willing to learn by example rather than sad experience. That we early birds had come through our first blunders relatively unscathed seemed a miracle to me now.

We shot our first story together that day, the laying of a steel mesh mat on the open beach for the landing of amphibious "ducks" bringing in supplies from the ships in the harbor. I watched Kreider's technique of "cutting in the camera" and liked the way he worked; but on a story like this, I could see no difference between his treatment and what Lannigan would have used. I didn't believe I would notice any great difference in their treatment of combat footage either, such things being largely in the hands of chance.

We were interrupted in our work several times by the intrusion of large enemy artillery and angry German fighter pilots. Big shells steadily pounded the harbor. We saw at least one ship and a duck receive hits. All the while, three ships, one a Liberty that had been beached before it could sink, were burning away, with long plumes of boiling, black smoke. The lighted and unmistakably-marked hospital ship, the St. David, hit by bombers on the second night, was on the bottom of the harbor.

I considered it all good experience for Kreider, including the quiet admonition given him by an engineer corporal after he had unconsciously backed ten yards out into a mine field while making a long shot.

We finished the story in about four hours and were heading back toward town for chow and a quiet afternoon of letter-writing when, once again, ack-ack opened up on all sides of us. As we dived over the sides of the jeep, we were able to snatch a glance at the spot directly over Nettuno where black bursts of ack-ack blotted out a large patch of sky. There above the earth patiently glided a formation of black bombers.

As we lay flat, scattered in our stubble field, we rolled easily with the shuddering earth as an opposing hell was let loose from the ground below the planes. Then, the stoic formation banked to the left and took a direct line back in the direction from which it had come. As we watched them soar out of sight, one of the planes began to trail a plume of black smoke, which gradually grew larger and darker as the plane dropped slowly out of the formation.

Just before we reached the road to our house, we noticed a column of smoke growing larger and larger, from what seemed to be the center of town. We decided to go back into town and at least take a look before going home.

As we drove down the main street, large chunks of smoking metal began landing close around us, so we stopped the jeep behind a building and left Snuffy with it. Kreider and I ran four or five blocks toward fire. Whatever it was, it was still burning and exploding and should make good pictures. When we got close, we saw that the bombs had made a direct hit on a convoy of trucks, and it was the ammunition load that was burning furiously and exploding over and over.

From behind the protective corner of a building, we tried to figure out how to get closer. We were in range of danger but not quite close enough for good pictures. We noticed there was a slight pause in the series of blasts after each big explosion, so, immediately after we had waited for the smoking pieces of steel to finish falling after one of the blasts, we dashed a half block to the positions we had spotted beforehand. Mine was behind a set of heavy marble steps at the entrance to a building. Kreider took up a more dubious spot behind the wheels of a truck that had not been hit, but whose driver had prudently left it to its fate.

From these positions we could get a clear view to shoot our pictures without exposing more than our heads and shoulders for a few seconds at a time. We could now see five trucks, all blazing from bumper to bumper. Each seemed to be loaded half-and-half with 155mm projectiles and powder charges. The powder charges were shooting out forty-foot jets of fire as they exploded out the ends of their cases, harmless except for the intense heat they created. The blasts we had seen and heard were from explosions of projectiles that threw out, not only their own shrapnel, but large pieces of truck as well.

Crouched low behind my invulnerable steps, I wondered if I was going to get anything worthwhile on my film, since my hands were trembling badly as I pulled out my safety slide. I hadn't realized just how far gone my nerves were.

The first shot I made was a cover-up in case I got nothing else. I took it while the trucks burned peacefully and safely—a good shot, but not spectacular. Next, I set the image in my finder, held my breath and waited for the explosion. When it came, I saw with one eye a whole front fender of a truck flying directly into my camera. Ducking and shooting at the same time, I cursed myself for blurring the shot as the huge chunk of metal crashed onto the opposite side of the steps from where I crouched.

My anger at myself calmed my shaking hands considerably, and I was able to record two more shots of the blasts, which I considered enough.

Kreider, in the meantime, was grinding off spasmodic scenes with his Eyemo, and alternately ducking behind a set of large dual wheels on his truck. He was, at last, getting a taste of combat photography and, as I sat, slumped against the wall of the building, I admired the way he held his head out to get the last frame of film possible before he was compelled to duck for cover.

Finally, he lowered his camera and looked at me. We both smiled without a word. I motioned for him to come over to my slightly safer spot and he made the dash between blasts. I slid over to give him room, and he dropped into the open space, panting.

"Did you cut it in the camera?" I asked, smiling.

"Are you kidding?" he answered with a laugh.

Regaining his breath, his face grew serious again. "No hard feelings, Bell?" he asked.

"Hell, no," I answered.

Lying there on the rubble-covered sidewalk with the heat of the fire streaking filthy sweat down our faces, and with occasional pieces of hot steel ricocheting above us, we twisted to a position where we could shake hands.

We reached home tired, dirty and hungry, but personally I felt good. A chow of corned beef, canned peas, hard crackers and instant coffee satisfied our hunger. Poor but necessary baths out of our helmets took care of the itchy feeling. We spent the rest of the afternoon writing letters home and rereading a few of the old ones we had saved.

We had not received any mail since we hit the beach, but even though the Army placed a high priority on mail, we hardly expected any yet. We were eager to know the opinions from home on our new front, though since we were not allowed in our letters to mention our location, those at home had no way of knowing we were in the thick of things.

We learned that enemy paratroopers were expected that night. Most of the guards on the beachhead had been quadrupled. We, being near a guard post of an ack-ack outfit, took only the extra precaution of closing the two doors to the outside and placing an empty water can against each. Normally we were in the habit of leaving the doors open to insure an unobstructed way out when the dive bombers showed up. Tonight, our crude alarm system seemed advisable.

After several flights to our foxholes before midnight, we were all so exhausted that we were sound asleep when the blast to awaken the dead came. My first sensation was only the jolt of a terrific concussion and the sound of empty water cans tumbling across the floor. I was out of bed and halfway across the room with pistol in hand before I realized that the glare of light coming through the windows was from the explosion of a ship near shore. Next day we learned that it had been a Liberty ship, the Samuel Huntington.

The sleep knocked out of us temporarily, we stood outside the house talking for a while and watching the ship, broken in half by the violence of the blast, burn its guts out. Finally, chilled, we went back inside to examine the new cracks that had appeared in the walls, and to scrape the chunks of plaster off our beds before crawling back in.

At breakfast, Kreider explained in painful detail the sequence of a story on the collection and burial of bodies that Herbert wanted. I explained to Kreider why some of the shots could not be made, but agreed to go along with him on the project because, as I had seen before, there would be very little photographable activity at the front in daylight. Gen. Clark had us stopped, and everyone was dug in deep and holding the status quo while the Germans took the opportunity to scrape up reinforcements.

We looked up the red-faced Ranger chaplain and got a promise of assistance, directions on where we could find our material, and the location of Lannigan's grave.

In the yard of a little farmhouse where we had been told we would find a pick-up station for bodies, we saw a group of Italian women and children kneeling beside a line of uncovered mangled flesh and blood. We were able to distinguish the remaining upper half of a man's body with the shreds of civilian clothes still plastered on it with dried blood. The group made a good shot so we silently set up our cameras and unobtrusively moved into position to take our pictures. We were ignored, so we moved in for close-ups and a better angle. I focused a close-up of a young girl kneeling close beside a badly mutilated G.I.'s body. The girl's smooth, clean profile made a powerful contrast with that of the corpse, whose lifeless wide open eyes stared as if horror-struck directly into my lens. Just as I was about to trip the shutter, I suddenly swore and lowered the camera.

"What's the matter, Bell?" Kreider asked as he saw me walk away without taking the shot.

"What the hell's the use of shooting stuff like that?" I said with disgust. "That's the kind of stuff they won't use because they think it's too gory for the sensitive American people!"

The funny thing was it didn't seem gory to me. It just looked like a good shot, the same old contrast stuff like the priest saying mass in a bombed-out church—surefire stuff with stateside editors. Maybe at one time I would have been shaken to see a dog run over in the street, but now a half-gone body with bloody entrails oozing out into the dust had no effect on me. I was just getting used to seeing death in its various forms. A new set of values on human life seemed to be settling inside my mind.

Another peculiar effect was also fermenting in my head. Though the sight of blood no longer caused any sensation other than curiosity within me, the thought of blood was always with me. A tracer bullet in a belt of machine gun ammunition looked as if the point had been dipped in blood. A piece of red cloth on a fence post looked like a shred of bloody flesh. The red tail of a fighter plane made the machine look as if it were bleeding to death. Whenever I closed my eyes to the light, a red blanket of blood covered me. Often, too, I saw the image of a pair of G.I. boots reaching out from a dark pool of blood beneath an olive-drab blanket. I knew I needed a rest as I had never needed one in my life, but since I saw no possibility of getting one, I did my best to ignore these disturbing images.

At the cemetery, where we had followed the truck carrying the stack of expended bodies, we made pictures of them being lined up with over a hundred others for identification and eventual burial. A large crew of civilian workers was busily digging neat little holes in a large, marked-off field.

When the light began to fail, we packed up our equipment and headed back to the house for supper. As we walked in the door, we were greeted by the very welcome smell of something cooking. Bernie had appointed himself cook and was brewing up his specialty, cheese rarebit. His uncomplicated recipe consisted of K-ration cheese melted with canned milk into which were dipped K-ration crackers.

The tantalizing smell compelled us to try to sneak a sample but we were stopped short by the point of a bayonet.

"Whenever you guys get that hash heated up and some coffee made you'll get this stuff, but 'til then, nobody comes within six feet of it," Bernie warned, still waving his weapon. We began pumping up another Coleman stove.

Art came in and stood silently at the door watching us. I asked if he was feeling better.

"Sure, I feel O.K.," he answered listlessly.

I didn't believe him. He looked incredibly tired. His hands shook violently as he lit a cigarette, and the flare of the flame illuminated dark circles around his eyes. He looked like one of those who were surely heading for a crackup.

As we ate, I looked at the men sitting around the table. With the exception of Kreider, all of them wore a tired look on their faces. Their eyes were approaching that dead, blank look. The conversation was an excellent attempt at belying the facial expressions, but the pauses were much too long, as if the speaker just forgot, temporarily, that he was talking. I knew I must present the same appearance as the others, and for a moment a feeling of desperation swept over me.

Art was silent all through the meal and ate his small portion slowly and mechanically without looking up from his mess kit. After supper everyone, with the exception of Art and me, went across the wheat field to a large house where the neighbor artillery battalion had a radio. I stayed to write up the captions on the day's shooting, and Art wanted only to lie quietly on his bunk.

When I had finished, I blew out my candle and went to Art's room. The room was dark but I could see him lying in his bunk with his face to the wall. When I said his name he jumped wildly and then answered with my name.

"What's the matter, fella?" I asked as I sat down on the edge of his bunk.

"My God, I don't know, Cliff." His voice cracked.

"We all need to take it easy for a couple of days, that's all," I suggested.

"I don't know," he repeated vaguely.

He and I had always been pretty close and I hoped it would help if he talked it out with me. After a pause, he went on.

"I'm O.K. when I'm here," he continued, "jumpy as a cat, of course, but I guess we all are. It's just when I try to work. I swear I can't hold my camera, my hands get to shaking so."

"You want to go back to the company?" I asked.

"No."

"Capt. Herbert would send you back as a courier. He offered it to me."

"I don't want to," he said, emphatically.

I tried hard to persuade him. "Look, Art," I implored, "nobody's going to say a damn thing if you go back. You've been here five days now and the roughest part is probably over. Before this you had four months at the front. Even the infantry get to go back for a rest. Nobody's going to say a word."

"No," he said and turned back to the wall.

"O.K., fella," I said and left him alone again. I felt a complete breakdown was close, but there was nothing else I could do. And as a matter of fact, Art held on. Most of us did, but as I said earlier, for many the wounds were deep and slow to heal.

When the others came back, I asked for the BBC news, but the news from London was far less important than the news from Anzio. The others had learned from the artillerymen that the beached Liberty just below our house had not been sunk by German artillery. The enemy was now sending in what became known as "glider bombs." These were launched by a bomber, guided to the target by radio control and probably propelled by a rocket motor. According to reports, they carried a thousand pounds or more of explosive. It sounded bad for our crowded little beachhead, which had been growing smaller nightly.

The civilian correspondents had by now scrambled aboard ships and run back to Naples while their frantic screams of "another Dunkirk" were being stopped cold by the military censors. We Army types had no choice but to stay and take whatever came, but we didn't really have the inclination to run out.

We went to bed that night even more prepared than usual to make the scramble from our beds to our holes at the first opening of the fifties. Instead of removing my shoes and placing them fireman-fashion on the floor beside my bunk, I merely loosened the buckles and laces and went to bed with them on. Later I was thankful I had done so as the raids came much more often than usual. I was unable to sleep more than a few minutes at a time. Lying down, I was asleep almost as soon as my head touched my rolled-up field jacket; but with the sleep immediately came all sorts of garish nightmares and I would awake, often sitting up. I wondered seriously if Art was in any worse condition than I.

The roar of the fifties, punctuated by the frantic, deep-throated pounding of a nearby Bofors (anti-aircraft gun), was already at its most frightening height as I came out of my bunk on the run. Seconds later, I looked back over the edge of my hole and saw Bernie make a swan dive into his. That seemed to be the cue for the whine and crash of the explosions: one-two-three-four, each one closer than the last. The ground heaved, dirt fell on me at the bottom of my hole, and hot steel whizzed down to bounce off the tile roof of the house or thud into the ground.

Gradually, the steady roar of the planes overhead trailed off and the firing from the ground stopped, except for a few parting shots from the heavies. We crawled out of our holes, beating away most of the mud from our clothes, each one counting the others.

Again we lay down in our beds and pulled our dusty blankets over us. It was useless to go to sleep, I thought, and probably dangerous, too. Then I was asleep.

This time when I awoke, not only were the guns at the height of their desperate thunder, but the rumble of bombs falling on Anzio was loosening plaster and dust from the ceiling. As I bounded for my slit trench, a blinding light burst overhead, illuminating the area with a blue-white intensity. The daylight brightness, contrasting with the inky shadows it left, gave everything the ghostly quality of an infrared photograph.

This first flare was accompanied by three more, and others came as these burned out. The invisible plane that was dropping them circled again and again, seemingly invulnerable to the enveloping holocaust.

We knew we were in for it this time, as the flares were directly overhead and all coming in approximately the same place. Then, as I had before and would again, I repeated a series of short, to-the-point prayers.

Even with the seconds seeming to expand into hours, we did not have long to wait until we heard the rumble of many engines growing louder and louder as they approached. The rumble increased to a roar easily discernible through the constant din of thousands of explosions. The mounting tension made me feel as if I would stand up and yell to the bombardiers to drop their bombs now or forever be damned. Instead, I dug harder and harder into the mud.

Suddenly, above the oppressive din, I heard an un-recognized swishing sound that rapidly grew louder. The swishing took on a rasping viciousness that reached such an intensity I felt as though the noise alone would crush my body. Then, in a split second, flash, noise, light, life and death were wiped clean from my mind. Only one thought existed: how was

Mother going to take the news of my death?

The concussion was a violent yet gentle thing. Soundlessly, I was crushed from all sides and felt my senses go numb. My body was lifted from the dirt at the bottom of my foxhole to almost the top of it. Then I was released to thud back into the mud.

There I lay, limp and half-conscious. The raid was still going on and occasionally I was rocked from side to side. Dirt fell into the hole, threatening to bury me, but somehow it didn't matter.

Slowly I began to tremble. I shook till it seemed that my bones would fall apart. I was cold as if my blood were frozen, and yet perspiration bathed me from head to foot. When the spasm had exhausted itself, I was too weak to move. I lay there dazed for what seemed like hours.

Finally, I felt stronger. The sounds of the raid came back to me. The glare of the flares was gone but the firing of the guns around me continued. Now, however, they seemed far away and not in the least frightening.

I twisted myself over on my back and, disregarding the danger of falling flak, watched the display of brilliantly colored fireworks forming a garish umbrella overhead.

The show died slowly and I climbed laboriously back to ground level with the ecstatic feeling of one who had died and been miraculously restored to life. As I stood and watched the others crawl out of their holes, I was in a state of happiness I had never known.

We did not go into the house immediately, but gathered silently beside the wall of the building and sat on the ground.

"Must have been a glider bomb," someone suggested.

"Yeah," someone else agreed.

We were each reluctant to leave the vicinity of our holes and each reluctant to admit it. At last Snuffy broke up the farce by going into the house without a word and reappearing with an armload of blankets. As he passed, he announced to no one in particular, "I'm sleeping in my hole tonight."

It was cold and damp as well as hard and cramped in our rugged refuges that night, but we all got at least three hours of blissful sleep for the first time since we had left Naples. There may have been more raids before daylight but, as far as my body was concerned, the whole world could have collapsed once I had closed my eyes and I would have remained totally unaware of it.

At dawn we took a look at the glider bomb crater about a hundred yards out in the wheat field, and began work on our slit trenches with renewed interest. The crater was about hundred and forty feet across by some sixty to seventy feet deep. This time I stopped digging only when my hole was chest deep and wide enough to accommodate my set of bedsprings. I lined the sides with two shelter halves, dropped in the bed springs, covered the top with heavy boards over 4"-by-4" beams and shoveled dirt two feet deep over the whole thing. At one end I dug an entrance approached by a short angled trench that protected me from fragments in case a small anti-personnel bomb should drop into the uncovered space. At the other end, I installed a hollow tile in the roof, at an angle, as an exit for concussion and, also, for fresh air. As a finishing touch, I dug up weeds and carefully transplanted them to the top of my covered cavern for camouflage.

After I had installed my bed roll, a candle, a couple of magazines, and an attractive "pinup," I felt that, though the war was still going on I, at least, had it licked.

When we had all finished, we invited each other to crowd into our individual safety zones to compare the little original touches and innovations. We all enjoyed much better sleep from then on.

A couple of days later we ran into the CAT team of Hershey/Blau/Boone. This team and another had been living together in a large stone house near the center of the town, using the reinforced cellar as an air-raid shelter. Now, however, they were using a large cave on the outskirts of town. The reason for their move, as they explained with great animation, was that the house no longer existed, a large bomb having been dropped on it while they were luckily bumming chow at Corps CP a couple of blocks away.

"Why don't you guys move into the cave with us?" Sid Blau suggested. "It's big enough. There's a bunch of Quarter-master officers coming in, but we'll hold you a spot if you want."

It sounded like a good idea, especially when they mentioned that the Quartermasters' outfit had a kitchen close by that handed out pretty good chow.

The next morning when we arrived at the cave entrance, our jeeps were loaded down with all our equipment. In the darkness of the narrow tunnel, we took up residence along the damp limestone walls. The cave had two entrances, one near the top of the cliff beneath which the cave lay, and the other lower down, where we set up housekeeping. Near the top entrance was installed a medical detachment aid station, made up of black soldiers. Our part of the tunnel was the shallowest—there could not have been more than ten feet of crumbling limestone above our heads—but we put our faith in the scant possibility of a direct hit.

Here we slept for nearly five months, damp and un-comfortable but with a feeling of relative safety, while our extra clothing and equipment molded away. Days we spent in a little house on top of the hill, except during the time we were out on assignment or in the cave sweating out a bombing raid or artillery barrage. Eventually, all the members of the 163rd detachment, numbering about twenty-five men, took to gathering here.

The day came when Capt. Herbert was called back to the company and replaced by Lt. "Pappy" Brinn. The captain took Art Elliot, Snuffy and, against his will, Bernie Kline. Within two weeks we heard the sad news of Bernie's death on the southern front. I always hoped, but never knew for sure, that Art made it.

"Pappy," at first glance, seemed to be a tough character.

Our cave away from home.

His rough-chiseled face seldom cracked a smile, and he gave his orders with the intonation of a Foreign Legion drill sergeant. But he had a kind heart, as we all came to know.

Some of the men had been with him through the Africa campaign and, though he tried to conceal it, he showed a fatherly affection for them. But he would not permit this to be interpreted as favoritism.

Pappy had been a newspaperman, and when he volunteered for the Army, he vacated the chief's chair in a large picture syndicate's West Coast office. He introduced a newspaper-style city desk operation that left us a little aghast at first. All semblance of our three-man teams vanished, and all assignments were made from Pappy's chair on the front porch of our little CP house on the hill, a sort of subsidiary to the main CP. There he sat, from dawn till dusk, shooting personal pictures of air raids and shelling, with a Leica and 135mm lens. A field telephone hung outside the window, and the number of story tips that came through it was a constant source of amazement to us. He spent relatively little time at Corps CP and yet he seemed to be on intimate terms with all the right people.

After a full minute of ringing, Pappy would lift the phone out of its leather case without taking his eyes from the unobstructed panorama of Nettuno below him.

"Brinn talking," he would growl into the mouthpiece. Then, either "O.K., I'll send a man," or "Hell, no. It ain't worth nothing to me." If the tip was a good one, the first man available would get a one-sentence summary of the whole story with time, place, and rated importance, plus the instruction, "Go and get it."

Brinn's personal influence on those under his command was an amazing thing. Undiluted respect and admiration for this hard-cussing, middle-aged tyrant was shared by every man alike. He dissolved friction by the sheer weight of his personality. A happier bunch under such unpromising circumstances could not have been found.

One day we heard news from Caserta, where our company HQ was now located, that Capt. Morehouse was gone and our company had a new commander. The monarch we had cursed from Fort Sam Houston to Anzio was out and the old despotism was dead. We had never heard of the new Capt. Smith, but we welcomed him with open minds.

The first we knew of his presence in Nettuno was when someone stumbled onto him in conference with Brinn in the room designated as office in the subsidiary CP house. Later in the day we were summoned to the CP'S "day room." There, we got our first good look at him.

He said the usual things: he had been assigned as company commander of the 163rd, we did not know him and he did not know us but he had heard good things about our work, and so on. He touched on nothing controversial and committed himself to nothing. If anything more important was scheduled to be included in the speech, we never found out what it was. A rapid series of heavy explosions loosened dust and plaster from the ceiling. Before it had time to drift to the floor, the room was emptied via windows and doors. Smith immediately grasped the situation and joined the flying wedge formation into the mouth of the cave.

The next day the captain took an LST for Naples, and life on the beachhead settled back into its normal abnormality. We never saw him in Anzio again.

By now our position on the semicircle of our battered beachhead was at least fairly secure so long as the Germans failed to further reinforce the troops surrounding us. They seemed content to leave their manpower at the same approximate strength since it was already sufficient to stop cold any attempted advance. That was the fault of Gen. Clark and his indecisive beach commander, Gen. Lucas. The Wehrmacht brought up larger and larger artillery to dump on the towns, docks, and harbor. There was never a time when they were unable to reach any spot on the beachhead. They used us as guinea pigs to try out any new weapon their scientists and engineers happened to produce. We received not only glider bombs but miniature tanks loaded with explosives guided by either hand wires or radio control; rockets; a huge shell with what was rumored to be a booster charge in the rear end; several new types of "window" for jamming our radar; and new types of butterfly anti-personnel bombs.

In the meantime, Allied supplies and men were pouring in. Coming ashore were tanks by the hundreds, more anti-aircraft, large guns, sophisticated listening devices, a ready-made airport with steel mat runways for part of a fighter squadron, and dozens of barrage balloons to help block the enemy's strafing runs. The entire 34th Division arrived in spite of the constant pounding from air and ground that greeted them as they landed.

We got to try out a few new weapons including the first T72 tank destroyers and the first M4A1 medium tanks. We also wore the first of the new uniforms designed for cold weather

Tanks being unloaded at Anzio beachhead. Taken from one of my newspaper clippings.

fighting.

We were given first priority on such necessities as food (two fresh eggs for every man on the beachhead on one occasion), tires, gasoline, and ammunition, of which much was lost by bombing and shelling for lack of a safe storage place.

*****

Heller, Lapidus and I went one day to visit the artillery boys we had met while living in our house across town. We were greeted royally and invited to sit in on the same poker game that had been going on when we left. As we were leaving, B.B. Eyes said to me, "Hey, Bell, before you go I want to show you something."

He led me over to the little house we had lived in. It looked just the same except for a few new and wider cracks and a little more tile gone from the roof. The place was still empty; I wondered about that. When we walked around it, I saw that something had caused a radical change in the landscape. The little frame servant's house was gone, with hardly a trace to indicate where it had been.

"Bomb," B.B. Eyes explained, "the night after you guys left."

I walked over and looked reverently down at the spot where I had so lovingly carved out a foxhole. Now it was only a depression in the ground, full of loose dirt, completely caved in.

*****

When we discovered that our extra clothes, shoes and equipment were growing a thick coating of ugly green fungus, and that everything we owned that contained iron was rapidly rusting away, cave dwelling became less appealing. One day a fellow named Bonnard approached our group with an interesting proposition. He had a place he wanted us to see. Due to the location most of us responded in the negative, but I and a couple of others were interested enough to take a look.

When we drove into the rear courtyard of an eight-story hotel facing the waterfront in the heart of Nettuno, Bonnard pointed out a small garden house.

"There's a good place to keep the jeep, see?"

Entering through the rear door of the building, we picked our way down a rubble-strewn flight of stairs to the basement, which had served as servants' quarters. There had the advantages of the position pointed out to us.

"You see? There's a whole apartment here with a kitchen and two walls between it and the Krauts. Two-thirds of it is below ground level and we're defiladed on three sides by buildings. We've got nothing to worry about from above. The only possible spot they could get to us is with a bomb coming straight down and landing in the street in front of the building."

We looked out the small barred window near the top of the wall. Across the narrow street was a three story house that we saw would offer even more protection. Figuring the angle at which a bomb would have to fall in order to throw shrapnel through the window, we decided that an enemy bombardier would have to hit an area hardly larger than an average room. It was hard to see why the place was unoccupied.

Convinced that the possible risk would be more than outweighed by the gracious living offered by this battered servants' quarters, we went to work industriously with the brooms we had brought along in anticipation. We took turns choking, coughing, sneezing, and gagging in the dense clouds of unbreathable dust we raised, and finally got the three rooms we had chosen into a livable condition.

The job of furnishing our new living space brought out innumerable hidden talents in all of us. They were mainly those of taste, diligence, agility, and the willingness to carry the furniture down anywhere from one to eight flights of stairs. Many a tough decision was made between leaving a beautiful marble-topped desk, full length mirror or king sized mattress and carrying it down hundreds of steps.

All morning we struggled and sweated to outdo one another in furnishing our few square feet of space. At twelve we knocked off for chow, then resumed our labors until dark. Lying on the bare springs of our individual beds, we talked over the question of moving in immediately or waiting until the following morning. It was decided that, since it would take time to gather up our equipment that was distributed between the cave and the CP, and since it would take more than one jeep-load for the move, we would wait until morning.

None of us had ever made a more fortunate decision.

One of our number, Max Campbell, had always been fascinated by the terrible spectacle of an air raid. That night, as usual, he went to the cave entrance to watch the display when we heard the guns open up. The rest of us, lying comfortably in our warm bunks, listened to the raid's progression from the deep pounding of the heavies down to the hollow thumps of the thirty-sevens as the planes came within range. Finally, the frantic hammering of the fifties started and we waited tensely for the inevitable crash of the bombs.

It wasn't often that the whine from the fins of falling bombs reached into our cave, but tonight we heard them plainly. The earth rolled like a ship in rough weather as the explosions ripped at it and we held our blankets over our heads to keep the dirt from falling in our faces.

Campbell returned, stumbling over cots in the dark, and was greeted with friendly jeers.

"What's the matter, Maxie? Getting rough outside?"

"Yeah," he returned. "Looks like they found out where the one-sixty-third lives."

It did seem as if our area was the center of attention that night. Listening, I heard a dull "whomp" near the beach and waited for the other three that invariably walked like giant footsteps over an area of about a quarter mile. The second was definitely closer. The third gave a low-pitched whine as it drove toward the ground. Its crash released a flood of dirt particles as the earth pitched violently.

I never heard the fourth bomb, nor even realized for several seconds what had happened. A cyclone-like breath of air rushed through the narrow passageway of the cave, pushing over mosquito nets and scattering bits of light equipment and clothing before it. I found myself half off the top of my cot with my head hanging toward the ground. Instantly, we were all choking on the heavy atmosphere of dust and powder smoke.

"Hey, somebody come over here and help me," a voice called out in the dark. Several of us groped our way to his bunk and, bare-handed, dug off several hundred pounds of rock and dirt that had buried his legs and lower part of his body.

The word was passed back that the entrance at the top

had caved in and the aid station was buried. Fearing that the cave's mouth had been sealed, we went up to investigate. We found the mouth still partly open and the medics digging in the ruins of their dispensary to salvage enough medicines and equipment to treat the wounded who were being brought in on litters over the backs of other men.

A direct hit on the trench shelter occupied by about fifteen quartermaster men had left seven or eight wounded who were brought into the aid station. The dead were left to be gathered up in the morning. Two men from a nearby ack-ack pit staggered in alone, blood gradually soaking their shirts. They sat down on the dirt floor and leaned back against the wall, waiting for their turn for treatment. One died in this position.

We could do nothing to help except donate blankets to cover the wounded, so we went back to our section of the tunnel and sat listening to the sounds of the raid, wondering if it was ever going to end. Sometime much later, the noise of the firing died away and we lay awake the rest of the night listening to the groaning, crying and cursing of the wounded men lying in rows along the walls of the cave.

Early in the morning, we crawled out into the chilly fog of the dawn to survey the effects of last night's firestorm. Fourteen paces from the spot that I estimated to be just above my bunk lay the center of the bomb crater. Our CP house was polka-dotted with large shrapnel scars. It had taken the full blast of the bomb. The ragged pieces of metal that had entered the glassless windows had gouged chunks out of the walls, and a sliver had found the oak cabinet in which we kept our supply of film and extra camera equipment. The most valued piece of equipment there had been a ten-inch telephoto lens, used only on special occasions by the movie men. It now looked as if someone had punched a pencil through the center of the barrel.

Bonnard, Galbraith, Campbell and I met after breakfast to compare opinions on the completion of our housing project. We were a little less sure of the wisdom of our plan, but figured our position in town was at least as safe as a crumbling limestone hole in the ground.

Within an hour we had our gear together and were ready to start out with the first jeep load. We drove into the hotel garden by the side entrance and filed in through the back door to gloat over our lavish suite.

The rooms had been a filthy mess when we first set eyes on them but what we saw now rocked us back on our heels. Our gaudy furniture lay tumbled and broken about the rooms and everything was half-hidden under building stones and dirt. The little oblong window looking out over the sidewalk was now a gaping hole in the wall. The upper halves of the walls were pockmarked with shrapnel holes of various sizes.

The area out on the street hardly larger than an average room which could be reached only by a providentially placed bomb had been reached. By unanimous consent, we hurried back to the cave to reclaim our spots before somebody else snapped them up.

The beachhead front was now in more or less the same conformation it had acquired during the first two weeks following the landing. Activity was generally confined to subjects of small photographic interest. During this time, our shooting encompassed occasional spectacular shelling or bombing, celebrities visiting the beachhead or feature stories on everything from pet milk cows to home-made liquor stills. There were times when there was nothing more important than the poker game in the CP office.

To offset the poker game, the losers organized a volleyball team that consistently defeated all contenders, a washer pitching game, and a horticultural society. The membership of the latter consisted of Sid Blau and me.

The hard caliche soil could support no more growth than scrubby weeds and the hardiest and ugliest of wild flowers, but Sid and I had discovered a rock-bordered patch of dark earth near the backdoor of the CP. This we took to be a long-abandoned flower bed. Thus encouraged, we made long hikes through the open fields at the edge of town, searching for tiny plants that we hoped would turn out, in time, to be flowers. Spring was just around the corner and our imaginations had overwhelmed our good sense.

With our trench knives, we carefully extracted the weeds from our flower bed and dug and crumbled the hard clods. Then we set out twenty or so of the drooping little plants that we had dug up with a good amount of dirt still around the roots. Last, we carried scarce water in our canteens to pour around them.

Nearly two-thirds of the unhealthy little sprouts died of indigestion in their unaccustomed luxury. The remainder lingered on the brink for several days and then began to stretch out their leaves.

As Sid and I dutifully made the rounds each day, issuing to each hungry little mouth its ration of water, we examined each for signs of pregnancy, but it seemed we were doomed never to see a bloom. Quite possibly our lack of botanical knowledge was at fault: we couldn't distinguish between weeds and flowers. But despite the jeers of the other men we began to enjoy being called "landscape artists."

At about this time, Brinn announced that the drought was over. He had managed, by some devious machination, to get a truck and crew to haul a five hundred gallon wine cask from town to set up a private water reservoir. Now we would be able to take a bath whenever we itched and even wash our stiffening clothes. Also, for Sid and me, it meant the end of hauling water, canteen by canteen, to feed our garden. Unfortunately, both of us were out on stories when the truck arrived. Had we been present, we would have at least had the satisfaction of screaming our lungs loose in vain desperation. When we returned we saw the ugly, obese wine barrel snuggled down squarely on our pitiful, flattened flower garden.

*****

The Germans had begun to use anti-personnel bombs in ever increasing numbers. These tiny bombs, no more than six inches long, were a very effective way of putting a man out of action, though they seldom caused death. Every night thousands of the little manglers rained down on us, the pops of their small explosions all but drowned by the firing of the anti-aircraft guns. In the morning we found the duds lying dangerously about as well as the empty shells of their carriers. The carriers, as big as bath tubs and similarly shaped, held the hundreds of little bombs while they were still inside the airplane. When they were released into the air, a mechanism inside caused the two halves of the shell to come apart and release the clusters of bombs, which then scattered like shotgun pellets among the men below.

The foot mine also became a favorite of the German engineers. These tiny charges were sown in open fields by the thousands, making it almost impossible to walk more than a few steps before setting off one or more. The result of an unfortunate step was a foot blown off cleanly at the ankle, and a trip home.

Booby traps could turn up anywhere. A dirty piece of broken bottle stuck in the ground could spell death for an unsuspecting soldier. A tired man could sit on an apparently empty ammunition crate and lose his life. Opening a drawer filled with explosive sent another to his grave. The pressure of a foot on a step, the opening of a door, the lifting of an obstruction, even the moving of the dead killed many a man.

*****

The First Special Services Force (SSF), aka the Black Devils, was another of the supposedly elite units of the military services, along with other publicity-bloated outfits such as the 101st Airborne Division, certain Marine units, the British Commandos, and even my beloved Rangers.

Max Campbell, who covered the Black Devils, had promised to introduce me to this Canadian-American outfit. One

The intrepid photographers of the 163rd. I'm second from left on bottom row, Yale Lapidus on my right, Kreider on my left. Bob Heller sits behind Lapidus, Sid Blau behind me. Max Campbell is second from right on second row. Pappy Brinn is at middle of back row, with dangling camera. Peterson, with whom I would later work, is third from left, back row.

morning, at least an hour before daylight, he and I, with the driver named Pratt who had worked with Bernie Kline, were the cause of grunts and complaints of sleeping men as we pumped up a Coleman stove to make coffee. We were preparing to leave for the front to shoot a story and it would have been unthinkable to leave before we expelled the damp cold with a cup of the boiled brew.

Once on the road, our teeth stopped chattering and, as the first pale light began to fan over the mountains, we felt good. It was beginning to look like spring on our beachhead and the air was pushing its fresh smell through the dust. Small fires along the way announced the coming of chow as men began to crawl out of their holes in the ground. Here and there the smoke generators had begun to send their snowy, silhouetted plumes into the gray sky and the bundled ack-ack crews along the road were wiping the dew off their guns while they watched the morning sky.

At the CP, the SSF company commander was heating a can of K- ration eggs, and after offering us a package of crackers with steaming coffee, he told us that the raiding party we had hoped to accompany had already left.

Against his advice, we left the jeep behind the farmhouse serving as the CP, and cameras in hand started walking down the road in the direction of the departed patrol. About half a mile down the road, we balanced our precarious way across the Mussolini Canal on the broken timbers of a blown bridge and arrived at a crossroads without the slightest notion of which way to choose.

At a house beside the road, we saw two men sitting on the ground, talking, with the muzzle of their machine gun sticking out a window.

"Did you fellows see a patrol go through here a while ago?" we asked.

"Nope. Not this morning," was the indifferent answer from one of them.

Seeing our hesitation, the other said, "One of 'em went down that way yesterday," pointing straight ahead.

"Should we take it?" I wondered aloud, looking at Campbell and feeling more than a little doubtful.

"Let's try it a little way if you want to," he answered, not looking too certain either.

The first man looked up again from his seat on the ground. "It's all Kraut from here on," he warned.

As we walked back out into the road, I automatically

cocked my .45 and slipped it loosely into its holster with the cover flap tucked inside, out of the way. I noticed that Campbell, five paces ahead, was doing the same, and the click of Pratt's tommy gun behind me had a comforting sound.

For a while we stepped carefully around the dark spots of our own road mines, but after that we had a clear straight road and flat open country from the sea to the mountains. The only signs of civilization were some scattered farmhouses set forty to fifty yards back from the road. As we passed them one by one, our eyes were fixed as if hypnotized on the dark windows, from which we constantly expected a stream of machine gun fire. Down the center of the road we strode, quickly and nervously, afraid to trust the weed-filled ditches that were probably mined, feeling very much like three small boys passing through a graveyard at midnight. Not a sign of life did we see in any direction, nor did we hear so much as a distant shot. The silence bore down upon us until the vast expanse of land and sky began to feel as small and as close as a tomb.

As our nervous pace carried us deeper into enemy territory, I began to wish for the blessing of at least a mortar shell or a sniper's shot to stop our advance. The sound of our boots scuffling over the pavement became like the sound of an express train. On and on we marched, spacing ourselves farther and farther apart as our expectation of the inevitable trouble increased, and still nothing happened. Hope was gone for meeting the raiding party. Still, to turn back now, to give up and return empty handed with a story of walking down a smooth, wide highway, seeing nothing and hearing nothing: it was unthinkable.

After what seemed like days of mental exertion, we reached an intersection. The crossing road was as wide as the one we were on and just as deserted except for a burned-out American halftrack standing like a charred corpse in the center of the intersection.

Squatting beside the heap of twisted metal, we agreed to

make our way back toward friendly lines, now over three miles away. As we walked toward American territory with our backs to the enemy, I had the feeling that the entire German army was watching me, waiting to pounce like a cat on a mouse.

I looked at Campbell several paces ahead of me. He had suddenly stopped in his tracks and now stood frozen, his eyes on a house some fifty yards to the left. His hand rested gingerly on the butt of his pistol.

Jerking my eyes in the direction of his stare, I caught a glimpse of a quick movement at an upstairs window.

I dropped to one knee, drew my .45 and set my camera on the ground. Pratt, behind me, was down also, and I heard the click of the safety lock as he readied his tommy gun. We waited, ready and expectant, like cornered animals. We crouched in our wide open position in the center of the road for well over a minute and still the fire did not come.

"Must have been a curtain," Campbell finally said, standing up and replacing his pistol in its holster.

"Could have been," I agreed, doing the same.

I was far from convinced, since I had not seen the slightest movement since that first undeniable glimpse. Quickly we resumed our march, looking back frequently until the house was out of easy rifle range.

Our answer to the dilemma of the disappearing curtain came soon enough, though we were almost within sight of the American outpost at the crossroads.

The first indication we were not alone was the sharp, rocket-like swish and quickly following crack of an exploding eighty-eight no more than twenty yards to our right.

All three of us broke into a dead run, hindered only slightly by the weight of cameras and weapons. We longed to dive into the comparative safety of the shallow ditch beside the road, but the thought of mines kept us on the bare pavement.

Violent noise, ripping explosions, the swish and flutter of shells, the whiz of shrapnel broke out on all sides of us. It seemed that in addition to the eighty-eights, large mortar shells were also dropping in. I even imagined I heard a machine gun somewhere.

We ran blindly, all our strained attention on the road before us, our eyes straight ahead. With our mouths open, our burning lungs gasping for air and our bodies bathed in perspiration, we finally managed to stagger to shelter in the rear of the outpost house, safe, miraculously unharmed.

Later, when a PRO scribe, eager to add to his number of words published in hometown newspapers, wrote about it as a news story, he embellished our experience with a tank battle and a company of German infantry. He failed, however, to describe our feeling of gratitude to a providence that had brought us through unscathed.

*****

At the airfield on the beach at the southern edge of Nettuno was part of a fighter squadron that probably lost more planes on the ground from artillery fire than in the air from other causes. To uninformed observers, it seemed their main duty was to shoot down escaped barrage balloons and keep the field in readiness to receive the crippled planes that limped in nearly every day.

From our CP on the hill, we could watch the smoking, coughing planes circle the field and go in. Then, likely as not, we would see a cloud of dust, and sometimes black smoke, arise to indicate another failure to make a successful landing. At the end of the steel mesh runway, a great boneyard of smashed airplanes, from P40s to a B17, was piled high.

The appearance of a crippled fighter plane usually caused a spurt of excitement at the 163rd's CP. The first photog to lay hands on a camera and the first driver to get a jeep started usually combined to make a frantic dash to the beach in an attempt to beat the last dive of the plane into the water.

Most of the pilots of the limping fighters made a

series of circles over the beach area until they spotted the covey of "ducks" and small harbor craft heading out into the harbor. Then, a half roll in which the pilot ejected while the plane was in the inverted position, to float down in his parachute while the plane, pilotless but still powered, invariably fell into a vertical dive and hit the water with a huge splash.

Seldom was the photographer able to get the picture, and seldom was the pilot pulled out of the water.

We never saw American planes during enemy raids over the beachhead, and after the first four or five hundred attacks, learned not to expect them. After a while, though, we began to see large flights of friendly bombers passing overhead. The cheerful sight was watched as closely as that of the enemy.

The German air defense was a formidable thing. Many times we cursed sadly as we watched our big silver friends in the air fall in flames or disintegrate in a huge, silent explosion.

To enhance the protection of Anzio and Nettuno and the harbor, our anti-aircraft defense was aided by a barrage balloon battalion, and the big fat sausages soon formed what looked like an impenetrable web of dangling wires overhead.

Assigned to cover the complete story of their application to beachhead defense, I worked for several days until I needed only shots of the repair phase to make my story complete. My opportunity came when one of the frequent breakaways came and the balloon was perforated with bullet holes by the playful fighter pilots from the field down the beach. Throughout the entire procedure of retrieving the collapsed bag, patching the holes, and refilling it with gas, I made a long series of detailed pictures. Lacking only a couple of shots of the re-ascension, I sat down in front of the unit's kitchen tent to wait out the final preparations.

Without warning a crash of noise broke loose about me as every anti-aircraft gun in the area cut loose with a hail of fire. I looked up to see a German fighter plane in an almost vertical dive, roaring down with complete abandon through the deadly network of balloons and trailing cables, machine guns blazing. Staring transfixed for a second, expecting to see the plane disintegrate as it inevitably struck a wire, I was suddenly galvanized into action as it began to level off close to the rooftops and head directly toward me.

What I took for a foxhole appeared in front of me and I dived at it head-first. Landing with a stunning jolt, I realized that the small patch of dug-up ground was the first attempt by one of the balloonists who had abandoned it after striking solid rock some six inches below the surface of the ground. Before I could even think of bettering my position, the deafening roar of the plane had rolled over my head and trailed off to the tune of fifties following it out of slight.

Rising shakily to my feet, I saw the balloon standing on its nose, its big tail straining for the sky as gas leaked slowly from the many holes punched in its huge belly.

From behind me a stream of profanity began to smear the whole German army. I turned around and walked to the kitchen tent from which the colorful language was coming. The large, red-faced cook, his face redder than usual, was searching through his supply of pots and pans, selecting some and throwing them savagely on the ground. With each new one he threw, he repeated his entire vocabulary of maledictions. Looking at the stack of utensils in the middle of the floor, I saw that each had at least one bullet hole in it.

The successful conclusion of our war on the ground owes a large debt to the "grasshopper" pilots. There could hardly be a front-line ground soldier who was not intimately familiar with the sight of the little olive-drab airplanes slowly circling at no more than a thousand or so feet above the front lines. These were the artillery observation Piper Cubs and L5s that continually stepped just across the enemy line, then stayed there, unprotected, to direct and report the progress of our artillery's work.

One of the Cub outfits, with which I became well

acquainted during our sojourn on the beachhead, used a cow pasture, complete with cows, for a landing field. In spite of a large gully trisecting the field, and the whole thing being on a slant, it was a very good landing field according to the standards of these outfits. Windstorms, holes in runways, enemy artillery, bombings, strafings, and accidents all took a toll on the planes, but they were seldom out of the air for long.

From the beachhead cow pasture, I was taken on flights to photograph the ammunition dumps, the hospital area, the towns and harbor, as well as the front lines, and learned to love and trust the little airplanes and the men who flew them.

From the air, the grand scale of the beachhead became apparent to me for the first time. In spite of the camouflage in the advance positions, I could see thousands of men and guns forming what seemed to be an impregnable line. Behind this, on the outskirts of the charred rubble of the two towns, were acres and acres of stacked boxes of food, of bunkers piled with ammunition, and mountains of cans and drums of oil and gasoline.

From the ground only a part of this was visible, but we knew that enemy artillery or bombers had scored an effective hit when we went a few meals without bread or when the gas dump limited us to five gallons. Occasionally at night we could hear the rumble of explosions coming from the ammo dump long after an air raid, or see from the top of our hill the flames from the gasoline dump leaping fifty or sixty feet in the air.

The losses were terrific, but the supplies came in faster and faster, and as they piled up we knew we could not now be pushed back into the sea in spite of the eight German divisions in the mountains above us and the bungling egomaniac behind us back in Naples.

On the beachhead there was never any real "front." The whole beachhead was the front. At the line facing the enemy, infantrymen died by small arms, mortars, mines, and light artillery. In the towns, men died by bullets from strafing airplanes, by bombs and heavy artillery. For the port battalions and Quartermaster supply men, the danger was the same as for the men at an outpost machine gun emplacement. The huge hospital area, equally subject to bombardment, comprised some four or five units. It received the wounded day and night, and evacuated the more serious cases by the shipload back to Naples. Here, side by side, in the long, bunkered ward tents, would be found front-line infantrymen, a shot-down German fighter pilot, and black Quartermaster supply men.

These Quartermaster troops, beside whom we lived, seemed to possess a sixth sense that warned them of raids and shelling in advance. We could always tell when to duck by watching the flashing dark line of them as they came over the ridge of the hill and passed by the entrance of our cave on their way to their own hole. This uncanny ability on their part failed to help many of them, however, and their casualties ran high.

One morning, as a fellow photog named Stanley Ross and I were brewing up a can of coffee just inside the cave entrance, we heard the pounding, scuffling noise of running men. Looking out, we saw the line of black troops streaming over the ridge in a full-out dash. Hearing no sound of air raid or shelling, we stood at the entranceway and watched.

Out of nowhere, a blinding flash exploded before us, the concussion hurling us backwards into the cave. As our stunned senses began to recover, we could hear, through the ringing in our ears, the pitiful cries of wounded men.

From the other entrance of the cave, Sid Blau had seen the shell land in the soft dirt of a small bank, uproot a tree with shrapnel meant for Ross and me, and knock down two of the black soldiers who happened to be passing the spot at that inopportune moment. As soon as he saw the two men fall, Sid was running for them in spite of the barrage, which was now coming in like rain. He and one of the black G.I.s dragged the wounded men into the safety of the cave. There, we could do nothing but watch them die.

8

The Road to Rome

So firmly were we rooted in the routine of our life on the beachhead, so acclimated to its claustrophobia, that we had almost come to accept, as a normal state, the limited confines of our tight little domain. We had almost begun to lose interest in what lay beyond the semicircle of mountains. As impossible as it may seem in such circumstances of ever-present peril to life and limb, we had become accustomed to the fairly easy life. With the lack of exercise and three good meals a day served up by the Quartermaster cooks, I now weighed more than I ever had. Even our musty cave had a certain homey feeling for us.

But our routine suddenly ended, and we were thrown back into the uncertainties of war. Word came that a large-scale Allied push had begun across the Rapido in the south, and on May, 23, 1944, we began to throw at the Germans everything that had collected on the beachhead for nearly four months.

Villetri, north of us in the Alban Hills, had been a stubborn German position that held us up by repelling frontal assaults from its well-placed location on the side of a steep mountain. But now word reached us that a link-up between engineer units from north and south had been made on May 25, and the town was soon outflanked. The next day Clark was on hand to make it official and have his picture taken shaking hands with officers from both fronts.

At last we were able to climb out of our pocket of cozy devastation and onto the well-paved Highway 7 leading to Villetri. It was there, on the first day of the breakout, that Pappy Brinn earned a Purple Heart. He, a lieutenant named Johnny Vita who had survived a passion for taking pictures of air raids from rooftops, and I tried to navigate an open stretch of road on foot for the third time. Each time the German eighty-eight gunners that were still in place had refused to allow it, and we had to make the headlong dash to the safety of a foxhole under the treads of an M4 tank parked beside a stone house. The third attempt had provoked the enemy gun crews to the extent that they continued blasting our area even after we had given up the effort to travel their road. Pappy had allowed the rest of us to dive at the hole first and, therefore, was still exposed when a shell almost got our range. He took a sliver of shrapnel in the hand, but refused to bother an aid station in a gully across a field from us. Later, the infection that resulted almost cost him his hand.

As we crawled out from under the tank after the German gunners had wasted fifty or sixty shells on us, we saw an ambulance move out from the shelter of the house and turn into the road we had attempted to take. We joined two other men at the corner of the building and watched the daring ambulance's progress across the long open stretch of road. No sooner had it passed a small clump of bushes at the edge of the road than large masses of dirt began to jump into the air all around it. At full speed, it raced the sights of the gun and, until it was out of our view, remained untouched.

"Dirty bastards!" I mumbled.

"Yeah, the sons of bitches," one of the other men standing there echoed. "Imagine 'em shooting at an ambulance."

We were all highly indignant.

"Good thing they didn't hit it, too," the man continued. "It woulda blowed to hell and back. The thing's loaded with ammunition."

This prompted a good laugh. The thought of a picture I might make showing a well-marked American ambulance being loaded with belts of machine gun ammunition and mortar rounds prolonged my own fit of laughter longer than the original sally deserved. Once again I was wondering what the effect would be if, somehow, a shot like that were allowed to pass by our company censor, the field press censor, the War Department censor, and the individual censorship of the various Stateside newspaper editors...to actually reach the American civilian public.

Across a field in a cramped little gully just below a machine gun emplacement, I found a perfect setup for a shot of an aid station in the field at the height of its activity. Its staff consisted of one captain (the doctor), one aide, and litter bearers who stumbled in and out all the while bringing in wounded men for treatment and then taking them on toward a rear collection point after they had received all the care that could be provided in this place. An ammunition box contained bandages, morphine, sulfa powder, bottles of blood plasma, distilled water, alcohol, and a few other things that might have been used if there had been more time.

The space was so small that I had no trouble including everything in my finder without exposing my head above the level of the embankment. At the bottom of the gully, a sluggish little stream ran across the feet of the wounded men as they lay quietly while the doctor dressed their wounds.

Noticing the doctor preparing to make a plasma transfusion, I lined up the shot and was about to trip my shutter when he began to put the things away again.

"You're not going to give him the stuff, Captain?" I called, disappointed.

"Nope," he answered. "He's dead."

It was a good shot and I hated to miss it. "Well, how about just holding up the bottle like you were doing it anyway? Just for a second?" I pleaded.

He lifted the empty bottle and placed the tube against the man's arm: the aide went on with his work of copying the name from the dog tag. I tripped the shutter and had what I consider to be one of my best shots of the war. The caption I sent in with the film carried the true story with the dead man's name and serial number, but the several times I saw it reprinted, he was always unidentified and described as "wounded."

"Staged" picture of already-dead soldier. I would see plenty of the real thing.

*****

We tried approaching Villetri from another direction and were stopped at a two-thirds-blasted farmhouse near which several tanks were lined up in a grove of trees, firing as a battery into the town about a half mile away.

After taking pictures of the tanks firing, and telephoto lens shots of the stuff landing in the town, we walked back to the farmhouse where a company CP was set up. Here we hung around their G-2 radio for the possibility of hearing that some other road had been opened so we could go in.

As we waited, I became more and more nervous about a lone wall of the house standing without support, high above the CP room. That heavy stone wall was all that remained of the second floor of the house and, at every blast from the guns of the tanks firing from the nearby woods, bits of loose stone would shower down on the roof above the occupied room. It was plain to me that if the wall should fall on that flimsy wooden roof, no one inside would come out alive. No one besides me seemed to give it a second thought, however, so I shrugged it off and soon forgot it.

Around noon, I rummaged in the bottom of the jeep and found a can of C-ration hash, and joined several other men sitting on rocks against a wall where there was a partial protection from the wind and dust. It was then that I realized we were sitting just outside the CP room and above us loomed that high, tottering stone wall.

With another shrug, I began opening the can of cold hash, only to be interrupted by the approach of a low-flying P-51.

"Watch him!" someone breathed tensely, but every eye was already glued on the plane. An American plane was no more to be trusted than a German one in such a place as this. All military equipment, we knew, would look alike from the air, and our fly boys were never too careful anyway.

Suddenly, the nose dipped slightly and the ripping roar of its machine guns slashed through the air. Then, with a slight bank to the left, it headed for us.

There was a mad scramble to get inside the remains of

the house and behind its thick stone walls. The plane, however, did not fire at us. It continued its low streaking flight over us and on in the direction of the French sector. There, we learned later, it and others completely cut to pieces a French convoy—another tribute to air-ground support.

A crash that rocked the ground like a shell from Anzio Annie[4] sent dust flying from the ceiling and walls of the old house. Back outside, I breathed easier when I saw nothing but clear blue sky where the old wall had been standing and a dusty pile of large stones where I had been sitting. My abandoned can of C-ration hash was buried under five feet of large building stones.

After a couple of days of following the last defense of Villetri, we were given the go-ahead to go ahead. Brinn had called together Joe Chiappino (movie), me (still) and Reno Frate (driver) and told us, "Tomorrow the infantry will be in Villetri. Get it. After that, follow the 36th. I'll see you in Rome."

Just how he knew the exact time the infantry would break the stubborn resistance that had repelled several previous assaults, or how we could manage to locate each other in a large city in the midst of a war when none of us had ever seen it, we didn't have the slightest idea. But when Pappy said something it usually happened that way.

Next morning, as our battered jeep struggled back up the mountainside on a now nearly-deserted road, we took a moment to look down and pick out the dwarfed scenes that had become so familiar to us. Remembering that those same scenes must be just as familiar to the Germans who had watched us down there from this almost impregnable grandstand seat, we wondered how it happened that any of us was still alive. Bill Mauldin's cartoon where Joe is telling Willie, "Here they wuz and there we wuz," really hit home with the full realization of the sitting ducks we had been. Our resentment against the official

---

[4] *Name given to two long-range railway guns that bombarded the Anzio beachhead from 20 miles away.*

command that put us in that position so needlessly, when we could have occupied these same advantageous positions practically without opposition during the first days after the landing, was momentarily drowned by the upsurge of morale springing from our final release.

We drove on and at last rounded a curve, and were just in time to see the first house in Villetri that came into our view lose a large chunk of roof. And here we had thought it was all over.

There being no other cover available, Frate headed the jeep at full steam for the off side of that same structure and, sliding to a dusty stop, nearly ran down a couple of crouching Signal Corps wiremen. The shelling was working into a full-dress barrage, hacking the stone house away and occasionally sending hot shrapnel our way from an explosion on the sides or rear.

When the shelling finally died down, a long column of tanks with infantrymen riding on them began to pass, heading along the highway that ran through the edge of town.

We vacated our hiding place with the urgency of men out to beat the swarm of civilian photogs who had, by now, crawled back to the beachhead at Nettuno, finally convinced that we were no longer in danger of being pushed back into the sea. We joined the tank column and rode wide-eyed into the fallen citadel. The Germans had pulled out during the night.

Nowhere before had we seen so many dead men lying strewn along the streets. Besides the dozens of Wehrmacht soldiers in varied, but usually advanced, stages of putrefaction, there were many dead horses and mules. The odor was overwhelming.

We took pictures of the road sign at the edge of town, riddled with machine gun slugs—tanks in the background—a picturesque, dust-covered corpse at the roadside, with tanks in the background, more corpses in groups with more tanks in the background, and wrecked buildings everywhere. We left the jeep to wander through the town on foot to look for anything we might find worthy of a picture. There was not a soul, American, German, or civilian to be seen. The tank division we had been following had moved on, and we were too far from the highway to hear them passing. There was now absolutely no sound. It seemed unreasonable to think the Germans would pull out without leaving at least a few snipers, and we knew from our conversation with the wiremen at the edge of town that there had been only one foot patrol through the town so far.

With the short hairs on the back of our necks crawling a bit, we advanced open-eyed through the streets. While stopped at an intersection to look over all the possibilities for sniper positions, I glimpsed what could possibly have been a man's outline in an upstairs window.

Without waiting for a formal invitation, I blasted away with two shots from my .45. When the echoes from my shots had died away, I was able to hear the sound of scuffling feet behind me. Whirling around to meet the whole German army, I faced a squad of infantry led by an American lieutenant who asked, "Whadda ya see?"

"Something in that window up there, Lieutenant," I answered him in a voice that had suddenly grown hoarse.

Turning to the men, he said, "Couple of you fellows go take a look."

A few minutes later a G.I.'s head stuck out the window and reported, "Kraut, Lieutenant. He's dead."

*****

Having explored and vanquished Villetri, and equipped with maps of all territory on the three possibly-available sides of Rome, maps of the city itself, a full tank, and two extra cans of gasoline and one of water strapped on the jeep's hips, we joined the race for Rome. We also carried miscellaneous K-and C-rations mixed in with a few hand grenades rolling around on the floorboards, and every article of clothing, bedding, and camera equipment we had.

In those last few days of May and the first days of June, 1944, time was vaguely represented by days and nights of driving, wandering, pushing forward through strange little towns, along strange roads, through strange territory, usually without knowing the whereabouts of our assigned unit or any other. There was no "front," only columns of tanks and trucks with men sitting and hanging on them anywhere they could find a hold. As they pushed along the main highways, they met occasional resistance but bypassed thousands of German troops who were nowhere near the road.

The speed of the advance during the first few days far outdistanced the huge dumps of rations, gasoline, and ammunition piled up at Nettuno and Anzio.

Stopping at night to catch three or four hours of sleep, we would wake up the next morning to find that the column had pushed on twenty miles while we slept. We found no food except ripe cherries that grew in the fields along the road and we ate them by the helmetful to supplement our diet of K-and-C rations which we usually ate as we drove. When the Ks and Cs ran out, we ate only cherries. Our water supply was quickly emptied by the dusty foot troops we passed on the road. We were soon dead on our feet from lack of sleep, food, and even water. I lost a good chunk of the weight I'd gained, without much surplus to draw from.

The long truck convoys that had started out carrying the infantry soon stalled along the roadsides from lack of fuel, and the long columns of dogfaces who then hit the road soon exhausted the few boxes of K-rations and canteens of water they were able to carry. Up ahead, the tanks used up their supply of ammunition on the first encounters with the enemy and had to wait until more was brought up. Farther on, many were abandoned beside the road with worn-out tracks, for which there were no replacements.

Proof that the Germans were facing the same situation, or worse, were the thousands of prisoners who camped in large groups along the roads, waiting to be taken to POW cages. Hundreds of their trucks, many filled with the loot taken from Italian houses, lay along the roadside ditches.

*****

On the afternoon of June 4, Chiappino, Frate and I, while looking for the head of the column, any column, stumbled onto a task force of tanks and tank destroyers on which infantry were riding. As we reached the head of the column, we were astounded to find that the first vehicles were already in the suburbs of Rome, including the jeep of General Edwin A. Walker, commander of the First SSF, Third Regiment.

The column was stymied at the approach to a long causeway over a dry creek. Beyond the causeway ran a long, high embankment from which was coming occasional fire.

We waited while a patrol was sent out to investigate the situation. On their return, they reported the departure of the German gun crew.

The column then began to move on, first an M4 tank, then a tank destroyer, Walker's jeep, our jeep, and the long column of men and machines behind.

Across the causeway, sweating, a right turn, a couple more blocks, sweating, a turn to the left, through an archway and we were in Rome.

I wished Lannigan could have been there at that moment.

Down the street the column crept, slowly, cautiously, expecting at any second the burst of fire that was almost sure to come from the German rear guard left to defend the "open city."

At the first street intersection the lead tank stopped, waited, poked out a nose to feel for the situation, and received a hail of machine gun slugs. Unharmed but angered, the huge hulk of armor pulled out into the open, fired four quick shots from its big gun and the machine gun bullets ceased coming.

At about the same time, the tank destroyer commander just behind us, who had opened his turret hatch to obtain a better view of the disturbance ahead, beat a quick retreat to the interior of his vehicle as a stream of zipping slugs began to whip over the top of a stone wall beside us and ricochet around his head.

Once again the lead tank rolled forward a few yards and stopped behind a protecting building beyond which was a slight angle in the street. Then, slowly, it pushed its nose around the turn. A German anti-tank crew loosed a screaming shell that burst against the side of the building. The tank pulled back out of range.

Here the convoy stalled as an alternate tactic was considered and a foot patrol was sent out to try to assess the situation.

Safe from the continuing machine gun fire behind the protection of our high stone wall, we got out of the jeep and began to shoot a few pictures of the column.

Though we considered the situation highly insecure, a few Italians almost nonchalantly wandered the street carrying pitchers and jugs of wine that they poured into glasses and offered to the G.I.s crouched warily behind whatever cover they could find. I watched a group of elderly ladies, dressed in black, appear from somewhere with armloads of flowers with which they almost completely covered the body of one G.I. who had barely reached the "open city" before he was killed.

We sat on the curb tasting the wine offered to us. It did not relieve the mounting tension caused by the zipping and whining of the bullets passing over our heads. After a while they became almost unbearable. Frate backed the jeep close to the wall. By standing on it, we were able to peep over. We soon spotted the flash of fire coming from the camouflage of what appeared to be a haystack some three hundred yards away.

Frate and I, with M1 rifles, and an SSF man with a Browning Automatic Rifle, stood on the jeep and crouched below the top of the wall until we were all set and then, together, stood up and fired over the wall until our rifles were empty. While we were firing, a loud explosion, accompanied by a concussion that nearly knocked us off balance, announced that the Tank Division behind had decided to join us. When my rifle was empty, I grabbed my camera in time to make a shot of the Tanks firing. After that, we were bothered no more by the German machine gun.

Finally, with darkness not far away and no hope of progress in any other direction, Walker ordered the column to move on, forcing a fight with the German anti-tank gun and whatever else the cover of the buildings might be concealing.

Starting slowly, slower than before, the lead tank moved out of its covered position and disappeared around the turn. Immediately the sound of several terrific blasts came to us and we saw smoke begin to drift back.

Not knowing what had happened, we waited breathlessly until a ragged figure staggered around the corner, running and stumbling toward us. Screaming, gesticulating, and struggling, he was caught by several men and forcibly pushed into the general's jeep. As he sat there raving, cursing, and crying, we recognized him as the commander of the M4 that had just been sent to fight the German gun. His clothing was scorched and his face blackened but, other than being hysterical, he seemed unhurt.

For several minutes the lieutenant's ravings were pure gibberish, but after he had downed several glasses of Italian wine his words became more intelligible through the flood of tears. His wild eyes staring at the general, he yelled over and over, "It's all your fault they're dead." Then, holding his head in his hands, he sobbed, "I can still smell my driver burning! I can still smell my driver burning!"

The light faded as we sat in our jeep waiting for anything else to happen that we might photograph. Finally, the light was gone. We had our captions already written for what, as far as we knew, were the first pictures to be taken inside Rome by Allied photographers. Our only thought now was to get our film back to the lab and on the way to the States. To our knowledge our only connection with the lab at Naples was the P-38 courier plane at Nettuno, at least six uncertain hours of driving away.

So we drove it. A little after midnight, we were at the Nettuno airfield hunting for the courier service officer, who would not believe we had been in Rome, but who agreed to take our film.

At the time, Chiappino and I, thinking we had turned in the first pictures of Rome, were happy even though we were practically dead from fatigue. We later learned, however, that another team had entered the outskirts of the city from another direction, got pictures and returned to Nettuno an hour or so ahead of us. All 163rd photogs, early or late, beat the first civilian correspondents by at least twenty-four hours, which was, to us, important.

After about four hours of sleep, bedded down with our old neighbors, the officers of the Quartermaster depot, we were on Highway 7 headed back to Rome.

Strangely, as we drove down the broad street leading to the center of the city, we saw no other American G.I.s. There were even very few civilians on the streets at first, but as we stopped to consult our map of the city for directions to the Press Club, we were suddenly surrounded by masses of humanity crawling over the jeep, slapping us on the back, shaking our hands, shoving bottles of wine, loaves of bread, sausages, and flowers at us, and chattering at us in rapid Italian with an occasional English word thrown in.

Through all the confusion, I became aware of a persistent tugging at my sleeve and turned around to face a middle-aged woman who said to me in perfect English, "May my daughter kiss you?"

The idea of a slobbering brat drooling all over my face was not appealing, but I saw no method of gracefully escaping the issue. "Certainly, ma'am," I answered her, feeling much like a movie star must feel while humoring his adoring public, and looked around for the child.

Before I had time to grasp the situation I was clasped tightly around the neck and soundly kissed by a beautiful, dark-haired girl of about twenty years of age who promptly disappeared into the crowd.

This incident seemed to set a precedent, and we were grabbed and kissed by every soul, male and female, who could get near us. Protesting loudly, we managed to escape these smothering affections only by grabbing our cameras and climbing onto the hood of the jeep where we began to shoot pictures of the astounding sight.

Standing there, above the crowd, what we saw made us a little weak in the knees. Jammed tightly, the crowd extended over the entire intersection of the wide streets and at least a block back in every direction. Well over a thousand people were yelling, waving, and cheering. Whatever they were cheering for, our dirty, unshaved trio in a beat-up jeep were the only recipients.

With my camera focused and ready to shoot, I raised my hand and waved to the crowd. A thousand hands waved back. The cheer rocked me as I took the picture. A man lifted up a small boy. He placed the child's feet in the palm of his right hand and raised him high above his head. The boy held a rigid military salute and a very grave face while I shot the picture. I returned the salute as smartly as possible in my position. The hilarious scene appeared in *Liberty Magazine* and several other publications.

It took us over an hour to extricate our jeep from the mass of humanity. Once we had found the convoys we began to run across platoons of other photographers, both civilian and military. Feeling our own pictures to be somewhat redundant, we nevertheless made shots of the troops passing the Coliseum, the Royal Palace, and St. Peter's Basilica, as well as Clark in his jeep. We finally ended at the Press Club bar, where we found Brinn.

Slightly in his cups, working on the stock of good liquor that had been hidden from the Germans but had been quickly uncovered by the American correspondents, he took our film and informed us that if we didn't put our cameras away and go have some fun he would kick us in the seat of our pants.

Wandering aimlessly, we ran across a nice-looking bar and purchased, for three hundred lire each, three bottles of very good champagne. After more wandering, with an occasional pause to deplete the contents of one of the bottles, we came slowly to the realization that our meager supply would be unlikely to outlast that of the bar. It could hardly have been more than two hours since our first visit, but when we returned, we found that the price had already risen to seven hundred lire per bottle. (The next day it was priced at one thousand four hundred.) Leaving the well-cursed bartender with his twenty-one hundred lire, we took our additional three bottles of sparkling happiness and set out to find lodgings for the night.

We passed up several small hotels and finally settled on a large, modern mansion of a building. We found that the place was unoccupied by guests and staffed by only a handful of employees. This suited us very well. We were soon settled in the three best rooms, with chambermaids working furiously to prepare the long unused beds. The chef and waiters outdid themselves in turning out unbelievably tasty dishes from the ten-in-one rations we had managed to steal off a Quartermasters truck.

We invited the bowing owner of the hotel to have dinner with us in his large, glittering dining room. Happy to accept, he raved about the quality of the food and brought out a bottle of his best private stock of wine. We sat at the table, talked and drank far into the night. The next day we were informed that two of us were carried to our rooms, but which two we were never able to determine.

Around noon I struggled from the softest bed I had felt in untold months and groped my way to the water faucet. By the time I had satisfied my burning thirst with the third glass of water, I was feeling remarkably well.

Lacking the inclination to play tourist, we now felt only the urge to relax, and relaxation in this particular instance was provided by strong drink, warm women, and soft beds. All were easily obtainable, and we sank gratefully into a happy haze of unreality from which the entire warring world was excluded. Rome was to us the climax of all we had gone through, the reward for all our previous work and hardship. Since our first introduction into combat we had looked at every advance only as a step toward Rome.

Sometime later, we were assigned, as the team most nearly in working condition, to photograph the ruins of the large municipal airport that had been even further enlarged by the Luftwaffe, and then reduced to a pile of junk by American bombers.

Our next job was to photograph the pope as he made his speech of welcome from the balcony of Saint Peter's. This went off uneventfully, though another of our teams almost got into trouble. They made an attempt to invade the restricted halls of the Vatican disguised as monks, with cameras. I made my shots of the pope with a telephoto lens from a tripod mounted on the hood of the jeep parked amid the thousands of people at the steps of the cathedral.

The next morning we found Brinn cold sober and cursing. He had just received an announcement that the company HQ unit was on its way to Rome. This meant, of course, that if we were to have any peace, we would have to find it at the front. By noon the convoy of team jeeps was on the road, heading north.

Rolling along at a good, fast clip over the smooth highway, with no worry of running into enemy traps, we watched the warm sun shine down on green, well-farmed fields and wondered how there could possibly be a war going on. The traffic on the road consisted mostly of large trucks hauling huge loads of rations and ammunition instead of the tanks, halftracks, and jeeps that we were so used to seeing. This served to remind us just how far behind the rapidly advancing line we had fallen during our brief stopover in Rome. With the enemy in such an all-out retreat as this, we foresaw only a jubilant gallop through Europe, ending finally in the streets of Berlin. So, we uncorked another series of toasts to victory in the west.

Dusk found us still no more than half the distance to the front. Taking a side road into a forest, we soon located a natural picnic ground, and deployed the formation over a large area for the night. A group went out to scour the area for left-over members of the Wehrmacht. We swapped odd bits of chow— loaves of bread, sausages, eggs, liquor—and finally set up our cots and mosquito bars, and crawled in at the crack of darkness.

Sometime during the night our sleep was interrupted by the too-well-remembered crashes and flashes of exploding anti-aircraft shells and the steady drone of airplanes. There was the familiar whiz and thump of falling flak. Still and stiff in my cot, I looked up through the net of my mosquito bar at the thin covering of fluttering leaves above me.

An extra loud "whiz" and a resounding "thump" caused me to shrink further down under my blankets.

When, finally, the noise had faded off toward the north, I reached out with one hand and explored the ground at the head of my cot. My hand touched a still-hot chunk of jagged metal, but it was not until morning that I discovered the hole in my mosquito bar, almost directly above my head.

*****

By noon of that day we had reached the beautiful, modern town of Marabella, a rich man's resort on the Tyrrhenian shore.

Locating a house to use as headquarters presented no problem because the town was practically deserted by its civilian population even though there was no evidence that fighting had taken place there. We decided on a luxurious new house of two stories surrounded by flower gardens only a stone's throw from the beach.

When everyone had chosen a position and set up his cot, we pooled our food supplies and appointed the most willing as cooks. As the odd bits of food began to show up and take their place in the stew pot, some of us decided the dish could be considerably improved by the addition of fish. With a little luck we could find some in the deep water around the huge rocks that lay at the foot of cliffs farther down the beach. The lack of fishing tackle presented no major problem because we had a good supply of hand grenades. A kayak and a water bicycle, found unguarded, provided conveyance to the likely-looking fishing waters, and soon the echoes of our depth charges resounded from the rock cliffs.

The ones that got away were the largest. Those that didn't get away may just as well have done so. Our most strenuous efforts to reach them as they rose, belly first, to the surface were foiled as the poor, dead fish sank to the bottom again, just beyond our reach.

The next day the teams gathered at a wicker table in the mansion's garden beside which Pappy sat in the warm sun. Poking a finger at a map on the table, he explained the different routes we were to follow "as far as you can go," picking up anything in the way of pictures we happened to run across.

It felt good, in a way, to return to this informal, catch-as-catch-can work. The weather was perfect. We had had enough of celebrating, and the going promised to be easy. With all its uncertainties, it was the work we liked.

However, once on the road, it didn't take long for our three-man team to become lost in the turns, forks, and crossings of the small country roads. The thin thread of G.I. traffic disappeared completely. For miles we had seen no American soldiers, nor any sign of their passing. The vague tightness that I had felt so often before came back into my throat. Driving on warily, we scrutinized every deserted cave, house, and clump of bushes that might possibly conceal a man with a gun.

Suddenly we were driving through the deserted streets of a small town watching eyes peer at us from cracks in shuttered windows. Arriving at the town square after having glimpsed only an occasional person who immediately slipped into a convenient doorway, we stopped. As we sat in the jeep, looking over the ancient buildings for a sign of either American or German occupancy, an old man stepped in stiff-legged dignity from a building we took to be the municipal headquarters and walked solemnly across the square toward us.

Addressing me, he asked, "Deutsch?"

"No," I answered, pointing to the small flag glued on the windshield of the jeep. "We're American."

He stared at the little flag for a moment, then his eyes filled with tears and he burst into a babbling of Italian. I saw what was coming and dodged before he could plant a watery kiss on my cheek. He grabbed my hand, however, and clinging tightly, he covered it with kisses.

The jeep was soon surrounded by people, with what seemed like hundreds more dashing down on us from all directions. Flowers rained over us; even a vase containing a huge bouquet was set in my lap. Glasses of wine were thrust in our faces. It was Rome all over again, only on a smaller scale.

Abruptly the shouting crowd became quiet as the church bells began to ring, and the sign of the cross was made amid a brief hum of prayer.

Joe and I grabbed our cameras and climbed out of the jeep. Immediately a squad of helmeted Carabinieri appeared to make a clearing around us. The officer in charge made a deep bow and said, in precise English, "If we may be of assistance to you, we are at your service."

By now I was beginning to wonder if these people were not suffering a case of mistaken identity. I had seen such a welcome for General Clark, but for three unshaven G.I.s in a battered jeep?

Heading in opposite directions, Joe and I set out to explore the town in search of pictures. The Carabinieri escort split into two groups to accompany us, along with a crowd of sixty or seventy men. When I explained that I wanted to take pictures, I was taken to a cemetery where two American fliers were buried, to a church that had doubled as a German ammunition dump and was still filled with tons of shells and explosives, to a clump of trees under which was a stack of aerial bombs, and to several booby-trapped vehicles that I marked for the engineers who would follow. Last but not least, we were offered the opportunity to capture fifty Germans who were said to be living in a cave on the other side of the hill. We politely declined.

Driving on, somewhat reassured but still wary, we picked up an ancient hitchhiker who waved a large chunk of sausage in one hand and a rusty knife in the other as he sang loud and unmusical songs from the hood of our jeep. With the old man's vague directions and our own doubtful references to our map, we proceeded in the supposed direction of the enemy. The roads grew narrower, bumpier, and more confusing all the while, but still we felt reluctant to turn back before we had something worthwhile on film.

Eventually, we rounded the side of one of the mountains that were becoming steeper and more frequent. The jeep came almost to a stop as our new driver, Dorsey, suddenly lost interest in the difficult driving. We all gaped at the beauty that lay before our eyes. A valley, emerald-green, velvet-smooth, and as lovingly cared for as a flower garden, stretched at our feet. A sparkling stream twisted leisurely along the flat floor and, as if reluctant to leave, slowly faded out of sight. Miles beyond, a gentle upward curve blended the smile of the luxuriant foliage almost imperceptibly into the stern frown of the rocky, rugged mountain country.

Directly in the center of the verdant, oblong valley, like a magnificent jewel in an exquisite setting, was a grass-covered slope reaching steeply upward to a flat peak to form a symmetrically perfect hill. Atop this hill stood the most beautiful structure any of us had ever seen.

The spires of an ancient castle strained for the frame of fluffy white clouds. Its towers, buttresses, and walls glowed in the brilliant sunlight against a background of deep blue.

I set up my camera to take a picture, even though there was no way to connect the scene to war or news. But I had to try to record my feelings on film.

We crossed the valley and drove up a narrow road to the iron-studded outer doors, fully twenty feet tall. The overall immensity of the many-angled structure pressed down on us as we looked upward to overhanging watch towers.

When we came to a stop, our hitchhiker leapt from the hood of the jeep and ran to a peephole in a door through which he flung loud, rapid Italian while waving his sausage and knife in the air. Meanwhile Dorsey, Joe, and I walked to the edge of the flat peak and inhaled the cool breeze while looking silently down on the wide expanse of beauty.

Behind us, one of the huge doors slowly swung inward, smoothly and almost silently, as three men tugged and shoved at its mass of heavy wood.

There, behind the door, our eyes met another unexpected sight. Dignified almost to arrogance, a young woman of exceptional beauty stood with the sunlight glinting from her striking red hair. She stood with her long, boot-clad legs far apart and played idly with a riding crop while looking directly at us. Behind her stood a servant holding the bridle of a sleek black horse. Looking across the wide cobblestoned courtyard, we saw several other horses being cared for by grooms.

Plainly, she was waiting for us to speak first, so Joe, with his easy-flowing Italian and natural charm, explained that we had seen the beautiful building and only wanted a closer look at it. Here, the old man broke in, explaining, hat in hand, that we were the American liberators.

At this the woman's face relaxed and became more friendly. She called to an old servant who was standing in the arched doorway of the main building. After giving him instructions to show us anything we wanted to see, she said goodbye and left. We did not see her again.

As we were guided through room after room, up and down angled and winding stairways, past huge portraits of magnificently dressed ancestors and suits of armor standing in dim corners like ghostly sentinels, I remarked how nearly the scene resembled a Hollywood set. Contrary, however, to my previous concept of castles as dark, damp, and chilly, this one looked comfortably livable.

I wrote down the name of the place, Monte Po, but I knew I would never forget it.

*****

Our days of nipping at the heels of the fleeing enemy were ended by orders that called us back to rejoin the company HQ unit, now bivouacked in a cork forest north of Civitavecchia. There we set up pup tents suspended from the trees, with sides open to collect all the fresh air possible in the heat that was becoming more intense every day. This period, we were informed, was to be one of rest for us. It proved to be a time of intolerable boredom, which we tried unsuccessfully to relieve by reading any literature available, regardless of age or content, by occasional guard duty, and by dozing in an oven-like pyramidal tent while reviewing thousands of feet of movie "rushes" of the movie men's work for the last several months. One day we were unexpectedly called into formation and presented with our long-overdue stripes. We were so bitter about their tardiness that I did not, at first, even bother to draw my three-striped chevrons from the supply tent.

By the time I had nearly learned the trick of keeping cool and was beginning to get used to this life of useless loafing, I was somehow roped in with four or five other photogs and drivers, and bundled off to join the lab detachment that was still set up in Rome. It seemed that Fifth Army HQ had been moved to Rome and, therefore, the place was beginning to crawl with big shots. The lab was doing its best to cover the stories, but they were not supposed to be photographers and besides, they had their hands full with the processing, as usual. They were yelling for help.

In Rome, we found the lab detachment set up in a movie processing lab that the war had put out of production. Unfortunately, the building did not provide enough room for living quarters. Our noncombatant element, not having had much experience in requisitioning the necessities, had settled for a fenced-in area a half-block away and set up pyramidal tents. We were welcomed by the men already living there, who gladly made room for us. They brought out various bottles of wine, and told us where to go for a good time in town.

From the officer in charge of our operation, a captain we had not previously met, we learned that we were expected to take it easy around the area until something turned up for us to work on. In the meantime, we were given an adjutant general's pass that would allow us to roam the city that was now a full-fledged rear area with MPs on every corner and "Off Limits" signs on just about every point of interest.

Unused to rear area procedure, with its creased pants and clean-shaven jaws, I was caught with a two day beard when a driver dashed into my tent where I lay on my cot fighting flies and mopping perspiration off my face. He handed me a piece of paper signed by the captain under the words, "3:15—Airport—V.I.P."

"We can just make it," the driver said as I ran my fingers across the bristles on my face.

At the airport, I did my best to hide behind my camera as

Under-Secretary of War Robert Patterson stepped from the C-54, accompanied by Clark and several lesser generals.

My first bulb flashed as Patterson stepped through the door of the plane. At the click of the shutter, I saw Clark's head snap up as he shot a deep scowl in my direction.

"Were you expecting photographers, Mr. Patterson?" he asked.

I smelled trouble.

Mr. Patterson, however, quickly replied, "Oh, that's all right, General."

Thus encouraged, I arranged a group shot beside the plane, addressing my suggestions to Patterson.

A few less important jobs came up and were handled, but life at the lab was almost as boring as that at the company CP. The heat was worse in Rome than it had been in the cork forest. One morning the heat was more irritating than usual and I had been wandering around the lab trying to shake off a bad case of nerves brought on by inactivity and a hangover from a cognac party in Larry Jones' cubbyhole the night before. In the yard in front of the building, I came across Lt. Strock, the officer in charge of the lab operations, polishing his shoes at the edge of the concrete fish pond. After we exchanged "good mornings" and salutes, Strock invited me to sit down with him on the edge of the fish pond. I poked a finger at the gold fish as they swam by.

He asked, "How do you like it here?"

Here was the perfect opening, and I started to blurt out a resounding "It's a bitch," but I was on guard against myself that morning. I soft-pedaled it to a weak, "Pretty boring, Lieutenant."

Well," he replied. "In a couple of days you've got a pretty important job coming up that will give you something to do."

I eagerly asked what.

"A V.I.P.," he answered. "I can't tell you who it is yet, but he's a really big boy."

This kind of super secrecy seemed foolish to me, but I

was beginning to learn that this was just more of the rear-area SOP.

"Bell," Strock added, after a pause, "You know I see everything that goes through the lab." Another pause. "I just wanted to say that your stuff is always some of the best that comes in."

I spent the rest of the day trying to figure out a hidden meaning, or at least to find a reason for his saying such a thing. The idea of receiving appreciation for work accomplished had long since disappeared, along with the rest of the naiveté I had brought with me into the Army. The only thing to come of all my thinking was the conviction that, somehow, I was going to louse up my next job. And it came very close to that.

*****

A messenger told me that I was wanted by the captain in the lab office. As soon as I walked in, the captain handed me another of those little slips of paper. This time it said, "R.R. station—0900 hrs.—V.I.P."

This continuing vagueness was getting hard to take. Surely if this "Very Important Person" was going to arrive at the railroad station in less than an hour there could be no harm in letting me in on his identity.

"Who is it, sir?" I asked.

"Well," he answered slowly. "It's Secretary of War Stimson. The engineers have just finished the rail line from Naples, and this is the first train—trains, rather—to come in. One of them is the secretary's train, and the other is bringing the first load of American coal to Rome. There won't be much to shoot on the coal train, but you should get as much as possible on the secretary. He'll review the honor guard at the station, and then drive to the Piazza for a flag-raising ceremony. For your captions, this flag is one that comes off the White House and is supposed to be raised over Paris and Berlin when we get there."

On the way back to my tent I realized I had done it again.

My hand flew to my chin and stroked a beard of more than two days growth. Looking at my watch, I cursed myself and calculated the time. I had forty-five minutes and I could still make it.

I dashed to my tent, grabbed my helmet from under my bed and leaped for the door in quest of water. Halfway through the doorway I was stopped cold by the driver sent to get me.

"Just a second," I pleaded, "I'll be right with you as soon as I shave."

"Shave?" he repeated incredulously. "All the rest of the guys are waiting for you in the jeeps."

I could hear horns honking furiously and several voices calling my name and several other names, not exactly mine but meant for me. With a groan I gave up the idea of shaving and grabbed my camera.

At the station, the two trains, decorated with bunting and flowers, came rolling to a stop side-by-side while eight or ten shutters clicked, and as many more movie cameras ground out foot after foot of film.

I made a shot of a half-dozen star-studded uniforms grinning from the cowcatcher of one of the locomotives, then turned the story over to Porky McCroby, and concentrated on Secretary Henry Stimson and his retinue, which included Generals Clark, Devers, and a half dozen others I did not recognize.

Running backward to focus, shooting, changing film and bulbs on the run, trying to keep other people's heads out of my shot and my own head out of theirs, I covered the stepping down from the train, the march through the station, and the reviewing of the honor guard.

My driver did his best to follow the official convoy while I did my best to make notes for my captions.

At the Piazza yet more photogs appeared, until it seemed we would outnumber the battalion standing in formation for the ceremony. In addition to our own still and movie men, there were photographers from the division PRO, Army Command PRO, the Air Corps, the Navy, from *Stars and Stripes*, *Yank*, and every civilian news agency represented in the European Theater of Operations. It was a game of leapfrog the entire length of Stimson's course as he inspected the troops. Shoot, duck out of the other men's way, change a flash bulb, and go back to look for another shot, was the procedure. A bank of kneeling photogs formed at his every pause, with a second rank shooting over their heads. With such a number of photographers at work on one subject, courtesy and consideration were absolute necessities.

When the friendly-faced and slightly stooped secretary of war had fulfilled his duty of reviewing the troops, he walked to the spot beneath the flagpole where the color guard waited with the folded flag. As he took his position, a line of photogs took form to get the most important, and seemingly the easiest, shot of the day.

The mechanics of raising the flag had been well rehearsed by the men responsible for that duty, and they did their job quickly and efficiently. The flag was attached to the cord and a single pull was all that was necessary to unfold it completely. At this exact instant Stimson, for some unknown reason, made a quarter-turn away, obscuring his face from the forest of lenses staring at him. He then began to raise the flag, with his arms getting in the way of a good shot. He as good as turned his back on us. Several shutters clicked in desperation. The remaining men, I among them, decided to take the chance of missing the shot completely by making a dash to the other side of the pole. It was a gamble to get there in time to make the shot before the flag had been raised too high to be out of the picture entirely. To cut the time down by a split second, which might mean everything, I gambled again by giving my focusing knob an outward twist as I ran. Thus, focused on a shorter range, I was able to stop short, turn and grab a shot a fraction before most of the other men in the race could get set.

As the shutter clicked with both Stimson's face and the unfolding flag in the frame of my finder, I realized that my lens was pointed almost directly into the fiercely shining sun. On the other hand, all the other photographers I could see were still trying to get a focus as the flag slid up the pole and out of sight.

Back at the lab, my head ached and perspiration dripped on my caption blanks as I tried to remember the sequence of shots and names of generals. From the next room, I could hear the sounds of splashing soup as "Uncle" George Bialkowski, the resident genius of the darkroom, developed the film. If the negative was in focus, I had a shot—if I had enough exposure to print. With our lab and radio setup, we certainly had everyone else beat for speed. Whatever came of what I had—and in my whirling mind it seemed to involve the entire reputation of the 163rd—was going to be laid on me, since Porky McCroby had still been taking pictures of his coal train.

The door to the developing room opened and Uncle George called to me, "Bell, you want to see your stuff?"

One by one he lifted the dripping film hangers out of the hypo tank and held them up before the open safety light. Trains, people walking, troops standing at stiff attention—all O.K.

"The hell with this stuff," I growled impatiently. "Let's see the flag rising."

"This it?" George asked as he lifted another negative from the tank.

"Oh, Lord," I groaned as I looked at the reversed silhouette.

"This is the most important one?" asked George.

"Important?" I repeated. "It's the only one that matters a damn."

George held the hanger closer to the light and squinted so closely at the negative that it seemed to be in danger from the smoldering tip of his cigar.

"Well," he finally diagnosed, "I think I can get something out of it."

"I'll love you forever." I spoke from the heart.

By the time he had given the negative a quick wash and a forced drying, word had spread that Uncle George was about to perform another of his miracles. A small crowd, consisting of Strock, the captain, a visiting major, the radio man, and several others had gathered.

On the third try, a good sharp image with just the right amount of contrast for radio transmission came up. Uncle George lit another cigar while receiving congratulations from his audience and heartfelt thanks from me.

As the picture transmuted itself into radio waves and teleported its way to Washington, I collapsed on my cot and decided I did not have enough energy to shave.

9

La Belle France

I was sent back at last to the company CP. Here I ran into a veritable nest of rumors, all suggesting that within a very short time we would be sent out to join our assigned outfits for another jump-off. There could be little doubt that it would be France.

All photographers and team drivers were placed into two groups of about equal size and sent off in separate convoys to join other outfits. Arrangements had been made with them for our feeding and quartering. Our bunch was assigned to several vacant tents in a hemp patch owned by a Signal battalion near Aversa, a small town near Naples. Though some of the men took every opportunity to go into Naples, most of us preferred to go only when we had something particular in mind, such as sailing or attending the opera. We loved the Italian opera-goer's attitude, which included drinking wine and easting snacks in the box seats.

When the company's HQ unit moved to Naples and located itself on a bluff high above the harbor, they brought with them a movie projector. We were invited to come view the latest films with them every other night. Soon they added the attraction of a small private bar stocked with locally procured liquors and PX beer rations, which were just becoming available.

Our favorite form of entertainment, however, was drinking our beer ration in our own tent in the cool of the evening. We cooled the beer by dropping the cans into a container of water (no ice, of course) and leaving them while we boiled eggs to go with them. These eggs were rare treats, and were bought over the fence, at twenty lire each, from the old

Italian women who also took and returned our laundry the same way.

With nothing to do but wait, our wits were taxed to conjure up any kind of diversion. With an amphibious landing hanging precariously over our heads, it was impossible to relax completely. Therefore, when I received a V-letter[5] from Frank Cadena, my number one friend from civilian days, it was a godsend. Frank informed me, by hint and innuendo—due to censorship rules he could not come right out and say it—that his squadron was in Foggia, just across the Italian peninsula. All sorts of plans rushed into my head.

I inquired of Joe Chiappino, who was now the non-com in charge of our group, what my chances might be of getting away with a short trip in a jeep. He could see no real reason why I couldn't do so. He suggested I talk to Lt. Lueders, a company officer now assigned to our detached group. He had heard someone mention that the lieutenant's wife had some relatives living in the mountains somewhere to the east.

Lueders and I started out early in the morning, and by nine o'clock we were laboring through the inland mountains. By eleven we were struggling with sign language and a few Italian phrases to locate the house of his wife's relatives in a little village high on the peak of a mountain.

I sat and drank wine while old photo albums were perused and Lueders lied about remembering relatives he had never seen. When the last of the babies had been brought out for inspection, we were persuaded to stay for lunch, which turned out to be a tough beef and garlic stew, black bread, and red wine. We were relieved when we were finally able to break away.

As we neared Foggia, we began to see scattered Air Corps units along the highway, and my anticipation of seeing Frank, who was a flier, grew apace. At the same time, rather

---

[5] *V-mail consisted of one-page letters microfilmed at their source, then printed out and delivered.*

strangely, I began to wonder if we would find anything to talk about.

In the sixth-grade class at Page Junior High, Frank and I had first struck up one of those tight boyhood friendships that usually flame with intensity and then die out. Though the light flickered at times, somehow it lasted through the trials and errors of school days. It gradually became a mature relationship that enabled us to meet and part easily without any feeling of strangeness

But would our friendship be the same now? Would we still have common ground? I had changed. I was sure Frank had changed. Friendship for me had become something that grew to intimacy inside a five-minute mortar barrage. It involved a deep understanding without the need for words, and it was also something that neither party expected to survive outside the conditions that fostered it.

Now, with this realization in mind, could I face Frank with the same casualness our association had always enjoyed?

I drove with Lueders into the battered city of Foggia and asked an MP where I might find the 301st Bomb Group. Following his directions, I headed, hesitantly, out the road to the north. A pair of hitchhikers gave me more detailed directions and I at last pulled up in front of the headquarters building for the 352nd Bomb Squadron, of which the 301st was a part.

Leaving Lueders to doze in the jeep, I walked into the building and asked a clerk where I could find Lt. Frank Cadena.

"Lt. Cadena?" the man repeated. He looked off somewhere across the room and then back at me. "Lt. Cadena is M.I.A. since yesterday morning."

"M.I.A.?" My voice sounded flat in my ears. I had heard the term used hundreds of times, but the meaning was slow to dawn on me. "Missing in Action" was a war term that had nothing to do with boyhood friendships.

The clerk got up and walked around the desk to me. "You a relative of his?"

"No." I choked a little. "Just a friend."

Suddenly I realized that I was the center of a group of men. I looked from one face to another as snatches of meaningless phrases came to my ears. "...two engines gone..." "...going down..." "...heading for Switzerland. Don't know if they made it..." "...think they all got out..."

My face must have shown the numbness inside me when I returned to the jeep. Lueders asked, "Want me to drive, Bell?"

"No," I answered. "I'd rather."

As I parked the jeep that night, a wave of deep exhaustion, both mental and physical, poured over me. By the time I made it to my bunk, the best I could do was to take off my shoes and fall across my cot.

On returning to San Antonio at the end of the war, I was deeply relieved to find Frank Cadena alive, well, and as irreverent and humorous as ever.

*****

After nearly three weeks of living with the anticipation of an assault landing before us, we were given a job to do. We were to shoot pictures of the practice landings on a beach north of Naples.

I was assigned with Danny Powers, a nice fellow and good cameraman in spite of his Hollywood background, to a half mile or more of beachfront. Other than some low scrub brush and three empty houses spread at long intervals down the beach, the area was bare.

Informed that the landing barges were to be preceded by rocket barges that would saturate the beach with missiles to clear it of mines and possible gun emplacements, we decided to get our first shots from an upstairs window of the house nearest the end of the landing area. It was slightly inside the danger zone marked on our map, but no better place was to be found on the almost flat land.

We set up our cameras with telephoto lenses and waited

for the rocket barrage to start. As usual, the show was late and I whiled away the time lining up my shot more closely. The more closely I visualized the logical place for the landing, the more I became convinced that, from this position, I would not be able to get the shot I wanted.

I reached a decision, told Danny good-bye and walked the thousand or so yards down to the next house. There I found a good place to shoot from in the attic after knocking a few tiles out of the roof and sticking my head and shoulders through.

Almost immediately, the rumbling sound of the barges came across the water. I looked down on the beach through the finder of my camera. It would be just right if they threw the shells into the area I had picked as the most logical.

Apparently, though, the logic of the rocket bargemen had taken a different line from my own and, as I saw the large formation rushing in, it seemed they were coming directly at me. Then, for the first time, I realized what a beautiful target the old house would make from that direction, all alone and silhouetted on top of the bank above the edge of the water.

With no other place to go and pictures to make, I did the only sensible thing I could think of at the moment: I retired to the floor below, where the stone walls offered an illusion of safety in comparison with the flimsy tile roof.

Kneeling at a window on the second floor, I calmed my jumping nerves to a sufficient extent to make a shot of the formation of barges rushing through a froth of water, the banks of loaded rocket tubes now visible.

Suddenly, with the thunderous "swoosh" of a hundred locomotives opening their steam valves, the barges opened fire on the beach area, precisely where I had anticipated it in the beginning. The flaming rockets arced onto the beach with screams like those of wounded animals, and exploded there with all the fury of 105mm artillery shells.

The barrage that broke loose in that small patch of hell was the most frightening sight I had ever beheld. Not one explosion after another, as in an artillery barrage, but every yard of the beach seemed to be exploding at once. The air was thick with dust, smoke, flying bits of metal, rocks, and shreds of shrubbery. Behind the steady roar of the explosions I heard the sounds of other screeching rockets on their way in, and the thunder of even more as they left their launching tubes. On and on and on went the maddening noise while I mechanically shot one picture after another.

The madness relented as unexpectedly as it had begun, leaving a heavy pall of smoke and dust hanging over the beach. The silence now seemed as terrible as the noise had a moment before. I could no longer hear the drone of the engines out on the water, nor, as I discovered to my amazement, could I hear my own movements.

Standing up unsteadily, I stamped my foot on the floor, hard. My ears were rewarded with the return of a dull thud, totally unlike the sound of a stamping foot. I also realized that my camera and I were covered with a thick coating of white dust that had fallen from the ceiling.

By now I could see the formation of landing barges streaking through the water, heading for the mantle of smoke just down the beach. I saw that I had barely enough time, if I hurried, to get down to the beach and in position to get pictures of the men wading ashore.

Down at the landing area, I stepped gingerly around a number of dud shells scattered on the ground. The air was still hazy and thick with the stinging smell of burnt powder. Beyond a shell-torn mound, I walked out onto a wide area of white sand sloping down to the water. The first of the barges had dropped their nose ramps and the men were jumping out into waist-deep water.

I raised my camera and began to focus. The beach all around me exploded with a blinding flash. I felt myself being lifted up. Then I was jolted front and rear. As my senses began to return to me, I realized that one of the dripping infantrymen was slapping the sand off my clothes while another held me by the arm and asked, his voice sounding as if it were coming over a telephone with a bad connection, "Are you all right now?" '

"Yeah," I mumbled. "Yeah, I guess so. What was that?"

"T.N.T. mines. Just knocked you down."

I was feeling better, except for the unsteadiness in my legs and a loud ringing in my ears. I thanked them and they said sure, picked up their rifles and joined the others in the simulated attack. I picked up my half-buried camera and shook the sand out of it. The repair boys would not be happy to see this one.

*****

Finally the assault convoy pulled out and "Operation Anvil" was under way. We were both disappointed and relieved to learn that we were to be left behind to come in as support in a few days while the other detachment of photogs made the actual landing. When we heard that it had been an easy landing except, as usual, for the hard-luck 36th Division, we were more eager than ever to be on our way.

A week later we boarded a Liberty ship with trucks, jeeps, and equipment. We came in by LCM on the famed French Riviera in the little harbor between St. Rafael and St. Maxime, just ten days late. By now the German army was many miles to the north and east, and still running. After spending the night on the beach, waiting for our trucks and equipment to be unloaded, we formed into a convoy and headed for Grenoble.

Driving along the beach road, we could see why this small bit of France attracted the pleasure-seeking rich and royalty from all over the world. The deep green of the trees, grass, and shrubbery, mingled with the brilliant colors of millions of flowers in bloom, overshadowed the ugly blotches made by artillery shells on the seaward side of many of the palatial villas. Among the country's charms were the unexpected number of beautiful girls, wearing shorts and riding bicycles. Unfortunately, we were unable to get closer than a whistle as our convoy rolled through the unending fields of grapes.

*****

At a factory building on the outskirts of Grenoble, we caught up with a small advance unit from company HQ led by Capt. Smith, the same captain we'd seen neither hide nor hair of since his rather perfunctory speech back in Nettuno had been brought to an unseemly conclusion by a bomb raid.

In the factory building we set up our cots, shaved, changed to clean uniforms, and then were informed that we could not go into town. This rear-area type of "chicken shit" brought on the usual amount of squawking, but early the next morning we were rewarded for our patience by being given the whole day to wander about unmolested.

Grenoble was the first French city of any real size we had seen, so we were quite intrigued by the comparative normalcy of life there. The city was apparently unharmed by the war. The shops were filled with all sorts of merchandise, most of it of good quality, and we were drawn like magnets after having become accustomed to the empty shelves or cheap junk offered to us in Italy.

Besides enjoying the slight intoxication of fairly good liquor, and the sight of comparative prosperity, we invited seasickness by buying tickets on an old funicular that swung above the housetops, out across the river, and high up over the steep side of a mountain to an old fort and a closed tea shop at the top. Here we examined the tunnels that had been used by the Germans as an OP. We acted like real tourists as we gazed off into the miles of space spreading out to the distant mountains far beyond the city at our feet.

The next day our convoy, now enlarged by Smith's party, was on its way to our next step northward, Besancon, a few miles from the Swiss border. When we reached that ancient French city with the fighting only a matter of a few miles to the north, my anticipation of getting back to work rose to a fever pitch. It wasn't that I was eager to be back in the kind of a situation where I was constantly in danger, but rather that I knew I would be back in that situation sooner or later, and the waiting was harder than the actual fact. As it happened, however, there were so few combat outfits actually in contact with the rapidly back-pedaling Germans that the photo teams who had made the initial landings were sufficient to cover the area. This was despite the loss of one team, all three men having been seriously injured by a shell that caught their jeep.

As the days passed, we spent our time lounging around the town making black market deals with cigarettes and candy for watches smuggled in over the Swiss border. Even so, we began to complain of the inactivity. Smith seemed to have heard us as he explained my new assignment to me one day in his office.

"Since you seem to be pretty anxious to get out, Bell," he said, "I'm going to give you a story with an ordnance recon outfit. They're salvaging captured German equipment and turning it over to the French. They're sending a jeep over for you this afternoon, so get your stuff together. Come back when you finish."

For the next few weeks I lived in the congenial atmosphere of the officers and men of the 55th Ordnance Group, temporarily set up in an abandoned warehouse a few miles outside of Besancon. After being greeted warmly by the captain in charge and having a sleeping cot assigned to me, I met a lieutenant with a grease-covered face who was, at that moment, practically standing on his head as he worked under the hood of a souped-up jeep, complete with red lights and siren. With this young lieutenant, who drove like a demon and christened each new jeep "Fireball" in honor of the wreckage of the last one (the current incarnation was "Fireball IV"), and with a British major with a large red mustache, who didn't seem to mind the lieutenant's driving at all, I covered hundreds of miles working on this story. We discovered many tons of machinery, artillery, trucks, and whole trainloads of equipment. On one of our journeys we found a trainload of huge torpedoes, warheads attached, which had probably been destined for the submarine fleet in the Mediterranean.

One night, after evening chow, as I lay on my bunk reading a paperback novel I'd stolen from the orderly room, the lieutenant panted up the stairs and sat down on the foot of my cot.

"Bell," he asked, "how would you like to get some pictures of the link-up with the army from the west?"

"My God, I didn't even know they were close to a link-up."

"Yep. We just got word that patrols met up today," he affirmed.

Before daylight next morning, a sleepy cook served hot coffee and cold Spam sandwiches for three in the kitchen tent while a guard poured gas into the jeep. Thus fortified, Fireball IV zoomed through the warehouse yard and took the narrow road toward Paris. Inside bounced an enthusiastic lieutenant, a dispassionate British major, and a sleepy photographer.

We drove at breakneck speed over bumpy roads jammed with G.I. trucks and civilian carts, wagons, and bicycles. By one o'clock we'd found a ration dump and cadged a box of ten-in-ones, which the major, as self-appointed cook, prepared for us over a Coleman stove beside the road.

Finished, we wiped the grease out of our mess kits with toilet paper, and continued our journey through the now almost-deserted countryside. The farther we went, the fewer people we saw and most were civilians. After we had driven for a good half hour without seeing a sign of military occupation, we stopped and studied our map. We discovered we were in the middle of a gap that was supposed to have been closed yesterday.

It was with an eerie feeling that we drove down the deserted road, dense woods flanking us on both sides. We had checked our weapons and were prepared to meet German eighty-eights and machine guns with our armament consisting of the major's .38 Webley revolver, my .45 automatic, and the lieutenant's carbine. Of course, we could also throw K-ration crackers.

As we drove on, the country became slightly hilly, forcing us to a slower speed. At one sharp turn we were forced to slow down to twenty miles an hour. Here, the expected happened. From high up on the side of the mountain, we heard the crack of a rifle and the "zing" of the slug as it ricocheted off the hard surface of the road in front of us. Immediately another shot followed and the buzz of the bullet passed just above our heads. From then on, Fireball IV never rolled under thirty-five, curves or no curves.

We reached Troyes, and the town was swarming with French soldiers who made up the right flank of the western invasion force. We drove around hunting for a gas dump. When we found one and refilled the tank, we conferred about what to do next. I was all for going on to Paris, which was only a few hours away. But since the lieutenant had work to do the next day, we finally decided to head back toward Besancon immediately so as to be through the gap before nightfall.

We made the dash back through the nearly-deserted country in record time and arrived in Dijon just as the sun sank out of sight.

In Dijon we held another conference and decided that it would be sheer folly to drive, blacked out, the rest of the way to Besancon. There being no G.I. outfits set up in the town, life there was going on at a near normal pace, and it was not difficult to find a hotel that was still operating. After the hotel cook prepared our supper from our remaining ten-in-ones, I went to my room exhausted and ready to hit the sack. But I had a bath in the rusty tub at the end of the hall and felt so refreshed that I decided to go out and have a look at the town. I took the precaution of writing down the name and address of the hotel in case I should get lost in the semi-blackout. This later proved to have been a prudent move.

On the main drag, I dropped into a bar for a beer. While dividing my attention between my drink and a pair of well-shaped legs across the room, someone touched my arm and said, "Pardon me. Are you *Americain*?" in a faltering, accented voice.

The question came from a big fellow about twenty wearing a shiny blue suit.

"Yeah, I am," I answered, turning to the stranger as if he were heaven-sent to guide me out of my boredom. "You speak English?"

"I speak a little. I study in the school," he replied.

I drained my glass, slapped down a fifty-franc note and said, "Where's a good bar?"

It seemed the fellow was a little doubtful as to which was the best bar in town, so he proceeded to show them all to me, one after another. At each one we added at least one friend of his to the party. After the first stop, I was not allowed to pay for a single drink.

My newfound friends urged their favorite wines on me at every stop, explaining to me the names, ages, and location of their conception. I did my best to pronounce the names and remember the information, but I always returned to cognac. By 0100 hours, I welcomed the unsteady support they offered me.

The last stop on the list was a dingy little restaurant, closed and dark. It belonged to a Spaniard in the group with whom I had been discussing Mexico City in my broken-down Spanish.

Around a large table in the back, the hilarious merriment gradually died and became a solid-satisfaction, family-group atmosphere. I relaxed into my alcohol contentment and listened happily to the group softly singing old and beautiful songs while I ate a huge plateful of baked rabbit.

Soon, one of the men looked at his watch and said

something to the others. The restaurant owner got up and opened a closet door. As he stepped inside, he turned around, stood on his toes and reached high above his head. Soon the voice of a BBC announcer relayed a coded message to the French underground. It was explained to me that these men had been members of the Resistance throughout the war. When the men had guided me back through the maze of darkened streets and left me at the door of my hotel, I felt that I had found truly worthwhile friends.

*****

As soon as I had shot a passable amount of film, I requisitioned a jeep and driver to take me back to the 163rd HQ unit. This effort consumed an entire day, since that unit had moved twice and I had to track it down by rumor. It seemed the Wehrmacht had backed into the Vosges Mountains and dug in for the winter. In its efforts to dislodge it, our infantry was now providing enough activity to occupy our entire force of photographers and I was being sent, with a fellow named Peterson as movie man, and a fellow named Zidek as driver, to join another CAT team—Noah/Bornet/Tressel—who were covering the 45th Division from Bain le Bain.

It was love at first sight as we drove through the cobblestoned streets of the ancient town. Bain le Bain had long been a famous spa because of its naturally warm mineral springs. The town now lacked tourists and the economic effects of the war were clearly evident, but driving past the small shop fronts lining the irregularly laid-out streets, we noticed sausages, cheeses, and fancy pastries behind the many-paned display windows.

At the small hotel where we found the other team in residence, we were introduced to a set-up that had no parallel for luxury in my army experience. We were conducted by the genial Italian owner to the second floor where we were each shown to a private room. Mine, with a window overlooking a well-cared-for courtyard and garden at the rear of the building, contained a chair, desk, rug, pictures, wash bowl and pitcher of water with a clean towel on a rack, and a bed more comfortable than any I had found since leaving home. It sported a feather mattress at least a foot and a half thick. At the head lay a cylindrical pillow that I never got used to. Covering the whole bed was a huge two-foot-thick "pouf," that unique French innovation of the sixteenth century, which is basically a large square bag loosely stuffed with feathers. At first I considered the thing a nuisance and shoved it onto the floor whenever I went to bed. Later, after cautious experiment, I discovered that it gave the same warmth as several blankets with only a fraction of the weight. I used it as long as we stayed in this pleasant little hotel.

Overshadowing our sumptuous quarters was the astounding meal we were served that night. I had not realized until then just how deadened my taste buds had become from many months of eating hundreds of K-and-C-rations and mediocre B-rations. The festivities of this evening brought the memories of good food back with a bang.

Beginning with an aperitif, the meal continued through a feast of genuine black-market steaks, mashed potatoes that had never been dehydrated, vegetables seasoned beyond recognition from their ten-in-one origin, green salad from the nearby countryside with a dressing unduplicated outside France, and a dessert of the lightest pastry ever served. The feast was accompanied by the inevitable bottle of wine, and brought to a most satisfying close with a small *digestif*.

Credit for all of this goes to the large and cheerful daughter of our Italian host. She worked from morning till night keeping house for the six of us as well as her father and brother, while wearing an unfailing smile. Though we all felt a fond affection for her, we did not want to risk losing the good thing we had, so an unwritten law kept us from trying to seduce her. She already had a boyfriend anyway.

*****

While enjoying this comparative elegance, we continued to record our assigned portion of the war. Because of the static condition of the front, we were forced to look more for feature pictures than for those of action. Occasionally, however, the division would order a push and we would have a few days of shooting under rather warm conditions.

At Epinal, we crossed the Moselle River by climbing across the broken stones of a blown-out bridge, only to find that it was under enemy observation and we were unable to cross back to the other side without inviting a probable hail of machine gun fire. (Why we had been given free passage on the way over we could not imagine.) We began to wander warily about the town in search of something to photograph while waiting for the offending gun to be found and liquidated, or for the cover of darkness.

A civilian unexpectedly placed an M1 rifle in my hand and explained in pantomime that he had found it on the street. I took it and joined a small party consisting of a G.I. and some FFI men (French Forces of the Interior—men who had previously been members of the Resistance) who were on a sniper hunt. One of the Frenchmen got a foot wound and the sniper got away, but I got a few pictures. I also got a couple of shots off with the rifle.

In spite of the occasional action shots and the small supply of carefully doped-out feature stories, we knew we were not turning in enough film, even though we had not heard any complaints from the company. So when we discovered the 117th Cavalry Recon Squadron working in the division's area, Peterson and I began to concentrate on their activities, leaving the 45th to the other team.

Photographing the activities of a recon outfit did not really appeal to me except for the wealth of material it provided for my camera. At a time like this, when picture material was at a premium, it offered almost unlimited opportunities if a photographer could manage to stay alive. This could, unfortunately, be for a discouragingly short span. Should anyone ask me what army job I considered the most hazardous I would, without hesitation, say that of the scout in a cavalry recon patrol.

A recon patrol moves toward an objective until it reaches it, or else. The "else" can include sudden death, capture, or retreat. Its job is not to fight; it carries weapons only for self-defense. Its job is to feel out the enemy—bait offered to make the enemy divulge its strength and location.

The men with the 117th that we met were tough and deadly serious about their work, but friendly and willing to do anything necessary to help us. They brought back fond memories of my Ranger friends.

The captain in charge of the troop was dubious about our sincerity because he had never had any of our photogs work with his outfit. However, after a few days' shooting in which we covered all the outposts, some of them close enough to watch the Germans eating dinner, he asked if we would like to accompany a motorized patrol into a town thought to be held by the Germans.

I had known that sooner or later we would be doing this, but I swallowed hard as I accepted his invitation.

At a road crossing, barely defiladed by a low rise beyond which stood the town, we pulled our jeep off the road and behind a small stone building. On the other side of the road among a grove of trees we saw an armored car and another jeep with a machine gun mounted in the back. These three vehicles were to compose the patrol.

The sergeant in charge explained the simple plan of operation. "We go in slow, and if they open up with anything big we get the hell out as fast as we can."

It sounded like pretty poor odds to me.

"I'm gonna give you one of my drivers," he continued. "You can stay here, fellow," he said to Zidek.

"That don't make me unhappy." Zidek smiled. I had a spasm of jealousy.

The armored car backed out of the trees and a few yards down the road toward the town. The other cavalry jeep followed suit. As we came into line with our spare tire facing the enemy, I realized we were going to approach our objective backwards. I had never seen this procedure used, but it seemed to make good sense.

Slowly, our patrol crept down the road, which led in a perfectly straight line between a few scattered trees growing at the road's edge. Leading the well-spaced convoy was the armored car with a rifleman riding on the back (which was facing forward) scanning the road closely for any suspicious-looking spot that might indicate a buried mine. On the front deck sat another alert rifleman, his eyes searching the wide-open fields on both sides of the road for any sign of movement.

Next, about fifty yards behind, came the machine gun jeep with its rifleman, gunner, and driver alert and ready to act at the first sign of trouble. Last in line was our jeep, Peterson and I with both cameras and .45s cocked and ready.

Slowly we approached the town that we could see clearly now, making frequent stops to examine with binoculars anything that seemed suspicious.

The cry of "Mine!" was relayed back from the armored car, and by the time we had reached the tell-tale spot in the road, the warning had been shouted back from farther on three or four more times as other mines were discovered. There was neither the time nor obligation to remove the mines, so the patrol merely detoured around them.

The closer we got to the town, the slower we moved and the more often we stopped. The tension became almost painful and I found myself almost wishing the damned Krauts would open fire so we could accomplish our purpose and leave.

I got out of the jeep and walked up and down the creeping convoy to offer my hopped-up nerves at least that much release. While taking a few pictures of the patrol with the town in the background, I managed to get my mind off our position for a few seconds.

We passed a field in which lay the rotting bodies of about fifty cows that had probably been mistaken for men in the dark and killed by a mortar barrage. Just beside the road, in a shallow shell crater, lay the body of a cream-colored Jersey, her belly torn open by the blast of a shell. Beside her lay the body of her unborn calf.

As the armored car reached the first houses in the town, it began to round the slight turn in the street and then stopped abruptly. The two men riding on top of it jumped to the ground and took cover behind its steel bulk. We drew our weapons and held our breaths.

Nothing happened.

I couldn't sit still in the jeep and just wait, so I got out and walked forward to the armored car to see what the trouble was. Peeping around the steel side of the car, I saw that the street was barricaded by a roadblock made up of large stacked logs.

Inside the car, the sergeant reported the situation by radio and was ordered to hold his position until it was taken over by tanks that were being sent out immediately. A half hour later a tank dozer, two light tanks, and the captain's jeep arrived. After the removal of the roadblock and a perusal by the tanks, the town was found to be unoccupied except by a few suicidal rear-guard snipers. The captain apologized for the lack of action and extended a permanent invitation to join any of his patrols whenever we felt the urge.

*****

Slowly, winter sneaked up on us. For over a month we had seen almost no sunshine. It rained at some time nearly every day. The cool had turned to cold and the first snow lay unmelted over the half-frozen mud.

The engineers worked day and night to prop up the narrow highways that were rapidly dissolving under the tracks and wheels of heavy equipment. To add to their job, they had to build miles of new roads in order for the infantry that was now stretched thin over a wide front to be fed and armed. To prevent their efforts from being ground into the mud, the engineers reinforced these new roads with a foundation of stone from the most convenient source, the blasted buildings left by artillery fire. Thus, entire battered villages disappeared from the earth.

Besides the mud, from which our jeep had to be winched on numerous occasions, the hazard of icy pavement began to take a toll on G.I. vehicles.

The road to Epinal was familiar to us by now, and Reno Frate, who was back to driving for Peterson and me, had taken its tight curves many times before. This time, however, a two-and-a-half-ton truck was approaching on the wrong side of the road. Smoothly, we skated over the ice-encrusted pavement almost head-on into the truck.

There was a crash, a jolt, a twist, and then utter silence, in which I could hear the trickle of liquid spattering onto the road. I was lying across the hood of the jeep. Tentatively, I climbed to the ground and found that I was still in one piece. My legs didn't work quite right, but I dismissed that when I found I could stand on them. I saw Peterson getting to his feet from the pavement.

"Where's Frate?" he asked.

"I don't know."

On the other side of the wreck we found him lying on his back, out cold. A huge blue lump the size of a baseball was rising on his forehead. While we were slipping a folded jacket under his head, he came to and insisted on getting up. After one unsuccessful try he was content to lie quietly for a few minutes.

The driver of the truck was shaken but unhurt.

By this time we were surrounded by jabbering French civilians, including an old lady with a pitcher of wine and a glass.

Frate refused the offer (for a change), so Peterson and I split it.

Several of the people brought us an assortment of pots and pans. On smelling the contents, we found that they had caught the leaking gasoline from the punctured tank of the truck and were returning it to us. We told them to keep it and received grateful "*merci's.*" Gasoline was a commodity of great value and would bring a good price on the black market.

A major in a civilian car stopped to investigate and was prevailed upon to take Frate to the nearest aid station. I accompanied him as I had discovered that both my shins were raw hamburger. We left Peterson to take care of our equipment and the salvage of the jeep.

*****

A month and a half passed, during which the front shifted back and forth but made little progress in either direction. We had become much too fond of the hotel and its people in Bain le Bain than was good for us. We had never stayed this long in any one place and it was possible now only because of the nearly static front. Nevertheless, there was a gradual forward movement and we knew we could not remain this far from the front. We kept postponing our departure because we were convinced that we would never find another spot that would offer us comparable living conditions.

Finally, though, we decided that, should the division begin a large-scale push, we would be left behind if we did not find a place closer up. Also, we were now spending as much as four or five hours of our twelve-to-sixteen-hour days doing nothing but driving to and from our scenes of shooting.

As we left our old digs, the Italian owner of the hotel, his son and their two dogs stood on the sidewalk and watched sadly. The girl, to whom we had just bequeathed a large supply of ten-in-one rations, stood at the window and sobbed into a handkerchief.

Our hunt for a new billet led us to a monastery high on a

hill overlooking Epinal. Here, we were welcomed with open arms by the poverty-stricken monks and promised the best accommodations they were able to offer. We should have known better.

While we were unloading our duffels and carrying them to a dreary-looking schoolroom, the dinner bell rang and we were invited to eat at the table of the abbot. The meal was exceptionally poor, consisting of clear soup, stew with a medium sized piece of extremely tough meat (species unknown), dark, heavy bread (two pieces for each of us and one for the monks), and deeply watered wine.

The abbot was surprised to find that we were photographers. He explained why. On the day the town was taken, he had watched through a window of the monastery as American troops crossed the river under fire early in the morning. Finally, at about ten o'clock, he had seen two men, carrying strange objects in their hands, leisurely climb across the wreckage of the bridge and reach this side of the river without a shot being fired at them. A few minutes later, these same two men had nonchalantly strolled across an open street straight down the hill from his window. Somehow, and to him it seemed a miracle, a German machine gun just below his window, set up behind a low stone wall there, had been taken off-guard and had not fired a single shot.

It was then that he had been able to identify the objects the men carried in their hands as cameras. As Peterson and I looked at each other, I felt the short hairs on the back of my neck crawl. I recalled every movement we had made that strange day. They were just as the abbot had described them.

10

The War Slogs On

And so began the push.

The bloody, muddy, miserable, freezing Battle of the Vosges Mountains was just beginning, and, had I known what was to come in the next few months, a shiver worse than what the sloppy, wet and bitterly cold weather could produce would have shaken me to my toes.

There was a surplus of action now, and we spent all the light hours of the day following the leading elements of our newly assigned division, the 100th Infantry. It was back to the old grind of driving, plodding, dodging, running, eating when we could, and sleeping when we could, with the bitter weather making life even more miserable.

The 100th was new to combat, and I felt the dread of working with inexperienced men. More than once, Peterson and I squeezed out of a needlessly tight situation that would never have occurred with a more seasoned outfit. It seemed criminal to us that men were sent into combat insufficiently trained and without competent leaders.

At about this time I had an ominous premonition. It told me that my luck had run out, that no more close ones were going to miss me, that no more imminent disasters would be deflected by some supernatural force.

One night while I was sitting on my cot, blankly staring across the room (as I had found myself doing all too often of late), my gaze happened to rest absently on my helmet lying on the floor. Over the battered steel shell was stretched the tattered bit of camouflage netting that I had put on many months before to minimize reflection from the bare steel where the paint had worn off. On the left side, the unraveled ends of several strings showed where they had been cut as a bit of shrapnel had glanced off the hard metal while I pressed my face against the dirt beside a road somewhere near Baccarat.

It seemed very "lucky" that the piece of sharp metal had not gone through my head, the netting suffering the damage instead. It occurred to me that from now on, all I had to do whenever I felt impending catastrophe was to remind myself that whatever violence was meant for me would be suffered instead by the lucky piece of netting. I should probably have laughed at myself, but at the time I welcomed the thought as a counterbalance to the idea of my inevitable demise, which was no more logical.

*****

Slowly the Germans were pushed from the wooded and snow-covered mountains, leaving behind thousands of mines and throwing artillery and mortar shells as they fled. Snow fell for days without ceasing, leaving a deep white blanket over the ugly scars in the ground cut by exploding shells. As we moved from newly-taken town to town, following closely on the heels of the forward elements, our requisites for a sleeping place for the night dropped from consideration of beds, hot water, and possibly an occupant who could cook, to only a stove over which to thaw out after a day of plodding through two feet of snow.

Warmth was all we were looking for when we ran across a big house on the outskirts of a small Alsatian town. It was tucked along the bank of a small river between the mountains. We decided to spend the night there, provided that the German opposition on the slopes above was cleaned out by nightfall.

The squad I was advancing with on foot ran across a machine gun set up inside the solid walls of a rock spring house. The Germans refused to be budged by rifle fire. When a bazooka was sent for and brought up, the Germans were quickly routed, and I got minor face burns from shooting my pictures too close to the rocket launcher's exhaust flames.

It was nearly dark when Peterson, Frate and I returned to the house we had spotted earlier, and approached the occupants. Given two small rooms on the second floor, we carried in our cots, bed rolls, and a case of ten-in-ones. We turned the rations over to a big, hearty woman who delightedly began preparing our supper.

I finished my captions quickly in the cold bedroom and wandered out to the warm kitchen to thaw out beside the cook stove. There, for the first time, I saw an extremely pretty girl of about nineteen working diligently under the loud direction of our hostess.

I stretched my hands over the stove and absorbed the beautiful warmth. When the big woman saw me there, she burst into a rapid flow of French while fluttering about to get me a chair and open the oven door so I could get a maximum amount of heat. Finally, she spotted my water-logged boots and, by means of vivid pantomime and loud French, made me understand that I was to remove them immediately.

As I did so, the girl disappeared through the door and came back soon with a pair of very large and very old bedroom slippers. These, she handed to me silently and stood to watch as I tried them on. They were so much too big for me that I had to laugh. This brought out a small smile from the girl, too, and the strong contrast brought into vivid relief the sadness that I had noticed on her face before. The woman got me to understand that the girl was Spanish.

"Verdad?" I asked the girl in my own poor high school Spanish. *"Que dice la senora?"*

The girl translated the French woman's words, saying in Spanish, "She says that I am Spanish and my name is Celia. And that I was sent here when my father was killed in the revolution." Looking down at my feet, she said, "Those are his slippers."

"Oh," I said, feeling as if this were none of my business.

"Era un hombre muy grande." Truly, he must have been a large man.

"*Si,*" the girl said and looked as if she were going to cry.

Quickly, I tucked my feet under the chair and lit a cigarette.

After supper we said good night and went up to our rooms where we fought off female efforts to load us down with extra blankets. It was decided that Frate and Peterson would sleep in one of the cold little cubicles, and I in the other.

I lit a stump of a candle, set up my cot, and crawled in to read, for the fourth time, a two-week-old letter from home.

Later, as I lay awake listening to distant rifle fire, a gentle knock came on the door. With one hand on my flashlight and the other on my .45, I called, "Come in."

Slowly the door opened. A figure slid silently into the room and stood unmoving in the darkness. I pressed the switch on the flashlight and saw the troubled face of Celia. She was crying and looked frightened.

"*Ven aca,*" I said, softly.

Quickly she came to me and sat on the edge of my cot. I put my arm around her shoulders and she gave herself up to her tears.

Much later, when she left, I lay on my back listening to the persistent chattering of a machine gun far off and wondered how war and peace, happiness and unhappiness could sometimes get so thoroughly mixed together.

*****

Under the momentum of the push, the Germans were unable to hold the plug in the Saverne Gap and, as the Americans burst through onto the flat, frozen ground beyond, the Allied call went back for armor. One of the first to be put into action in the area was the 14th Armored Division, brand-new and raring to romp onto German soil without slowing down.

Since it seemed that now the big show was going to be

with the tanks, orders came from company HQ that Peterson and I were to turn over the 100th to another team and attach ourselves to the 14th Armored Division.

I hardly considered this good news as it was common knowledge that a photographer with a camera and a .45-caliber pistol was pretty well outclassed by anything designed to stop a tank. It would mean, though, that if I did manage to outlive my first story, quite a number of my prints would come back to the CPLO stamped as having been radioed to the States for immediate publication. The newspapers and magazines could never resist a picture of tanks in action.

Locating the division CP south of Saverne, we were given a brief review of the situation. The division was now separated into three CAT teams, one to remain as reserve at headquarters, one to fork to the north, and the other to the south. We chose the southern element as the most potentially picturesque, and headed for Molsheim.

Riding with lead tanks or plodding with small infantry units, we moved through Molsheim, Shirmeck, and many other towns whose names were neither goals nor benchmarks. We shot pictures of small pockets of enemy as they were either captured or pulverized, of burning American tanks when they were blasted by the deadly German anti-tank guns, and of the bitter life of the infantry in the filthy snow. We were again growing accustomed to a diet of K- and C-rations, and the discomfort of being continually cold.

While the shooting was going on in one small town, a group that included Peterson, Frate, and me picked a large house as the most easily defended position in the vicinity, and organized our doubtful defense to await the anticipated German advance.

No German advance came, so Frate, the inveterate souvenir hunter, climbed to the attic to see what he could find. What he found were four badly frightened German soldiers who were hysterically glad to surrender to him. Characteristically, before bringing them downstairs Frate relieved them of all interesting possessions including medals, belt buckles, and money. He later gave the money to a man who claimed to be collecting for a fund to help Alsatians who had been captured by the Russians while serving in the German army. Nobody believed him for a moment but the Nazi-issued money was worthless anyway.

One of those tanks the press was so fond of.

*****

Barr was a small industrial town that I remember mainly for a bloody night battle in which the 14th lost six or seven tanks, and for an overabundance of Rhine wine.

During the afternoon before the battle, the armored column was halted halfway through the town at a street blocked by the lead tank when it was knocked out by a shot from a huge German tank. The entire crew burned to death there, including the colonel in charge of the combat team.

Walking down the column of buttoned-up tanks stalled along the deserted streets of the town gave me an eerie sensation in the pit of my stomach. When firing broke out ahead, we ducked into an open passageway that happened to be handy. There, we found a tall civilian who greeted us profusely and dashed off to bring back a basket full of small bottles of English-labeled Rhine wine. After opening one each, we filled our large pockets with the others.

Returning again with another basketful of the bottles, the man climbed onto one of the tanks stopped in the street just outside the passageway. He pounded on the assistant driver's hatch until it opened up enough to permit a hand to reach out and take the bottles, one by one.

When darkness came, the column had succeeded in pushing forward only another block or so. Having seen no better place to spend the night, we returned to the wine warehouse.

During the night, the tanks advanced through the town and several miles beyond, but not without cost. In the morning, we photographed several mangled, smoking hulks, inside of which were the charred bodies of the American crews.

Out of these smoking wrecks, Peterson and I were each able to salvage a pair of good binoculars. Though these were quite valuable prizes and would bring a high price on the G.I. barter market, I almost considered mine not worth taking. Climbing onto the still hot metal of a burnt-out hull, I leaned down into the open turret hatch and reached for the rack where the tank commander's binoculars were kept. As I did so, I came face to face, eye to eye with the lieutenant who had owned the glasses. Half leaning, half sitting, his head was turned back so that he stared me directly in the face as I leaned down into the turret. The expression on his face, still showing the extreme agony in which he had died as the anti-tank shell tore away his leg and half of his right side, hit me with the force of a sledgehammer.

*****

As the American drive pushed closer and closer to the German border, the resistance became more stubborn, though never enough to stop the rolling tanks for long. Perhaps the Germans had been caught unprepared, but now there began to appear more and more Mark IVs to face the charge of our M4s and M4A1s. It was now necessary for the American anti-tank crews to follow the advance closely in order to consolidate every new gain.

In the sector we were working, an anti-tank outfit composed entirely of black soldiers arrived. We had never seen an outfit like this in combat, and were eager to work the story if it turned out to their advantage.

At a battered little town that the Germans were unusually reluctant to give up, we saw the gunners work for the first time. The town had been held on several different occasions by both the Americans and the Germans. Now the see-saw battle was at an impasse, with the Germans occupying half and the Americans half. The Germans held a slight positional advantage from which they were able to rake with machine gun fire nearly every American-held street leading from their zone. Therefore, no one crossed a street unless it was absolutely necessary, and then only at a dead run.

While we were attempting the almost impossible task of portraying a stalemate, the Germans undertook a tank charge against the defenses of the town.

I took a position behind one of the anti-tank guns, and began to record the action. Soon, however, the gun stopped firing and I found that the crew was out of ammunition.

The only thing to do was send a detail of men to the small dump across the street for more. The street happened to be one of the more dangerous ones, though, and I could not blame the men for hesitating to cross it in the face of the German machine gunners.

Suddenly one of the black gunners dashed across the street to the tune of whining bullets. He immediately crossed back with a 75mm shell in his arms. Soon, two more of the men joined him to form a continual procession across the slug-sputtered street. When the pile of ammunition was high enough, they went back to their job behind their gun and, with the others, turned back the advance. No one was scratched, though hundreds of bullets had searched for them.

On through Hagenau, Soultz, Lauterbourg, and many other small towns the tanks, backed up the infantry, drove against the ever-tightening German resistance and the hostile weather.

It was becoming a fast, heavy, continuous series of small fanatical fights with a furious exchange of firepower and heavy losses on both sides. The Germans were frantically determined that the Americans were not going to reach the soil of the Fatherland. The American units were equally determined to be the first Americans to cross the German border.

Even among the photo teams the determination to bring back the first pictures inside Germany kept all of us at the farthest point of our assigned unit's spearhead. This accounted for a head wound from a sniper's bullet for one photographer, a sprained leg for another when the tank atop which he was riding hit a mine, a shrapnel hole through the tail of my field jacket, and plenty of close calls for everyone.

By now our confidence in the combat judgment of our 14th Armored Division had risen from zero to extreme admiration. They had learned the facts of life and death through the loss of a great number of men and tanks. Time after time they had faced the crack German panzers and, though it was agreed the Germans had the mechanical advantage, the American tankers managed to inflict heavy wounds and keep rolling forward.

*****

From a high church bell tower, being used as an OP overlooking a large open space of cleared cropland, I saw and photographed the only picture-book tank battle I ever saw. From this exposed position, our team commanded a perfect view of the no-man's land between the advance American troops in the town and the enemy foxholes and machine gun emplacements a quarter-mile away at the edge of a wooded area.

The lieutenant observer beside us called for an artillery barrage on a concentration of enemy infantry grouped loosely around a concrete pill box. After the barrage ended, leaving some dead and the rest scattered in foxholes nearby, we were dumbfounded to see no less than fifteen German Mark IV tanks lumber slowly out of a clump of trees and form a single line abreast. Then, evenly spaced in a line a thousand yards long, they roared across the open fields toward us.

Frantically, the lieutenant called for artillery fire and the entire town around us roared with the sound of tank engines. As we watched, an opposing line of American tanks took form below us, some of them concealed among the buildings and trees of the town, others in the open field on the outskirts. With the frantic firing of the guns added to the explosions of the incoming rounds, the air soon became hazy and hard to breathe.

In front of us, a German tank stopped abruptly and began to burn. No one crawled from the hatches. An American tank, in a street to our right, stopped firing and lay dead for unknown reasons. An anti-tank shell sent a track flying from another German machine, and in a matter of seconds it was hidden from sight by the explosion of heavy artillery shells. When the smoke cleared, it was burning fiercely.

Still, the line of panzers came on, half-hidden within the smoky atmosphere. Abruptly, the tanks in the center of the line stopped and continued firing while the ones at the ends began to encircle the town. The firing from the town increased until it was almost impossible to see more than one or two of the enemy tanks at a time through the heavy haze of smoke and dust.

In the fury of noise and swirling smoke there was no time to think of personal danger while Peterson and I continued shooting film as fast as we could operate our cameras. The naked vulnerability of our position in the tower did not terrify us until later, in retrospect.

Suddenly it was all over. When it seemed the enemy tanks would surely have the town irretrievably surrounded, their formation broke. Scattering in three directions, the tanks turned tail and lumbered at full speed for the concealment of the woods, leaving behind the blazing remains of several mortally wounded machines, along with their crews.

*****

It seemed almost amazing to us that we reached the German border at last. Together Peterson and I photographed the American tanks as they rolled under the big arch at the border custom house. We followed quickly on foot and, keeping a nervous eye out for trouble, zipped open in the frigid breeze and let fly on German soil. Somehow the symbolic gesture was not as satisfying as it should have been.

Later, back at the CPLO, we learned that we were not the only CAT team to cross into Germany that day. It was never determined who had been first.

The next morning we stared into the early dawn skies searching for a promised flight of American dive bombers. Looking to the east from our perch in the observation tower atop the customs house, we could see the tops of the buildings in a town where, the night before, the tank column had run up against a pocket of German resistance.

The airplanes failed to appear on schedule, as usual, and I began to feel nervous One reason was the well-known occurrence of wild pitching by the bomb boys, enhanced by the knowledge that we were well within the red zone of their operation. Another disconcerting thought was that we were probably under direct observation by the enemy, and there were no friendly troops between them and us.

Finally the bombers showed up, dived, bombed, were duly photographed, and left. Before they were out of sight, the

German eighty-eight gunners began to vent their anger in our direction. Retreating to the stairwell, which appeared to be the most solid portion of the building, we sat down and sweated it out while the building dissolved around us. When the hail of fire and thunder slackened for a minute, we took out with heels flying for the comparative safety of a little group of buildings about two hundred yards behind the customs house. We were hampered not at all by the weight of cameras, weapons, mackinaws, and rubber boots.

*****

Now what we had was a slow, hard, dirty fight that seemed to go on forever. The whole line of the eastern front had been drained to the danger point to reinforce the crumbling lines in the north, where the Germans had walked through green troops and were advancing almost unopposed toward Liege in what would become famous as the Battle of the Bulge. More and more often the tanks were stopped at well-defended points for intervals that were longer each time. Again the job was handed to the foot soldiers and the tanks were relegated to a supporting role. Our cameras were now focused on a new type of warfare—that of the armored infantry. We saw the men digging in side by side with their big mechanical friends.

At one point I took up a position on the rear deck of an M4 firing into a strongly resisting town. As I hung onto the rim of the open turret to hold myself against the recoil of the gun, I spoke to the tank commander. I remarked on the accuracy of the tank's gun crew.

"This is easy shooting," he said. "You should see some of our targets."

"Well, Lieutenant, it would make a good picture if you could hit that Kraut OP there." I pointed out the tower of what appeared to be some sort of municipal building in the center of the town.

"OP, huh?" He smiled. "O.K. But just to make it harder,

we'll hit the face of that clock on it."

It took me only a minute to set up my camera with the ten-inch lens. When I gave him the word, the lieutenant called for three rounds of fire from the tank gun. Later, when we finally took the town, I noticed from short range that not one shot had missed its mark.

*****

Through the CPLO we were invited to rejoin the company HQ unit on Christmas Day. The main festivities were held in the evening to allow teams working on Christmas stories to drive the long distance from their assignments and get there without missing the wonderful dinner, the "Road Show" program, or the party afterward.

The reunion was a masterpiece put together with the odds and ends available. Never, though, could it replace, for any of us, what we had left behind some sixteen months before. Foto Facto, our little company newspaper, said, "What we were trying to do was re-create Christmas overseas in the spirit that we knew it at home."

And in some measure we succeeded. It was, on the whole, a nice Christmas holiday—about as nice as you can get in the Army. But we would be kidding ourselves if we pretended that was the whole story. After the fun, the food, the laughter and the songs, when each of us was alone with his thoughts, we felt the sadness of being away from those we loved. All the homesickness and yearning of the rest of the year comes to a head on this day, and no matter what you do, you can't forget.

*****

The going was getting ever rougher. Up in the north of France General Anthony McAuliffe said "Nuts" (as the word was sanitized for publication) to a German demand for surrender, and our front was bled dry for men and equipment to get him out of his predicament. The terrain was impossible for armor now and the slogging infantry came back into its own. CAT-1's new assignment, an anonymous task force, was a jumble of green and experienced outfits and parts of outfits sent up from other areas to bolster the thin lines facing Bitche. With them, we battled slowly and clumsily north through Lorraine.

Then the war machine ground to a jerky halt. The infantry dug in deep and the engineers sowed mine fields out ahead. Just beyond Phillipsbourg, our photo team settled down with a very nice family. The man, his wife and children all seemed determined to overpay us for the food we contributed to the household by waiting on us every moment we were in the house. Our host appeared to have the idea that Americans drank at least a gallon of coffee a day, and we hardly disappointed him. For breakfast we had two cups of coffee each. When we returned to our room after working all day, we were greeted by a pot of fresh coffee on the glowing coal stove. After supper we usually left to take our film to the CPLO and when we returned out of the cold night we found another pot of steaming black brew on the stove. Of course, it was our coffee and the old man drank his share, but we were grateful for the attention.

During the last days of December, we concentrated our attention on B Company, just down the road from where we were living. Unlike most of the other units, they seemed to be making slow but visible progress toward Bitche. Almost all other action in the task force consisted of night patrols and occasional mortar or artillery barrages. Finally, on the last day of the year, we were able to see, from B Company's outpost, the medieval castle perched atop a mountain with the town of Bitche scattered down its slopes.

Now that the town was well within artillery range, it seemed only a matter of days before we would be able to walk in. We marked New Year's Day with a bottle of schnapps at the CPLO's house, after which we returned home with the expectation of a good night's sleep.

At about midnight I was awakened by the sound of small-arms fire from down the road. I pulled the blankets up over my head and went back to sleep. It seemed like only a matter of minutes before I was again awakened. This time the sounds seemed closer. Certainly they were louder. Out of the darkness from across the room came a muffled, "Damn the bastards." Frate had his head covered with his field jacket. After that, it was no use trying to sleep so I lay awake till dawn listening to the sounds of the fighting and trying to figure out, from the difference in the sounds of the rifles and machine guns, who had the upper hand. We didn't know it at the time, but this was the beginning of a general winter attack the Germans called Operation Northwind.

By the dim light of the gray dawn, we started down the road to find out just what the disturbance had amounted to. Rounding the first turn, no more than a hundred yards from our front gate, we were brought up short by a half-track parked across the road.

"What gives?" we asked.

"Krauts got the road cut up there," was the answer.

"What about B Company?" we asked, fearfully.

"They got cut off last night," the man on the half-track called.

We drove the short distance back to Phillipsbourg and beyond that across the valley to the little town where the task force HQ was located. A sporadic artillery barrage was underway. Leaving Frate with the jeep under cover of the wall of a two story house, Peterson and I made our way the few blocks to the CP. Along the way we passed every conceivable stage of disarray ranging from men lying flat on the ground to others frantically packing up their belongings.

The area was being shelled a little harder now, but as we passed a truck parked on the street in front of the CP we noticed a young soldier sitting straight as a ramrod behind the wheel, staring straight ahead. His face was a pale shade of gray.

Inside the CP we found things much as usual except for

one factor: all business was being carried out on the horizontal. We crossed the room, stepping carefully over and between the prone figures. We found the G-2 officer sprawled full length on the floor, a telephone in one hand, a dozen colored pencils in the other and a map spread before him.

"...Tank column," he was saying into the telephone, "supposed to be heading down the road your way." A pause, and then, "Hello, Carter! Hello!"

He dropped the phone on the floor. "No answer," he said, looking at us.

"Capt. Carter of B Company?" we asked, knowing the answer.

"I heard him say, 'This must be them now', and then no answer."

"Where's the Kraut tank column, sir?" we asked.

"On the road from Bitche. Heading for Phillipsbourg."

Without another word, we dashed for the door. We lived on that road. As we crossed the room, concussion from a shell landing outside pushed in several windows. Outside, the kid in the truck in front of the building had, by now, crawled out of his cab and was standing on the running board, peering wide-eyed around him.

"Say, fellow," Peterson called as we ran. "You better get down from there. It's getting a little too hot for sightseeing."

Surprised, the youngster looked at him and answered simply, "The captain told me to stay with the truck."

"Well, for Christ's sake," Peterson yelled, "At least you can get under it!" A light came over the boy's face. "Yeah," he said and smiled gratefully as he climbed down.

Burning rubber, we dashed back toward "home," swerving around a furiously burning weapon carrier that had just caught an artillery shell in the main street of Phillipsbourg. We slid to a stop in front of our door while two German observation planes above us called the shots for Kraut artillery on the other side of the hill. I have no doubt we beat all previous records in the duffle-packing event, assisted by our weeping hosts. With last instructions to the family to go immediately to their cellar and stay there until the Germans occupied the house, we said goodbye, forgetting several pounds of coffee and sugar that we later could only hope our hosts discovered and hid from the Germans.

In town, we parked the jeep on a side street and prepared to await the oncoming tank column, along with the anti-tank crews who were setting up their guns to cover any possible approach. The green infantry had pulled out in a panic, which made one yearn for the cool heads of a mature outfit.

Peterson and I picked a shooting position where we could include in our viewfinders an M4 tank, an anti-tank gun and a long stretch of highway up which we expected to soon see the approaching German tanks.

Suddenly a slow-moving form came into view on the distant road. We waited tensely while the tank commander examined it with his binoculars.

"Wagon," he announced, and we relaxed again.

The heavily-laden wagon, stacked high with a family's possessions and several members of the family, rocked slowly along the ice-covered highway behind two plodding oxen. Absently, we watched it come down the road and swing wide around the muzzle of the tank gun.

Suddenly we heard the roar of a speeding engine and we watched as a big car swung crazily around the tank, then back the other way to clear the lumbering wagon. Skidding past me out of control on the icy pavement, the car spun completely around and came to a stop fifty feet away. As I watched, dumfounded, the doors flew open and out stepped five black-uniformed SS troopers.

Running toward them on impulse, I raised my camera and focused. As I clicked off my picture, the five lined up beside the car and slowly lifted their hands above their heads. Immediately we were surrounded by men who came running from all directions to complete the capture, and I was left with the problem of figuring out a caption for the picture I had just taken.

Still the enemy tank column failed to show up. The delay was hard on the nerves and we were getting tired of waiting when, from behind, came a column of American tanks to force the issue. There being no percentage in following a herd of tanks into a fight on the enemy's own ground, we held our position in the town until we lost the light of day. The situation, which had been building in intensity all day, fizzled to anticlimax as the German tanks decided not to fight that day. The only point of interest was revealed later when we found that we had been cut off and surrounded for ten hours. The task force command had given us up for lost, without our ever having been aware of the enemy troops in our rear.

Within a few days, the German army, supported by more air activity than we had seen in several months, crashed through our first two lines of defense and was driving again to seal the all-important Saverne Gap. Fortunately they were not quite strong enough to smash the defense of experienced troops who had been rushed in. Soon their advance ground to a halt just short of the town of Saverne. They dug in for a breathing spell while reinforcements, mainly in the form heavy artillery, were brought up.

We retreated to Saverne, where we became accustomed to the nightly barrages of heavy artillery shells reminiscent of the Anzio Annie railroad guns. The huge shells were now falling into what had recently been a secure Corps rear area. They quickly decimated the MP motor pool, the Quartermaster hospital laundry, the G.I.-restored movie theater and several more buildings before Corps HQ had time to pull out.

Assigned now to the newly arrived 101st Airborne Division, Peterson and I expected to find much colorful material in the outfit about which we had read so much. Instead we found a rather mediocre organization whose greatest occupation at the present was the continual reiteration of their valiant stand at Bastogne. Other outfits had been in similar situations, but had neither the time, inclination, nor public relations staff to publicly glorify themselves. The wonderful Ranger battalion at Anzio, the 36th Division at Salerno and B Company at Phillipsbourg were continually being surrounded by the enemy. Some fought their way out, some were cut to pieces, and some, like the 101st, were rescued (by the 4th Armored Division). Some replied to a German offer to surrender with words comparable to McAuliffe's much-touted "Nuts," but most were never given that opportunity.

With the 101st, we found little to photograph, the division merely performing a holding action at the time. Therefore, we made a series of excursions to the south of Saverne to assist the team covering the 36th Division. That division was engaged in several small, fierce battles for the possession of strategic towns. In this type of close infighting, a photographer was offered all sorts of unexpected pictures which showed, truly and intimately, the job of an infantryman in combat. Here, in unposed pictures, the tenseness and absorption in the important job of staying alive was written on a man's face and in his actions. These were the true portraits of the war, and the hardest to catch on film.

The most difficult job I constantly had was that of wrenching my attention from a tense situation long enough to attend to the conscious operation of a camera. That was when habit and instinct took over.

Oberhoffen was one of the small towns south of Saverne, no different from a thousand others but strategically important. It had been occupied repeatedly by first the Germans and then the Americans. The Germans now had possession, but the 36th was as determined to own it as the Germans were to keep it. A bloody, savage, house-to-house battle ensued, which went on from day to day with the gain or loss of a few houses every day. At the end of nearly a week the Americans seemed to have gained a slight advantage.

Checking in one morning at the regimental CP, Peterson and I were told that the mayor of Oberhoffen wanted a wagon sent into the evacuated town to pick up the bodies of civilians killed in the fighting. We drove immediately to the town only to find that we were too late. Since we were already there, we decided to investigate the possibility of action for the day. Walking up the street toward the houses that formed the "front line," we were suddenly stopped by a noise that sounded like a mournful cow. It was coming from the barn behind a house we were passing. We warily crept through the backyard of the house, detouring around three German medics, all quite dead, lying in the path. All three wore prominent red crosses on their sleeves and carbines slung over their shoulders. One lay across a bazooka.

In the barn we found four cows that apparently had gone days without food or water. I was in favor of turning them out to forage for themselves until I remembered that after dark anything moving in the town would be fired on without question or warning. We gathered up all the buckets and pans we could find and hunted up water. The cows drank faster than we could carry at first, but they finally seemed sated. We left a good reservoir of water and halfway clean hay. We were repaid by cow-eyed looks of gratitude as we departed.

We found the platoon CP in the cellar of a bombed-out house. The commanding officer there told us that he was expecting orders at any moment that would send them all on a general attack.

"You going with us when we move out?" a lieutenant asked.

"I guess so," I answered.

"It may be rough," the lieutenant ventured, looking me over.

"Maybe it'll make good pictures."

"Maybe it will," the lieutenant said. After a pause he

added, "You know, I don't think I'd like to have your job."

The radio began talking in a raspy, garbled voice and, after listening for a while the lieutenant turned to me and said, "Well, are you ready?"

I wasn't sure that I was, but I said yes.

Our objective was the church on the same side of the street and about fifty feet farther down, along with a three-story building just behind the church and another three story building just beyond the first. To take them, the lieutenant was leading two squads accompanied by an M4 tank.

Peterson had gone across the street to a building in which most of the men were waiting, so I dashed across the open space between house and building to let him know what was going on. We saw the tank move out into the open and stop directly in front of the church. My first picture was made as one of the squads dashed, man by man, out the front door of the building we were in to the cover of a low stone wall across the street from the church. As they ran, they received rifle fire from some high place, but we couldn't locate the enemy rifleman. Thinking the fire was probably coming from the church bell tower, two men took a position partly shielded by the tank and poured lead into the tower windows while the others advanced to positions at the side of the church. I ran for cover behind the tank, where I crouched and took another shot of the riflemen firing into the church tower.

By now, some of the men had entered the church by a side door and taken two prisoners from beneath the pews. I joined two men in investigating the bell tower, which yielded no results. The tank in front of the church had, after repeated attempts, knocked down a stone wall and climbed into the church yard from where it could be heard firing a long stream of machine gun bullets at several green-uniformed men running across an open field beyond the buildings.

The first three-story structure, set at an angle from the rear of the church, was the next target, and the other squad had been working up to it through a neglected apple orchard. Crouching low behind a wall that bounded the rear courtyard of the church, we worked our way to a gate at the entrance to the targeted building. The men approaching through the orchard had received no fire and now had the building covered on two sides. Cautiously, they—and we—slipped through the doorway. Almost at the entrance, a stairway led to a cellar. This being the most logical place for the enemy to hide, the infantrymen yelled down the stairs for them to come up. No answer came from the darkness below, so they threw a hand grenade down the steps as a precaution. There was still no answer, so two men with flashlights went down to investigate. The rest of us scattered throughout the building to make sure it was empty.

With two of the three buildings taken, and two prisoners but no casualties, the situation looked well in hand. Two riflemen were posted at upstairs windows to cover the advance to the remaining building. The path led through a narrow gateway in the rear wall of the churchyard, across another small yard to a door. Peterson decided to shoot his movies from one of the upstairs windows, while I chose a foot-square hole in the rear wall from which I would have a good view of the men after they had passed through the gate until they entered the building. The range was short; I was no more that fifteen feet from a window of the final building. I would have a good shot of any action.

The squad was ranged behind the wall, ready to go one by one through the gate and spread out around the building. I raised my camera to the hole in the wall to make an accurate range-finder focus. The lieutenant , leading the way, stepped through the gate. Through my range finder, I saw a German soldier lean quickly out a window, fire a bazooka, and duck back out of sight. It took only a fraction of a second and I was left dumfounded without a picture or an excuse.

The bazooka shell hit the wall just to the left of the gate and exploded inches from the lieutenant's head. He dropped and never moved. Demoralized, the squad pulled back and huddled close behind the wall. One man pushed in beside me and poked a rifle through the hole I'd used for my camera. He pumped several futile shots through the window opposite while others tossed grenades over the wall. The sergeant had two white phosphorus grenades, which he threw onto the roof in an attempt to set the building afire. They rolled off and showered the burning particles back over the wall onto us.

It seemed to me that a bazooka of our own offered the only solution, and I suggested it to the sergeant.

"It might work," he said, and sent a man back for two. By now the tank, through dint of more butting and ramming, had managed to pull up beside the church and was in a position to fire on the target building. The squad pulled back to the church and the tank began work. First, it fired several signal smoke shells in another effort to set the building on fire, but when these failed to produce a flame, it began the slow job of taking the building apart, stone by stone. Some of us stood on the altar and a nearby table to watch through a broken stained glass window in the rear wall of the church. Suddenly, out of the heavy pall of smoke and dust, some twenty yards away, staggered a wraith-like figure, blackened by burnt powder, his face blood-spattered and unrecognizable, with his left arm dangling like a limp rag.

"It's the lieutenant!" someone yelled, "He ain't dead!"

Staggering as if drunk, the ghastly apparition advanced a few more awkward steps and fell to the ground. He tried to rise again, unconsciously trying to support himself with a useless left arm. Again he fell, but this time he lay still.

"Get me out of this thing," the young radioman sobbed, struggling with the harness of his pack radio. Free of it, he ran for the door, only to be caught by another of the men who yelled at him, "Don't be crazy. You can't go out there now."

The radioman was not to be stopped, though, and dragging the other man behind him, he made his way out the door. Rather than let him go alone, the second soldier ran with him to the still form of the lieutenant, and together they dragged him into the church as 90mm shells from the tank's big gun ripped the air only a few feet above their heads before they crashed into the house.

While the medical aide held his finger on the lieutenant's tongue to permit him to breathe, the radioman called frantically for a litter. The tank gun persisted in its hammering fire until the building beyond the church was all but leveled. Four dazed Wehrmacht holdouts were routed from the cellar.

As I had not been expecting any extended action, I had brought with me only one pack of film. Later I learned that of the dozen shots in the pack, eleven were immediately flashed to the States by radio, a percentage that, to my knowledge, was never surpassed in that theater of war. I was later commended with a Bronze Star for my "meritorious achievement while engaged in military operations involving conflict with an opposing foreign force." I trust the radioman and his companion earned their Silver Stars.

11

From Paris to Dachau

The lacy black ironwork of the Eiffel Tower loomed above the tops of shabby houses as our small convoy of jeeps and weapon carriers drove carefully through the snow-covered streets of Paris. Chilled and shivering inside, we lifted the tarpaulin at the sides of our truck and peeped out at the famous city where we were to have three whole days of rest after the merciless jouncing of a two-day trip.

At the hotel we were sold G.I. coffee and G.I. doughnuts by the Red Cross and assigned cots in bare, unheated rooms. Some of us managed to find time to take the Metro to, and be left unimpressed by, the Eiffel Tower, the Arc de Triumph, the Army PX, Rainbow Corners Service Club, and some black-market perfume shops. The others, who believed literally in the "rest" angle, retired to Pigalle and relaxed in the bars and upstairs rooms. The sightseeing element soon gave up and joined them there to get out of the cold, gloomy weather, if nothing else.

Three days later, the convoy sloshed its way through the filthy muck of half-melted snow and headed for the Vosges Mountains. There was a sad lack of women and wine but the Germans were hardly more inhospitable than the Parisians had been.

Peterson was slowly sinking into a permanent alcoholic haze. He was thereby progressively jeopardizing himself and the other two members of the team. Though his condition had been apparent to me for some time, it was only when we were placed in close contact with the Corps Officer that it came to official attention.

So, I lost another partner with whom I had worked out a

mutually satisfying relationship. With Peterson pulled back for a rest, I was assigned to cover the 103rd Division with Joe Chiappino. We had worked together briefly back in Italy, and he was now a brand-new second lieutenant. He was a man of high intellect with a touch of aestheticism. He was also easygoing and impossible to dislike. I judged myself lucky to be teamed with him.

The 103rd was just beginning to form a solid crust of experience. At present they were performing a holding action with large-scale patrol activity and an occasional local push. Pictures at this time were at a premium and we had to content ourselves with occasional actions and whatever feature stories we could dig up.

One of these features concerned Georges Kieffer, an FFI district leader and self-titled "Tallest Man in the World." Since he was eight feet, six inches tall, he was probably not far off the mark. He and his rather small mother had us in for "tea," and they proved to be delightful, friendly people.

At division G-2, the colonel informed us that a night attack was planned on a certain small town, but the uncertainty of the enemy's strength made the outcome doubtful. He had requested recon pictures from the Air Corps but had failed to receive cooperation. This was a strong hint that I could not ignore.

After a phone conversation with Lt. Strock at the company lab, it was arranged that I should take to the air that morning to make the pictures, which would then be printed and delivered, if possible, that evening. The flight in the L5 was uneventful, though we flew deep into enemy territory. After this I made several other flights for this division on a less-urgent basis, thus contributing heavily to our stock of good will and cooperation from the division's officers. Also, I enjoyed the flying.

From this ideal setup of complete compatibility between division officers and photo team, I was suddenly switched to the

71st Division, of which I had never heard, to work with Joe Dieves, whom I knew only slightly. At about this time the front broke loose and sent us charging down toward the Rhine. All thought of anything behind the front lines was forgotten.

Pushing rapidly through a series of small-town delaying actions and sporadic holdouts, we followed the Germans' orderly retreat. We took up a two-day residency in the fairly large town of Speyer when the division's advance was temporarily checked. Rumor had it that there was a large champagne winery in town, and we set out to find it. After locating our objective, we were temporarily stymied by a high stone wall with only one gate. The gate was fastened from the inside and bore the confiscation label of the division general with "Off Limits" signs.

By standing on the hood of the jeep parked against the wall, Dieves and I were able to hoist our driver, Harry Tressel, over the top. It was only a matter of minutes before he had the gate open and we had the jeep backed up to the loading dock. Here we were met by a surly civilian workman to whom we explained that we had come for two cases of the best champagne in the house for the general's party that night. With a shrug of his shoulders and a wave of his hand, the man indicated a stack of cases on the dock.

But no, it had to be the very best for the general.

Well, if he had to he had to. The man led us down a winding stairway at least a hundred feet underground. When he switched on the lights, we were amazed to see a huge chamber filled with thousands of bottles of champagne stacked in labeled sections. As he led us through the aisles between the racks of bottles, the man stopped at intervals to exhibit samples. Each time we refused the offer, and the dates on the labels became older and older as we went.

Finally, when we were satisfied that we had the oldest, if not the best, champagne in the vault, we filled two cases and loaded them into the jeep. Dieves signed the invoice as Col. G.I.

Shitz. We and our special friends were well supplied for several days.

The Military Government (MG) moved in fast on this agreeable town. Their first action was to comb the town for all weapons and cameras. When we heard that they had collected a whole roomful of cameras, we decided that a picture story on the workings of the MG was indispensable to a complete record of the war.

Next morning we arrived early at the MG office, but the major in charge was not yet in. While waiting outside the door, I was surprised to find myself addressed by a passing colonel as "Say..."

"Yes, sir?"

"Say," he said again. "Aren't you the photographer who was with the 103rd?"

"Yes, sir. I was for a while." I was wondering which old sin was catching up with me.

"You made some aerial pictures for me, didn't you?"

"Oh, sure. Yes, sir, I remember now." It was the G-2 colonel from the 103rd.

"That was a good job you did. We found several gun positions on your pictures and changed our plans to flank the town instead of hitting it head-on. Probably saved the lives of forty or fifty men."

Nothing, utterly nothing, anyone ever said to me made me feel as good as that one statement.

While I was talking to the colonel, the MG major arrived. The colonel took Dieves and me in for a formal introduction and build-up, after which he left.

"Look, you fellows are photographers," the major said. "How about going in there and picking out a good little camera, not too complicated, for me. And," he winked, "while you're there, pick out one for yourselves."

If ever a deal had been served up to us on a silver platter, this was it. When the major opened the door, we saw before us a five-foot-high, glittering pile of cameras of all descriptions. It covered nearly half the room. Perched at the very peak lay two Rollieflexes.

"Well, there you are, fellows," the major said. "When you finish, come on back to my office." We barely heard him. As the door clicked shut behind us, we dived as one for the Rollies, then began a frantic pawing through the huge pile. A Kodak 35 caught my eye and fit nicely inside the big pocket of my field jacket. A little yelp came from Dieves as he discovered a Leica. Soon I uncovered another. Finding these beautiful little mechanisms was all very fine, but we thought we would never be able to walk out with more than two each. The thought of leaving the others behind was heartbreaking.

A tapping on the window at the rear of the room revealed Tressel, who, bless his soul, had thought we must be having problems and hunted us down. We made three successful trips to the jeep before the major reappeared to ask if we had found him a camera yet.

"Yes, sir," Dieves replied without batting an eyelash, and showed him the box he had just picked up to look at. After showing the major how to operate his camera, we thanked him for the Rollies and left his office whistling. Later we figured the approximate value of each of the eighteen cameras and divided them into three equal splits. Then we left town.

With very little action to photograph, we decided to make a quick story on the wreckage of the huge chemical plant of I. G. Farben in Ludwigshaven. In the large administration building, we found plans of the gigantic factory and planned a shooting schedule to include what we guessed were the most important processing plants. Once started on the job, however, we were overwhelmed by the fantastic proportions of the layout and asked permission from our company to stay until we could do justice to the story. The vast amount of damage done by bombers to the factory area presented a pictorial paradise for an artist. As photographers, we were a little awed. The wreckage of the large buildings, exposing mazes of pipes, machines and scientific apparatus, was spread in a complicated array over many acres. Wonderful picture material was presented in any direction the camera was pointed. We knew our pictures would probably be labeled "Secret" and never published, yet the artist in us compelled us to use every camera trick we knew to bring out the feeling of the devastation. That we had no real understanding of what we were seeing made little difference to us. We were the reporters, not the scientists. The technical details could be recorded later by those who knew what was of scientific rather than pictorial interest.

Another team was sent later to help us, and together, we worked on it for a week. During that time, the scene was invaded by a dozen or more high-ranking army officers and civilian scientists who came to explore the secret processes of the chemical manufacturing, including of synthetic gasoline and alcohol, which the Germans had been using.

Some of the last shots we needed for our story were of the big loading facilities with their tall cranes reaching out over the waters of the Rhine. We begged the use of a "duck" from an outfit ferrying supplies across the river now that Mannheim had been taken by Allied troops. We were warned that the Germans had been launching floating mines onto the river from upstream. A lookout with a rifle was posted on the bow to watch for the drifting T.N.T. As we rolled off into the water and moved upstream, we saw that tanks and machine guns had been posted along the bank.

With one sweep, we made our pictures and headed back to the landing. Without warning, we were suddenly surrounded by zipping machine gun slugs and roaring explosions. Face down in the bottom of the duck, I tried to remember how far we were from the shore and wondered if I would make it swimming, if I were left alive after the duck sank.

Then, as quickly as it began, it was over and we climbed to our feet to look at the pieces of a shattered log floating on the water beside the duck. Lookouts on the bank had mistaken it for a mine. Needless to say, if it had been a mine we would have been blown out of the water.

Later, back on the road again and trying to catch up with the infantry, we pushed on through Mannheim, Darmstadt and Aschaffenburg. We paused long enough at Aschaffenburg for me to fly back to Ludwigshaven and Mannheim for the finishing air shots of the I. G. Farben plant. I had also been asked to get some aerial shots of Ludwigshaven and Mannheim themselves, and the blown bridges over the Rhine. Then it was time to move on, through Bishofsheim, Neustadt, and Schweinfurt, where we made pictures of the local civilian fire department, mostly women, trying futilely to extinguish fires after an incendiary bombing. With their exception, the entire population of Schweinfurt was gathered together in a huge pen while a group of CIC (Counterintelligence Corps) investigators worked at finding Nazis among them.

Next we dived into the story of the five large ball bearing plants at the edge of town. The plants, essential to the war effort, were huddled together in a group which made them a perfect bombing target. To thwart this, a long-term project had involved moving the entire complex of factories into a huge, unfinished underground facility.

Dieves and I knew we were missing an important part of our story by not going down into the deep shafts, but it seemed unlikely that the Germans would have left without first installing booby traps and mines. The engineers had not yet checked any of the area, so we decided against the effort.

As was often the case, however, my curiosity overcame my good sense. Warily I wandered into one of the angled corridors which led from an entrance. When I rounded the first turn in the narrow tunnel, the light from the entrance disappeared. I moved forward slowly, feeling ahead of me to keep from running into a wall. By cautious shuffling, I moved past three or four turns in total darkness. The deeper into the concrete blackness I pushed, the more convinced I became of the folly of this venture. I decided to turn back. Before I did, I fished my cigarette lighter from my pocket and flicked it open. In front of me I saw nothing at all, as the weak light faded into the distance. Then I looked down. There, also, the light faded into black distance. My toes were poised two inches over the edge of a shaft, whose bottom I could not see.

Wurzburg was the next important town on the itinerary of the charging Seventh Army. Without a pause, the advance elements rolled through at top speed, pursuing the fleeing German army. Dieves and I soon learned the reason for the unusual attention. The town, with several bridges across the Main River on one side and a German tank school on the other, had been subjected to one of the most complete fire-bombings on record. It had absorbed a blanket bombing of incendiaries, and according to MG estimates was ninety percent destroyed and ninety-eight percent damaged. It was a sad destruction of an entire town.

Dieves and I quickly shot the coverage required, with a few extra shots of beautiful Marienburg Castle perched on the crest of a steep hill just across the Main. Though the town was gutted by fire, we found it hard to show the full extent of the damage because, in most cases, the hollow shells of the buildings still stood, hiding the charred interiors. We decided to shoot the long rows of hollow stone hulks from above. We first tried shooting from the bell tower of an ancient monastery on a hill just outside town, but the distance was too great. We finally turned to our old friends, the "grasshopper" pilots, and were rewarded, as usual, by cheerful and efficient cooperation.

From the air, the horrible sight of the destruction Wurzburg had suffered was enough to touch the heart of even a bombardier.

*****

The assignment changes continued. I was switched to XV Corps to work more special coverage with Johnny Vita as movie man and a fellow named Bartlett as driver. The first important job was Nurnberg (Nuremberg). The famous old city presented a scene of bomb and artillery damage that somehow softened the contrast between the ancient walls and towers of the Inner City and the Hitler/Speer modernism of the Sports Platz, Congress Hall, and S.S. Kasserne. By this time I considered myself a connoisseur of destruction and had photographed the remains of billions-of-dollars-worth of burned and blasted property. I had begun to yearn for the satisfying pleasure of some beautiful, unmarred work. But I felt a primitive pleasure when the engineers blasted Hitler's massive eagle and swastika ensign from its pinnacle atop the Sports Platz.

Schwabach, Wissembourg, Eichstadt, Ingolstadt, and on and on. The infantry was out of touch with the Wehrmacht again, and it was possible to drive for hours without knowing whether the road belonged to the Americans or the Germans. "No man's land" had lost its meaning.

Thus we drove, passing entire German convoys, wrecked, burned, and blasted, mingled with the bloated corpses of men and horses. Hundreds of bedraggled German soldiers trudged, unescorted, toward our rear groups, in pairs or alone. Some hailed us, but we could do nothing but wave them back toward the rear elements where they would, eventually, find someone who would take them into custody. Whenever we stopped, we were assailed by beaten and hungry members of the Aryan super race looking for a POW cage.

On a narrow highway winding through a wooded area, we topped the crest of a hill and skidded to a stop just short of a machine gun on a tripod set up in the middle of the road. Behind the gun, pointed straight at our heads, a three-man crew crouched in a business-like attitude. I am sure all three of us gave up hope for an old age at that moment. But the expected blast did not come. The three Germans picked up the machine gun, carried it around and dumped it in the back of our jeep. They then proceeded to climb aboard. At this point we waved them off and pointed back down the road where, we assured them, they would find a POW camp with lots of C-rations.

*****

When we first entered Germany we were not aware of the prevailing attitude toward Jews. Therefore, when we passed through the first German towns we did not understand why so many people stood beside the road and watched us with their hands cupped over their noses. We soon learned the meaning. The symbol represented the hiding of a "Jewish nose," and implied that all Americans were Jewish or at least closely allied with Jews. We were to witness the full impact of this German attitude later.

Of course, they could not really believe that all Americans were Jewish because we were soon followed by the black support troops. Some Germans then began to shout at us, "Nay-gah, nay-gah." They seemed disappointed when this did not provoke the expected reaction from us.

On April 29, 1945, we arrived in the town of Dachau with the Corps officer and two other teams. We quickly requisitioned a house, giving the occupants two hours to move out. (The Germans usually gave the Italian and French civilians fifteen minutes.) An investigation of the house revealed a large cache of fresh eggs in a tub, and a barrel of them soaking in brine. These were the first real eggs we had seen in several months. We had eggs fried, boiled, and in omelets at least four times a day.

Just outside town was the infamous concentration camp. At the time we were not aware of the significance of the place, but Hershey and Blau, who were assigned to coverage of the 45th Division, entered the camp with the first infantrymen and were now working up a complete story. When they returned to the house that evening, bringing stories of almost unbelievable horror, Johnny and I decided to visit the place the following day. We wanted to take a few personal pictures and see for ourselves if it could possibly be as bad as they said.

What we saw left us stunned for days. Without the pictures I took there, I do not think I would now trust my memory, so far was the scene removed from human experience. Many books, articles and memoirs have been written about this hell on earth, and about its liberation by American forces, so I will not attempt to describe everything we saw and heard. But I must write about some of it, if for no other reason than to exorcise it.

Even before we reached the entrance to the camp, we came upon a railroad siding where some twenty freight cars of all descriptions were standing. Piled inside each of the cars, in an incredibly filthy tangle, were the twisted bodies of forty or fifty human corpses. Here, during the long, brutal trip to the camp, they had died of starvation and exposure or from beatings and shootings by their S.S. guards.

We learned that on those trips, the number of those who reached the camp alive depended on the distance they had come. They were not given food, water or sufficient clothing to protect them from the cold. When a trip took as long as three weeks an entire train, hauling nothing but dead bodies, would still be delivered to the camp. The crematory ovens were weeks behind.

Along the road leading to the camp we passed rows of clean, modern little houses. These, we learned, were for the camp guards and their families, and were some of the nicest in the town.

Inside the camp we saw nothing at first to substantiate the terrible tales of Hershey and Blau. It was, to outward appearances, a comparatively nice place. There were green lawns and paved streets and a well-cared-for little canal running outside the high, electrified barbed wire fences restraining the prisoners. We learned later that Dachau was made into a virtual showplace among the many concentration camps in Hitler's Reich because it was close to the Swiss border, and therefore one of those most likely to be inspected by the International Red

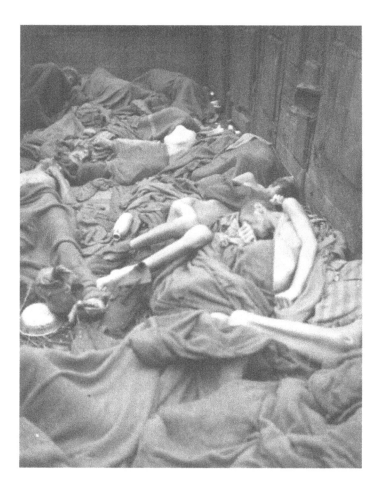

Starved and frozen prisoners on a Death Train

Cross committee from Geneva.

On the inside, we could learn the true story only from those who had actually been interned there. It was not difficult to find a prisoner who spoke English because many of the political prisoners were men of good education, and all were eager to help us in any way possible. We chose the most persuasive of those who swarmed around us to be our guide. He informed us that he had been a university professor and had been influential in the Communist Yugoslav government. For this latter crime, he had been condemned to death. His mother and father had died in the camp's gas chamber and his brother was, at that moment, dying of a bullet wound to his chest, inflicted by one of the guards.

We were led through the barracks and "hospital" wards, where an epidemic of typhus was raging. The barracks were of a flimsy construction, about the same size as those used by our Army at home. The bunks were triple-or-quadruple-decked and as narrow as those we had endured on troop ships. The difference was that these were made of wooden planks and most had nothing resembling a mattress. Also, the number of inmates crowded onto each bunk was usually four. When disease, such as the current typhus, broke out, it usually meant that the whole ward died of the infection. The bodies were collected at infrequent intervals, and the sick and dying often lay for days beside the bodies of their fellow inmates who had died.

Probably the greatest cause of death, which claimed about five thousand a month, was starvation. It wasn't clear just what the prisoners were fed, but several said there had been some cannibalism. Riots over potato peels, which the S.S. burned in sight of starving prisoners, were quelled by beatings, shootings and the use of vicious guard dogs.

At times, water was withheld as punishment. One prisoner described to us a system whereby he was able to salvage rainwater from the gutters. He would soak his coat in the mud and then twist it until water dripped into his mouth.

Our guide showed us an area used for "target practice." It consisted of a path of sharp, fist-sized rocks that led from small mounds of dirt where the guards rested their rifles. At the end of the path was a fifteen-foot concrete wall topped by barbed wire. At a given signal selected prisoners were forced to begin running barefooted along the rocky path. If they reached the wall it proved that the riflemen were poor shots.

One tree in the camp was reserved for hangings. There

were also tall wooden frames that had been used to suspend naked prisoners by their arms four or five feet above the ground. Ropes were used to ties their legs far apart and huge, vicious dogs were encouraged to snap at the prisoners' genitals until they were torn away.

We saw the very elaborate extermination center. This contained the gas chamber, where prisoners were taken in groups and told to strip for a bath, then given a "shower" that consisted of piped-in gas. Our guide told us this was called The "Death of the Angels" by the prisoners because rumor had it that, before death, the victims heard the angels singing. In an adjoining yard we photographed huge piles of sorted clothes taken from the victims.

The largest and finest building inside the camp proper was the crematorium. Here, the huge stacks of bodies awaiting cremation were piled in disorderly heaps nearly to the ceiling of the holding rooms. Prisoners, under the supervision of guards, had performed the labor of cremation.

When battle-hardened infantrymen of the 45th Division—men who had been through more actual hell than almost any other American soldiers in this war and, were accustomed to gory sights—first passed through the camp following a furious small-arms fight put up by S.S. guards, they were crazed with anger. Some of the S.S. men who surrendered to them were cut down by machine gun fire in the same manner they had so enjoyed using on their own prisoners

Our guide told us that when they were freed the inmates turned on those guards they could get their hands on. Not one of the guards, including some who had put on prison garb to escape detection, was allowed to live. The freed prisoners had no weapons but they used their bare hands to deal with these personal enemies. The corpses lay scattered around the camp grounds for nearly a week with their faces and heads beaten to a bloody pulp. A few were castrated before they were killed. An especially brutal guard, who had beaten many prisoners to death, had his right arm twisted completely off before he was killed.

German guards killed by prisoners. Johnny Vita in the background with his Rollie. Prisoners mill around behind the barbed wire fence.

Of the roughly six hundred Catholic priests who had been interred in the camp, thirty were still living when the Americans arrived. Speaking of the S.S. guards, one of the priests told me, "I have always taught that killing was a great sin, but now I would gladly kill any of these men with my bare hands."

Visiting Dachau was easily one of the worst days of my life. The memories of this terrible place I have tried to set aside, to the best of my ability.

12
Peace and Other Ironies

With no specific assignment and no great desire to stick our necks out with the war so near a conclusion, our team spent the next few days driving through the countryside near Dachau, picking up whatever small feature stuff we happened to run across. The Germans were putting up a futile fight to hold on to Munich, a few miles to the south.

Finally, Munich fell to our infantry. That battle had not been our team assignment, but Johnny Vita, Bartlett and I were now sent in to do a feature story on the once-vital railway hub which lay in ruins from repeated Allied bombings. It was May 6, 1945, as we walked through the station and out under the huge overhead canopy of thousands of broken panes of glass, dodging sharp splinters that showered down with every puff of wind. In the rubble-strewn yard, I turned to line up a shot of the battered station building with blackened hulks of railroad cars in the foreground. Thus occupied, I failed to hear the first roar of airplanes approaching at an unusually low altitude. By the time I did, the fleet of several big B17 bombers was almost overhead. I looked up just in time to see that the bomb bays were open and dark objects were beginning to stream out. With an unconscious reflex, born of more than nineteen months' practice, I dived head-first into a convenient bomb crater. To protect the camera in my right hand, I took the force of the fall on my left and a searing pain shot from my wrist to my shoulder. As I lay face-down in the bottom of that hole, every muscle tensed against the blast to come, I heard a series of small explosions high overhead. Ack-ack was my first thought. But no whistle, no whine, no explosions came. Puzzled, I looked up and saw a stream of "bombs" fall a hundred feet below the airplanes and then explode in the air with small puffs of smoke. From these puffs, thousands of leaflets fluttered down over the city. I caught one and read the English translation telling the people of Bavaria that all German armies in southern Germany had surrendered unconditionally. It was not surprising, but certainly welcome news.

After a quick survey of the railroad marshaling yards, we decided it would take a full two days, at least, to cover the story. Therefore, we began to look for a place to sleep. On a side street on the northern edge of the famous *Englisher Gartens*, we found a small private hospital that had been abandoned. Living in the three-story building were two young women of about twenty. They were former nurses and had stayed on when the hospital closed because they had no other place to go, their families having fled the bomb-torn city to live with relatives in the far north of the country. We made arrangements with them to cook our meals and wash our clothes, and went on to photograph our wrecked railway equipment.

Next day, while Johnny and I were deep in the tangle of wreckage in the freight yard, which looked as if it had been hit by a giant Mixmaster, we saw driver Bartlett climbing over the scorched debris toward us. When he got within hailing distance, he yelled, "Hey, you guys. The war's over. I was just talking to a guy who heard it over the radio."

"Yeah? Official, huh? The whole thing?"

"European theater, yep."

"How soon you suppose we'll get home?" I wondered aloud.

"Two or three months, at least," Johnny guessed.

"Probably so," I agreed. "Hey, Bart, how about standing over there like you're looking at that engine? I gotta get some life in this shot. "

We were obviously pretty unimpressed with the official announcement of the war's end. It seemed almost impossible that this thing could be finished, though we had not seen any fighting for several days. It was as if we were just having another of those infrequent breathing spells and would soon be back in the familiar pattern of destruction.

That night, however, we sat down to begin the inevitable letter home in which so many men would say, "Well, it's all over now, Mom, and I will be seeing you soon." I wrote something similar to this and then read it over again. It sounded flat and foolish and I tore it up. It wasn't real.

*****

As we drove through the battered streets of Munich every day, we became more and more aware of the wealth of modern history which passed before our eyes. We made a brief outline of a story on the effects of war on the many famous Bavarian sights, both old and new. When the railroad story, the reason for our extended time in Munich, had been milked dry of material, we had to report to the company with our film. Without too much effort we persuaded the captain to allow us to work on the history story indefinitely, since there was little else for us to do.

We met a young lady named Margaret, who was quite taken with Johnny. We mentioned in passing that we had become unsatisfied with our current living situation. She suggested we move into the house where she was living with two other former nurses, in the suburb of Solln. We settled easily into a life of good, well-prepared food, soft beds, pleasant surroundings and companions. We worked leisurely on our picture story, making it last as long as possible. I was content to relax and absorb the atmosphere of relative luxury for a few days, but before long I began to get itchy feet. I suggested to Johnny that we finish our Munich story and move on to Berchtesgaden to shoot Hitler's private mountain retreat. A young woman named Mariana distracted me, and we remained where we were.

Eventually our story of modern war's effect on the historical sites of Munich and vicinity had been dragged out, amplified, added to and redone until there was nothing left to work on. Before returning to the company, we came up with another idea to prolong our stay. From Munich, with the cooperation of the district PRO, we would be able to cover newsworthy events throughout Bavaria. That ninety percent of these would be outside our zone of operation we passed over as lightly as possible.

The fact that there was little to keep the photo teams occupied played no small part in the captain's decision to grant our request. In the next few weeks we searched desperately for any idea for a picture story that would justify our continuing assignment. We roamed as far afield as Innsbruck and Berchtesgaden, Salzburg and Brenner Pass. Among the stories we covered was the recovery of millions of dollars' worth of Swiss railroad bonds and other securities along with an incredible array of jewelry from a hole in the ground behind a house belonging to a German baron. He had been entrusted by the Nazi government to hide them before the arrival of American troops.

Berchtesgaden was set on a crystal-clear lake among the Bavarian Alps and was the most beautiful town I saw in Europe. Looking at the quaint, traditional timber-frame buildings, the lederhosen and peaked hats some of the men wore, the mural-adorned walls and steep cobblestoned streets, it was not hard to see why Hitler chose this spot as a refuge during the war.

With the war over, the censorship rules were relaxed and I received a letter from my brother Bob who was able to give me his location near a town two hundred miles north. We hadn't seen each other since he joined the Air Corps and I joined the Signal Corps. I decided to take the team's jeep and make the trip AWOL, since there was no legal way I could make an excursion outside the Seventh Army area.

Long before daylight I started out, well supplied with

road maps and extra gas cans. After crossing the territories of two Armies, making hundreds of detours around blown-out bridges and fighting continually with carts and wagons on narrow dirt roads, I arrived at the outskirts of the town I was looking for, only to be stopped by an MP for speeding. I racked my brains for a sob story, which fortunately had the MP on the verge of tears as he let me go with a warning and directions to the airfield.

The three years since our last meeting had been a long time. After our first greetings, my brother and I found little to talk about. Perhaps the truth was that during the time we had been separated we had both grown up, and did not recognize one another's adult mind. But after dinner, Bob showed me his souvenirs and let me ride his German motorcycle. We compared family pictures and had ours taken in front of one of his outfit's planes, for the papers back home. When it was time for me to begin the long drive back, I had the feeling of having launched a new and promising friendship.

*****

It had been more than two months since our team had first driven through the streets of Munich, which now seemed as familiar to us as those of our own home towns. It was almost like leaving home to have to go. But the order had finally come for us to pack up and return to the company. Even the fact that we were to be sent to Paris for a week in a color technique school failed to lessen the regret with which we said our final *auf weidersehenfs*. The tears we left behind were genuine, we knew. I had agonized over it, but knew I would not be coming back for Mariana. Several weeks later my guilt was eased when I heard that she had taken up with an MG officer.

In Paris, we were assigned bunks in a hotel used by the HQ unit and swished through a demonstration of color film processing. After this, we were assigned a camera, issued film and told that we had the rest of the week to go out and use it up.

Paris in the spring was much the same as Paris in the winter. The orange and lavender haired girls still wiggled when they strolled down the Champs Elysees, the *pissoirs* still stood on the corners, the same books filled the *rive gauche* stalls below the Pont Neuf, and the Eiffel Tower had not grown an inch. This time we made a few more pictures, drank a little more cognac and rode a few more Metro trains.

We rejoined the company in Augsburg. I was anxious to get back into the field and expressed such a desire to the right people. Since Johnny Vita was on a list for shipment home, I was assigned with a new man, Jandt. We were assigned the 1st and 12th Armored Divisions. Although this was the first time I had had so much territory to cover, there never appeared more work than we could handle. As usual, the real problem was finding sufficient work to keep ourselves occupied. Once again the bulk of the film was shot on medal presentation ceremonies, training programs, Displaced Persons and USO shows. I photographed and met Jack Benny, jazz harmonica player Larry Adler, singer Martha Tilton, and Ingrid Bergman, even lovelier in person than on the screen.

I didn't have Jandt as a partner long, as he too was transferred out, on his way home. Everybody was leaving but me. Jandt was replaced by Morochnik. With his arrival, our assigned units were changed to include the 12th Armored and the 36th Infantry Divisions. On August 14, the day before the anniversary of their landing at St. Maxime, the 36th Division sent a group of men to southern France to participate in ceremonies arranged by the French people to express their gratitude for the liberation of the area. We were sent to record it on film.

After spending the night in a large beachfront hotel in Nice, reserved for transient G.I.s, we set out for St. Maxime, where we would have to stay the night in order to be on hand for the daybreak ceremony. We stopped at Cannes for a couple of hours, and were greeted by the welcome sight of beautiful young women in daring swim suits on the beach.

At St. Maxim we could not find one empty bed. Even the bawdy houses were full. What sleep we finally got was in the cramped seats of the jeep or on the dewy sidewalks.

The unveiling ceremony, with the troop review afterwards, was actually a brilliant affair and well worth our efforts. I even got the opportunity to be bawled out by General Charles DeGaulle for moving around too much trying to photograph him during the playing of *La Marseillaise.* But it was all over too soon. Back in Heidenheim, life seemed almost unbearably dull as we went about our job of shooting a Jewish Displaced Person story. The only thing to look forward to was that day we would finally get the word to go home.

It was raining nearly every day now and one particular afternoon we were trying to find something to take our minds off our brooding. Morochnik was sewing a new Seventh Army patch onto my brand-new Ike jacket, which I was saving to wear for my triumphal return home.

There was a knock at the door and a man, dripping water onto the floor from a soaking raincoat, stood there with a soggy piece of paper in his hand.

"Hunnert Sixty-Third Signal?" he asked.

"Yeah."

He came across the room and handed me the wet scrap of paper. It read, "Pack your things and proceed to Company. All of you are going HOME." "Home" was underlined twice.

I looked at the wet man and said, very sincerely, "Thanks a lot, Mac."

The next few hectic days were spent in the sad job of breaking up our close-knit company. Cameras and lab equipment were turned in and shipped to a Signal Corps depot, leaving us feeling empty-handed and a little lost. We said good-bye to the men who did not have quite enough points to qualify for separation. They left for service with another Signal outfit in Vienna. Feeling uncomfortable and a little foolish, wearing crumpled ties which had been fished from the bottom of barracks bags, we went through a simple ceremony to receive a few belated medals. Mine was the Bronze Star from Oberhoffen.

Early one morning, several trucks appeared in the company area and we were called into formation with all equipment. After a short farewell speech, the commanding lieutenant went through the ranks to shake hands and say good-bye to each man individually. With this, the 163rd Signal Photo Company, recognized as the best of its kind in the entire Army, was officially disbanded.

I am sure that at that moment every man present felt a pang of regret at the loss of our organization, which had grown into more than just another army "outfit." The friendships that had developed through periods of trouble and danger, hard work and hard play, had brought together men who would never have lived and worked together in civilian life. Now, after more than three years of living the same abnormal life, we had become friends regardless of age, background or education.

It was also a time to remember our seven friends who would never again see home, as well as twice that number who had preceded us homeward minus a leg, arm or other body part. (Fifty years later some thirty survivors of the 163rd met in San Antonio for another of several post-war reunions.)

It took the truck convoy three days to cross northern France to Camp Lucky Strike, north of Le Havre. On arrival, we were issued cots and extra blankets, assigned to tents and told that we would be out within two days. Rumor had us taking the Queen Elizabeth. However, the French October weather lived up to its reputation. Because of the rain, wind and rough seas that destroyed most of the temporary floating docks, the Queen was unable to dock at Le Havre. We missed our scheduled departure.

One day stretched into another and twice we missed our scheduled sailing as the bad weather continued. Finally, one week to the day after we had arrived, we loaded into big semi-trailer cattle trucks and were on our way to the port of Le Havre.

We were met by the beautiful sight of the West Point, the ship that would be taking us home.

The passage took five days, and for two of them we rode full speed through a rip-roaring storm. I pitied the hundreds of men who suffered and starved with seasickness, while I munched filched pork chops.

We were a little disappointed at not landing in New York but Hampton Roads, Virginia made an acceptable second choice, as would have any other port in the United States. On the dock, as we waited for our train to be brought up, we were given coffee and donuts by middle-aged, unpaid volunteer Red Cross ladies. We appreciated the sincere smiles they gave us even though the coffee was foul.

On the train I sat alone and stared out the window as we rolled smoothly along. I didn't want to miss a thing, not a rock or a tree. As I relaxed and the noisy bunch of happy men behind me settled down to their own quiet contemplation, I began to feel strange. I looked back down the car at the familiar sight of olive-drab uniforms and felt reassured.

Why, though, should olive-drab give me a more comfortable feeling than the green fields of my own country? What had changed? Everything I saw was apparently the same. Certainly I felt no permanent attraction to life in the Army. But now, as I was thrown back among things that had been familiar all my life, I seemed to see them clearly for the first time.

The train glided through the open countryside, across a bridge that was still intact, untouched; through the outskirts of a city which appeared strange in its efficient normality. We passed an unscathed cement factory where men worked peacefully and confidently. As the train moved slowly past a street crossing, I saw a man in blue overalls standing beside the tracks. He was not in uniform, nor was he armed. A little farther along another man stood in front of his house and waved at the train. He was offering a greeting, not making a sign asking for food or cigarettes.

There were millions like these men, I knew. I told myself that this was right, this was the way it should be. This was the way it had been all along and I was the one who was strange. I was seeing what I had not seen before, looking much deeper than before. The very air seemed cleaner. The smooth lines of buildings were soothing to the eyes; I wanted to touch them. The wide, straight streets in the towns gave off an air of generosity and plenty. Life seemed extremely good, and yet for the first time it frightened me a little. For the first time I really knew just what I had here, but I also was aware that it could all be lost.

As we climbed off the train at Camp Patrick Henry in Virginia, we were met by a band and escorted to our barracks where we were met by the pleasing sight of clean white sheets and pillow cases. At noon, German prisoners served us a wonderful "Welcome Home" banquet of thick, tender steaks in the main mess hall. Within forty-eight hours the Texas contingent of the old 163rd was on its way by Pullman to Dodd Field, now a separation center, just where I had started from. From there it took seventeen minutes to get home.

Three years, three months, five days, four hours and seventeen minutes, to be exact.

Lightning Source UK Ltd.
Milton Keynes UK
UKHW040045121122
412046UK00001B/303